CONSCRIPTS

LOST LEGIONS OF THE
GREAT WAR

To the memory of my mother

Lila Bet-El

CONSCRIPTS

LOST LEGIONS OF THE GREAT WAR

I l a n a R . B e t - E l

SUTTON PUBLISHING

First published in the United Kingdom in 1999 by
Sutton Publishing Limited · Phoenix Mill
Thrupp · Stroud · Gloucestershire · GL5 2BU

British Library Cataloguing in Publication Data
A catalogue record for this book is available from the British Library

ISBN 0 7509 2108 0

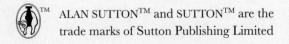

ALAN SUTTON™ and SUTTON™ are the
trade marks of Sutton Publishing Limited

Typeset in 10/13pt New Baskerville.
Typesetting and origination by
Sutton Publishing Limited.
Printed in Great Britain by
Biddles, Guildford, Surrey.

Contents

Plates

Preface

There are faces one never forgets, and faces one wishes to remember. Others come and go, weaving in and out of the fabric of a life; and some just slip away, lost forever. Then there are faces that seem to appear out of nowhere, demanding recognition, emanating familiarity. But one has never seen them before. The faces are not specific, nor is the location. This is not *déjà vu*; it is war.

I learnt the distinction in the former Yugoslavia, when I repeatedly encountered men who seemed familiar, but I did not know them. I was sure I had never seen them before. I was not of the Balkans and had never visited Bosnia, but these men struck me as old acquaintances. They were soldiers, Bosnian soldiers: Muslim, Croat and Serb. Garbed in uniforms supplemented by gym shoes and hand-knitted sweaters, often unshaven and with longish hair, a cigarette inevitably stuck between work- and weather-worn fingers. Hard soldiers and hardened men, yet not of a military demeanour. Once civilians, these men had become soldiers when Bosnia descended into systematic destruction – yet they retained their civilian essence. They had fought and would fight again, out of conviction and necessity and compulsion. They had become professional soldiers, with little interest in the profession. They were conscripts.

I saw many such men straggling along roads in a desultory fashion, on the way to or from camp; standing at crossroads with the patience of extended boredom; going through my papers and car at checkpoints, sometimes with a grin that was almost an apologetic smile, other times with distaste verging on disgust. Sometimes even worse. I watched them, and over time the observations led to recognition, not least of myself: I too had once been a conscript; transformed from a civilian into a soldier by a call-up notice and a uniform, disinterested but doing my duty. That was years ago and for a mercifully brief period, with no connection to war. But another, much larger part of me knew of many conscripts who had been in combat; men who did their duty in appalling circumstances, and eventually won a war. I knew of them because in my past I had spent some years discovering them: the conscripts of the First World War. And though long dead, they seemed to come alive – in appearance, attitude and role – through those men in Bosnia. Past and present, military and civilian, compulsion and duty: conscripts. The generic soldiers of the twentieth century.

There is an endless fascination with the First World War. Indeed, all wars seem to inspire huge interest, much as battle must be one of the most researched and documented of human activities. Merely from the specific perspective, military history appears to be one of the few niche markets that has more than sustained itself in an era of diminishing monographs. Since publishing is now apparently audience driven, the audience must want lots of books on wars and soldiers, if bookstores are any measure. The immense Blackwells in Oxford, for example, boasts a major department of general history, divided into subjects and countries – and a separate large military history department. And within this enclave there are many shelves given over to the First World War, packed full of classic and new studies, covering everything from chronologies of distinct battles to catalogues of weapons. Such is the array that it is worth pondering which is the more interesting phenomenon: the constant reprints of older works, or the stream of new research and analyses on an event that ended eighty years ago, and which can no longer be considered unique in a century of total war and atrocities. Which is not to say it is not interesting, merely to question why a consistently large audience apparently still finds it so.

The question becomes the more pressing after a stroll through the literature department of a bookstore. Once again there is a division, between the classics and modern sections. The former boasts a plethora of books written by those who fought. The First World War was also *the* great literary war, with the sustained popularity of Siegfried Sassoon, Edmund Blunden and Ford Madox Ford, to name but a few, possibly transforming it into the great bestsellers war. Theirs is largely autobiographical fiction; barely disguised descriptions of real people torn apart by battle and disillusionment. It is compelling stuff, which has formed into a canon; a focused and near monolithic testament to dire human experience.

A few steps further lead to the long colourful shelves of modern literature: those volumes that have convinced the literati of their worth in the last ten years. And there, among the ultra-chic narratives of post-modern life, nestle yet more books on the First World War. Not books inspired by the war, or reflecting on the war, but realistic books *about* the war, largely written as fictional biography. Books that get down into the grit and grime and disgust of soldiers' lives, and strive to recreate the awfulness of the Western Front. And, moreover, like their companions and inspirations in the classics department, bestsellers. Sebastian Faulks' *Birdsong* and Pat Barker's Regeneration trilogy stand out among these – especially the final volume, *The Ghost Road*, which won the Booker prize. The first, *Regeneration*, has now also been made into 'a major motion picture', as book blurbs so regularly put it.

The film is based on a good book. However, it is probable that the producers did not buy the rights only because of literary merit, but also for the story and the setting: Siegfried Sassoon's breakdown in and due to the war, and his therapy and relationship with the psychiatrist W.H. Rivers. The tale has received several artistic treatments, and clearly tantalises the creative imagination. But more significantly, it most certainly appeals to the collective English imagination in its depiction of Edwardian upper middle-class men dealing with crises of patriotism, duty and sexuality. Separately or in various combinations, these have been perennial themes of English literature in the past two centuries, but the First World War was a *real* event that combined and gave them all substance. It is a wonderful duality which *Regeneration* captures so well, skilfully spanning the fictional and the real, the personal and the public, battles and beliefs. Pulled together, these themes explain the appeal of the book, as also the other longstanding bestsellers: they all touch upon deeply embedded streaks of nostalgia, for what is perceived to be an era in which ideas and beliefs mattered to the individual and society alike, to the extent of going to war. In other words, in the public domain the First World War was, is, and probably always will be a war of ideology rather than necessity, fought by men expressing themselves as men, who viewed the ideology as a necessity – only to end up disillusioned or dead for their efforts. In this view it was a war of committed individuals; of men who expressed their commitment by taking themselves off to war; a war of volunteers.

But what of the soldiers who were not volunteers? What of the men who were not disillusioned, if only because they had no illusions to lose?

And what, for that matter, of those millions of men who did not have the time to dwell upon ideology or illusions, nor the ability to write about them poetically?

I initially liked *Birdsong*. It commenced as a tale of ordinary men who found themselves on the Western Front, trying to survive the situation and at the same time hold on to the last vestiges of their civilian selves, far away in England. Well researched and interwoven with many details of life on the front, it seemed to go beyond the classic images of that war, and reach out to the reality of the experience. But halfway into reading I realised I was wrong: Faulks was telling yet another tale of disillusionment; he had gone to the effort of side-stepping the upper middle-class subaltern heroes, but remained firmly entrenched in class and rank distinctions; he used all his skills to recreate a backdrop for anguish and battle, without realising that for the men who lived through it the backdrop *was* the anguish. For the trenches were a total life, focused on survival: of battle, and even more of circumstances. Though glorious and heroic to the civilian mind, fighting the enemy occupied perhaps a third of the soldiers' time; the rest was spent fighting the living conditions. In the simplest of terms, men of other ranks were hungry and dirty and lousy and scared – of dying, and often of living, if life was the trenches. And all this meant that trench life kept them both actively busy and mentally occupied – often far too busy and occupied to dwell too long on disillusionment.

There is a reason for repeatedly refuting the central role of disillusionment, as also the focus upon the volunteers. And the reason is that while all soldiers experienced the horrors of trench warfare, these images are relevant at best to just under half the soldiers of the First World War – since just over half were conscripts. Such men did their duty due to compulsion and had few illusions to lose. As of 1916, these were the men that joined the British Expeditionary Force, and by the end of the war they were the majority. In other words, the army that won the war was largely an army of conscripts not volunteers. They held the line, fought, conquered and survived – then they went home and instantly became submerged within the sweeping imagery of the volunteers. For despite their huge contribution, in public perception real men and real soldiers were volunteers who went out in search of masculine fulfilment, as an expression of patriotism and duty; not men who donned uniform thanks to a call-up notice. To civilians, and to the early volunteers, men took themselves off to war with all these illusions, only to have them shattered by the horror and futility of the event, leaving nothing more than the bitter taste of disillusionment. These perceptions, established in the first months of the war and pervasive ever since, totally negate any correlation between soldiering, duty, patriotism and conscription. They do not accept that men may be patriotic without wishing to express it through soldiering, or that men may see fighting as a job of duty rather than a great masculine illusion. They do not accept the existence of combat conscripts in the First World War.

Reading *Birdsong* in Sarajevo was a curious experience: here was a novel that sought to recreate artistically the awfulness of the trenches on the Western Front in 1915, when men were living and fighting in precisely the same conditions just a few miles up the road, in 1995. Rather than wonderful, this was a very bizarre duality of fiction and reality. Sarajevo was stagnant in siege, slowly being choked of life, living and humanity; and elsewhere around Bosnia the enemies were formulated in often stagnant lines, shelling, desecrating, killing, drinking, eating, retiring in the cold.

There is undoubtedly something symbolic in the fact that the two ends of the Short Twentieth Century, as Eric Hobsbawm recently defined it, have been marked by war in Sarajevo. The parallel is even more profound when one considers that while the murder of Archduke Ferdinand in July 1914 ultimately brought down the entire international system of the time, the latter-day round of murderous activities in the same location has brought in nearly every major player in the international system, with little benefit to their reputations. But the matter goes beyond profound symbolism to an awful irony (or possibly an ironic awfulness): that the nature of war, the methods of killing, have seemingly changed so little in eighty years. That for all the technological innovation, the invention of The Bomb, the amazing capabilities of SAM, Scud and Cruise missiles – that for all these and many more such impersonal and long-distance tools of modern combat, the method of warfare in the Bosnian conflict was not far removed from that employed in the First World War. Both lasted four years, with large offensives reserved for the warmer months and less intensive shelling in the long winter. In both the confrontation line was more or less established in the first months of battle, with subsequent and often minimal changes occurring at huge cost to human life. And the worst sites in both were near-stagnant, with close and very personal combat.

In Bosnia, one of these was in the north, in the Posavina Corridor: a flat but crucial plane that had devolved into nothing more than a grim setting for two parallel lines. In some places these were just 80 metres apart, the two sides eyeing each other with clarity before shooting. The clarity was enhanced by the totally stark landscape: there was nothing left. Not a house with a roof, or a tree beyond a trunk. Everything had been destroyed by the war, and for the war. Trench warfare is possible only on open ground, and this was vintage trench warfare. Not fiction, nor history, but a late twentieth-century reality.

As I toured a section of that line on a grey, cold day in autumn 1995, my own search for clarity in the face of the unknown-yet-familiar came to its terminus. Walking on duckboards between two man-high walls of mud and sandbags, water streaming beneath the planks and a forbidding sky above, I seemed to be walking back in time: these were the trenches, the landscape, the people I had spent so long discovering in the Imperial War Museum. It was Flanders in Bosnia, or Bosnia in Flanders. There were the pill-boxes jutting out and above the parapet for observation and shooting, the dug-outs in the sides of the wall, the name and direction signs, the appalling look of grubby makeshift permanence. There were the men, no less grubby, smothered in an assortment of coats and mufflers, brewing coffee on an improvised stove. (That was actually a significant difference: British soldiers in the First World War would have brewed tea.) But there was the grim set of their mouths, the combination of fatigue, fear, disgust and disinterest. Like the Western Front in the latter years of the war, most of the men were the lucky and determined survivors of dreadful bouts of battle in which close friends and comrades had perished. Like the conscripts in the latter years of that earlier war, these men just wanted to go home – but not if it meant defeat or relinquishing hard-won territory. They were temporary warriors who did not want to be soldiers, but they did their job, and did it well.

All wars come to an end. Even long, unremitting ones eventually arrive at a full stop – or at least at a semi-colon, allowing a generation or two to reassemble their gripes and troops into another round, usually defined as a new war. Within the great cycles of history, war is probably the most repetitive and linked. One leads to another. Such words seem a bit slick; an over-simplification of many issues and realities, yet nonetheless true. The First World War held the seeds of the Second, which in turn germinated the current wars of the former Yugoslavia. Some of these are still going on, others have now been halted – but another will inevitably start. If not there, then elsewhere. It is the nature of the beast: startling, luring, tragic.

Wars tend to start with a flourish. The shattering of mundane everyday life into conflict is undoubtedly dramatic: the sketch of peacetime is replaced by the theatre of war. However, in order to sustain audience interest, wars should be scripted very precisely: not too long, with some blood and gore but not too many victims, and some clearly defined heroes. Set-piece offensives should be kept to a minimum, in order to focus emotions and ensure heavy applause, with the best battle saved for last; victories are an imperative. The First World War started out well: it was to be the war to end all wars, and over by Christmas. In accordance with this script, within weeks there was much battle, blood, death and heroism; a huge drama, which men rushed to join. But then trench warfare set in, and the plot went wrong on practically every count: too much blood, gore and victims; too many battles with too few victories; above all – too long and drawn out, with an ill-timed and ill-planned climax. The Somme, in 1916, was billed as the ultimate battle of the war, but it was a colossal failure; even worse, it failed to end the war, which meandered on for another two years. Unfortunately for the conscripts, they were the heroes of this latter part of the script, but the audience had lost interest, despite another two major offensives and an eventual victory.

The conscripts were ignored because they arrived too late, once heroes had been defined and the crucial battle had taken place. Yet in many ways that is their greatness: they were ordinary men who became soldiers, fought, and – for those who survived – went home. From manual workers to clerks and solicitors, they were very *ordinary*, and they went to war and fought as ordinary men experiencing an extreme and unique event in their lives. And when the war was over they remained ordinary men. They were Mr Pooter, and his son and neighbours – the whole gamut of everyday white- and blue-collar Britishness. It is the essence of their charm and importance: the quintessential anti-heroes who plodded along. They may not have been dashing, nor did they dash off to volunteer, but they went when called and plodded through to victory. That is also their immense historical significance: like their counterparts in Germany, France and practically everywhere in Europe during the First World War – including the composite parts of what ultimately became Yugoslavia – they became the basic model of the twentieth-century soldier of total war: a civilian warrior, fighting for nation, survival and a return to civilian life. Since the trenches of Flanders, there have been millions of such men in Europe over the past eighty years. The latest generation, but the same model, were in the trenches of Bosnia.

Acknowledgements

There are happy debts to acknowledge for this book. The late Professor James Joll first listened to my thoughts on the subject, and was kind enough to point me in the right direction a number of times. Zvi Razi was a supreme mentor on the mysteries of methodology, and a constant prod on producing a manuscript. At various times, David Trotter, Martin Daunton, Keith Simpson, Doron Lamm and Avner Offer were kind enough to read parts of it. Billie Melman was extremely helpful in developing ideas; and Ron Barkai and Gabi Cohen were of great assistance. But all errors are, of course, my own.

The staff of the Imperial War Museum, and especially Nigel Steel, were exceedingly patient and helpful throughout the year I spent in the Department of Documents. The late and much lamented Alan Deacon called upon large reserves of humour and kindness in the face of my computer illiteracy. The Reuter Foundation Programme provided a wonderful writing environment, entirely enabled by Godfrey Hodgson. Rosemary Allan is the steadfast rock of us all. At Sutton, Jonathan Falconer and Anne Bennett were a revelation: they made the process of publication almost painless, at least for me.

Robin Denniston and Andrew Lownie made the book possible. But, as true and promised, it is sponsored by David Ish Horowicz and Rosamund Diamond. Al Feldmann cannot be thanked enough. Martin Bugelli, Anton Mifsud Bonnici, Ksenia Bobkova, Marian Hens and Emiko Terazono were great. Sandy Russell was, and is, the *non pareil*. And as ever, Dov, Ophra, Meira, Mike, Noa, Omer and Timna gave constant love and support.

Introduction

The First World War did not have much reality.

W.B. Yeats

The First World War ended eighty years ago, yet it still stands out as a unique and incomprehensible phenomenon. Atrocities had occurred before and certainly since, but the shattering realities of this war still render it in a class of its own. Indeed, judging by the perpetual flow of scholarship, popular books and films, the passage of time seems only to have enhanced both the importance of the war and the questions posed by it. Yet the salient facts were as clear then as they are now: a generation of men were mutilated, together with many cultural and social concepts that had been carefully constructed in the Western world throughout the preceding century. So obvious were the facts that as early as 1915 Freud wrote of 'The Disillusionment of War', claiming it 'tramples in blind fury on all that comes in its way, as though there were to be no future and no peace among men after it is over. It cuts all the common bonds between the contending peoples, and threatens to leave a legacy of embitterment that will make any renewal of those bonds impossible for a long time to come.'[1] It was destruction, whether through death or diminishment, which became the central cultural image of the war.

The events themselves created memory, which was transcribed into history, and from the combination of both evolved mythology. This is especially true of the trenches in Flanders, which, correctly or not, symbolise the First World War in the minds of most: mental images of long lines of trenches in a totally desecrated landscape; of much shooting and shelling; of patriotic men volunteering to fight for King and Country; of gallant poets donning uniform and entering battle. And in fact, these brave men of letters assisted most in the creation of the mythology of the Western Front. However, the British army was not

1

a society of poets and authors who could distil experience into poetic imagery; nor only of courageous volunteers. Rather, it was composed of an anonymous mass of men from all walks of life, whom we still perceive as no more than the 'Unknown Soldier' – a term coined in the First World War – of war memorials. Yet still so little is known of these men or of the realities trench warfare imposed upon them. And what has been discovered, both through literature and research, does not refer to the real unknown soldiers: the men who were conscripted into the army after 1916. Myth still insists that it was the war of the volunteers.

The conscripts were not a minority population within the wartime British army. Between August 1914 and December 1915 2,466,719 men volunteered; but from January 1916 to the end of the war 2,504,183 men were conscripted into the army. This means 50.3 per cent of all wartime enlistments were conscripts.[2] Indeed, by the Allied summer advance of 1918 a majority of the men fighting in the British Expeditionary Force (BEF) were conscripts, and it was this force which won the war. The subsequent disappearance of such a vast population and its achievements is undoubtedly a major historical and historiographical puzzle. Moreover, the conscripts disappeared while a minority of approximately 16,500 men pertaining to them, the conscientious objectors, have been widely discussed; whereas the regular soldiers and the volunteers have been documented in every scholarly and literary form throughout the past seventy years. It therefore appears that the conscripts were not forgotten but ignored in comparison with all the other singular groups of men who came in contact with the British army during the war.[3] As such, this situation poses two major questions: who were these men, these British conscripts? and why were they ignored?

Conscripts were British men, just as the regular and volunteer soldiers before them were. They were men from all walks of life who entered the army at a later stage of the war. The army, the British Expeditionary Force, remained essentially the same organisation, with the same objective of fighting and winning the war. The men were taken from the same towns, streets and sometimes even families as the volunteers, and apparently received the same equipment and fought in the same battles. There was only one difference between them and those who went into the army at the earlier stage: they were conscripted instead of volunteering. Their transition from civilians into soldiers was enforced rather than self-induced. In other words, it was the method by which they became soldiers that set them apart. And this was a crucial difference.

Conscription was always seen as very un-British: a measure that contradicted the essence of both an underlying national liberal ethos and the Liberal politics of the ruling government; one associated with the excesses of the Napoleonic wars and the brutishness of Prussian militarism. But during the war, Britain moved from the principle to the specific. It was a country that enshrined the concepts of 'sacrifice' and 'heroism' even as the war was unfolding; a country that projected images of cavalry charges to its civilians while men were shooting each other in trenches; a country that only got organised to fight a war after countless men – who had volunteered – had been killed and wounded; a country that created a context in which conscription was not only deemed unBritish, but also unpatriotic.

Put in this context, it is clear the conscripts stood no chance, as men afflicted by bad timing, and even worse imagery. They arrived after the image of the soldier had been established as that of the volunteer; after hundreds of thousands of volunteers had been killed and wounded; after women had stopped handing out white feathers, since duty and cowardice had lost any meaning. They were the heroes of the second half of the war, but by then the concept of heroism had become hollow. They had no adequate definition. Searching for the conscripts is therefore a process of sifting through the events of war they experienced in the army and the front line, and the images of war that surrounded them in Britain. It is an attempt to understand how they viewed their enforced transformation from civilians into soldiers, and their lives as soldiers – and to measure this view against their public image, both during the war and ever since. In other words, it is a search for their identity, as British men and British soldiers – and it is the subject of this book. With more than one thousand quotes from original sources, these men are revealed, in their own words, through their own experiences. It is their narrative, as much as possible – but it must be placed in historical and literary context, which is the purpose of this introduction.

Chronology was probably one of the most influential factors in deciding the imagery of the conscripts. Conscription commenced in January 1916, after the volunteers had been fielded – but also after the nation had been drained by a year and a half of war. As Lloyd George put it in his memoirs:

> Looking backward, there is no doubt at all that we should have been able to organise the nation for war far more effectively in 1914, and bring the conflict to a successful issue far more quickly and economically, if at the very outset we had mobilised the whole nation – its manpower, money, materials and brains – on a war footing and bent all our resources to the task of victory on rational and systematic lines. Towards the end, something approaching this condition was in fact reached, but there had intervened a long and deplorably extravagant prelude of waste and hesitation.[4]

The conscripts were part of the late attempt to mobilise the nation: they were a product of the war, as much as they were part of it. And understanding this element of their background is crucial to establishing their identity.

Britain was the only major power to enter the First World War with a force composed of its small regular army, mostly dispersed throughout the four corners of the Empire, and a 'part-time' Territorial Army. In all, it mustered approximately 700,000 men, of which half were not immediately available for service. In comparison, Germany, Russia and France each fielded conscript armies of millions from the very start, replacing their losses with yet more conscripts as the killing progressed. This was a result of Britain's interpretation of European foreign affairs, and its role within them as a dominant yet removed power. Pre-war planning was based mainly upon economic precepts: as a financial force Britain would become banker to the Allies; and as the nation that 'ruled the waves' its almighty navy would impose a blockade upon the enemy nations, especially Germany, so starving them into submission. This was a policy of 'business as usual', in which Britain would have retained her pre-war economy and population more or less intact, basically at the expense of all the other belligerents. As Lord Salter, the Director of Ship Requisitioning during the war, noted, it 'was contemplated that Britain's real contribution would be naval, industrial and financial, the Navy keeping the seas open against cruiser attack for Allied imports and trade, and denying them to the enemy'.[5]

Overall, any proposed war was deemed to be short and contained in terms of space and manpower. Within this view, conscription was considered costly and unnecessary, since Britain did not intend to field a large-scale army comparable to those gathered by the other warring nations. This strategy, however, did not really consider the nature of modern warfare, which entailed a prolonged and sustained effort in terms of manpower and ammunition. More significantly, it did not account for the complicated entanglement of international accords and agreements that eventually led most of the nations of Europe to war – nor for Britain's obligations within it. Indeed, even in 1914 most soldiers and civilians were not properly aware of Britain's commitment to France.[6] But the force of events quickly made its impact upon policy-makers, and in turn upon the nation. Faced with the reality of a full continental commitment, a call went out for volunteers, with a massive response that yielded an impressive army of over two million men up to January 1916. Yet this endeavour was still undertaken within the pre-war concept of Britain's role in the war, with the government constantly attempting to balance the national military commitment against the limited 'business as usual' principle. It was only when this balance became impossible to maintain – in other words, when it was clear that a viable military commitment could only be sustained with the backing of a full economic commitment – that universal compulsory service was enforced. In other words, conscription actually signified Britain's final departure from its concept of magnificent isolation and minimal participation in the continental war.

Upon this international background, and the raising of a volunteer army, it may be assumed that the introduction of conscription in the midst of the war was a sudden departure within Britain. But that was far from the case. The wider cultural context is explained in the Epilogue, but it is important to emphasise that the issue was already placed on the political and public agenda in 1901, because of the Boer War. For despite an eventual victory, the army at that time displayed severe shortcomings that amounted to a military failure. Both within and outside Parliament voices were raised in demand for a thorough reform of the military forces, a task undertaken in a series of measures by R.B. Haldane, Secretary of State for War between 1905 and 1912. Throughout this period the option of compulsory service was raised several times, but never too forcefully, and this for two major reasons. The first was financial: a national service scheme of any kind would have meant a huge increase in the army budget, and therefore an unacceptable drain upon the capitalist–mercantile economy of turn-of-the-century Britain. The second was conceptual, in that conscription was viewed as an infringement of individual civil rights, and a significant break with centuries of a tradition of volunteering – as well as a decisive step towards Germanic culture and militarism. However, this objection to compulsion was hollow, since forms of militarism – from membership in the Volunteer Force to various elements of Anglican and Nonconformist Christianity – were widely spread throughout Edwardian society. In other words, British militarism existed, but not as an organised political or state endeavour which could be equated with Prussianism.[7]

In the light of these obstacles, any pre-war debate on national service was doomed to failure. Yet there were debates, and they were persistent. In the political arena, the predominantly Tory pro-conscriptionist lobby slowly gained adherents, but the majority of MPs still felt the British public rejected the concept. Their hesitation was compounded by reticence in the higher echelons of the army, who never openly requested compulsion as a matter of military necessity or planning, and therefore a national question that could sway politicians. This also influenced the debate outside Parliament, which was dominated by the activities of the National Service League. Founded in 1902 in order to create a popular basis for its namesake, and headed by the ageing but universally admired war hero Lord Roberts, the League never gained massive support since its appeal was intrinsically to the upper classes of society. However, by August 1914 it had an estimated membership of 250,000 and a significant network of branches; it also boasted the support of well-known Tory figures, and its own journal, *A Nation in Arms* (previously the *National Service Journal*).[8] But ultimately the League never managed to bring about a significant political conversion to the cause of compulsory military service, since economic considerations always far outstripped its non-Liberal, and expensive, ideological proposals.

Public opinion, on the other hand, though intrinsically against the issue, was confronted by an intense quasi-ideological campaign for conscription from the rapidly emerging popular press. Fiercely nationalistic, the new tabloids apparently enshrined traditions of liberalism and volunteering. But at the same time, they quickly came to be characterised by a concern with peripheral or disjointed subjects, such as food supply in a future war, which were often removed from context and described in menacing tones. In this way, while *The Times* and the liberal *Manchester Guardian* reported on the conscription debate mostly within the confines of political interests, the new papers, led by the mass circulation *Daily Mail*, had no such scruples. Placed in the context of the German military threat, which was inflated by Lord Northcliffe and his editors to menacing proportions, national service was portrayed as a logical necessity that was being denied the country by politicians. It was not a muted campaign, nor was it short.[9] And combined with the political discourse of the time, and the work of the League, it makes clear that long before compulsory military service became a reality in England, the case had been squarely set before all elements of society and public opinion, and in a surprisingly positive way. Indeed, it could be said that the tradition of voluntarism had been broken with at least a decade before the first conscript received his 'call-up' papers in 1916.

The outbreak of war in August 1914 forced the issue of compulsory service to the very forefront of national life, lowering it from the lofty realms of principle and ideology to those of military manpower and national necessity. The initial burst of mass voluntarism that characterised the first two months of the war was followed by a steady decline in the numbers of men willing to put themselves voluntarily at the service of King and Country. Much has been written about the recruiting efforts under the voluntary system, yet it must be noted that it actually reached its peak in September 1914, with an immense 462,901 recruits. By February 1915 the monthly recruiting figures had dropped below 100,000, and continued throughout the year in a downward spiral.[10]

In May 1915 the so-called 'Shell Scandal' broke, which charged that the forces at the front were underarmed. As such, it really exposed the severe shortcomings of the British war economy and military organisation, and their combined inability to sustain an adequately equipped army on the battlefield. Since both issues were deeply rooted within the problem of manpower allocation, it became clear that aside from a growing failure to secure recruits, a basic flaw of voluntarism was its lack of method. Each volunteer decided upon his own enlistment, and so a qualified engineer or a miner could remove himself from the workforce, regardless of whether he would be of more use to the war economy if he remained in his civilian occupation. This was possible not only because of the personal nature of volunteering, but also because there was no contemporary data on the population as a whole against which an individual's value could be assessed. The first step towards any system of statewide manpower allocation therefore had to be a national survey of the population in its entirety – and one which would reflect upon the skills and size of the available workforce. For in order to single out an individual male citizen for conscription, or his placement in a reserved civilian occupation, his existence and availability for service had first to be established. The National Register of 15 August 1915 was compiled to do this.

The National Registration Act was passed on 15 July 1915. It called for the registration of every citizen and resident of England, Scotland and Wales, male and female, between the ages of 15 and 65, through a personal form which asked:

- (a) Name; place of residence; age; whether single, married or widowed; number of dependents . . . ; profession or occupation (if any), and nature of employer's business; . . .
- (b) Whether the work on which he is employed is work for or under any Government Department.
- (c) Whether he is skilled in . . . any work.[11]

A certificate of registration was to be issued against every completed form, so making each registered person responsible for notifying the local registration authority of his/her removal to a new address within 28 days of its occurrence.

The task of compiling a register was allocated to the 'Registrar-General, acting under the directions of the Local Government Board'.[12] This coupling reflects quite precisely the basic problem of the wartime manpower system: from the start of the war military recruitment had been organised on a local rather than a national basis. It was therefore imperative to involve the Local Government Board, both to gain the existing data on recruitment and to ensure continuity with any system to be introduced subsequently. However, any information pertaining to the overall population in Britain was within the jurisdiction of the Registrar-General. It was also the only organisation that could undertake a national survey, since it was responsible for conducting the national census every ten years, which was another form of population accounting. However, the previous census had been compiled in 1911, and was not only outdated, but also inappropriate for the task of providing continuous information on the population:

Registration differs from census taking in the important respects –
- (a) That it is concerned with individuals instead of statistics, and
- (b) That it must provide information as to the position at any time, instead of at a single appointed date.[13]

This definition was written by S.P. Vivien, Assistant Secretary to the English Commission of the National Health Insurance Commission, who was advising the Local Government Board on the compilation of the register. His experience from the Insurance Scheme initiated in 1911 made him exceedingly sceptical as to the effectiveness of such an endeavour. For while a census placed the responsibility for supplying the relevant data upon the head of a household, in the case of a register individuals were responsible for themselves. As such, he claimed, it would be virtually impossible to check up on each person, nor would threats or actual punishment by law be of any great use:

> The result will be that registration will be seriously incomplete, not owing to pat abstention, but from sheer inertia, indecision, and lack of guidance. . . . Few people have any conception as to the extent to which movement from one address to another takes place among the industrial population. One large Approved [insurance] Society has put it as high as one removal per member, per annum. The London Insurance Committee received, during 1913, 600,000 notices of removals affecting members of an insured population of 1,450,000 under a system which broke down *because removals failed to be notified.*

Vivien attacked not only the concept of registration as unviable, but also the specific wording of the Act itself: 'Every one of its features has a counterpart in some feature of the early system of registration experimented upon by the Insurance Commission, which was abandoned as unworkable as a result of dearly-bought experience.'[14]

Despite these warnings and reservations, however, National Registration day went ahead on 15 August 1915 in accordance with the guidelines laid down by the Act. In a memorandum to local registrars the Registrar-General gave instructions, which were somewhat complex, as to the tabulation of the completed registration forms, which were to be coded according to occupations, 46 in number.[15] When this process was completed in October 1915, the Register for England and Wales had 21,627,596 names on it.[16] Combined with further Scottish returns, which were administered by a separate authority, 5,158,211 were recorded as men of military age, of which 1,519,432 were starred as men in reserved occupations, i.e. those needed for the economic war effort in industry and agriculture. 'Further reducing the number available by the accepted average of 25 per cent for medical rejection, this left a [military] manpower pool of approximately 2,700,000.'[17]

Once the Register was compiled a policy committee was created, to advise on the best use to be made of it. Their most important suggestion was the creation of a permanent committee in order to co-ordinate the requirements of the army and industry. In October 1915 this evolved into the Reserved Occupation Committee, which was also responsible for tabulating the forms. This indicated a degree of order, but it also masked deep shortcomings in the effectiveness of the Register. Since his overall criticism of the scheme had been rejected, in a second memorandum Mr Vivien had suggested putting the onus of notification of removal upon employers, given that the 'industrial classes change their address many times without changing their employment. . . . [and those] who employ the bulk of the employed population are relatively few and responsible.'

The major drawback of this plan lay in securing the returns from small employers, since this would be dependent 'upon the zeal of the local registration authority'. Domestic employers were deemed unimportant.[18] However, according to the final report written after the war by the General Register Office, this suggestion was also not implemented, nor was any other effective updating system introduced. However, 'at a later date (May 1916) an Order in Council amending the Defence of the Realm Regulations required all employers of males of military age to make and to exhibit on their premises lists of all such employees'. Overall, the final report criticises the wording of the Act, since 'the provisions for its maintenance did not secure the constant revision necessary to keep the Register strictly on its original lines. Thus, although every person between the ages of 15 and 65 years . . . was included at first, by the lapse of time the register at the end of 1916 related to persons between the ages of 16 years 4½ months and 66 years 4½ months. Moreover, the Register excluded men who had been discharged from the naval or military forces and, owing to the absence of any legal obligation in the matter, had purposely refrained from registering.'[19]

It therefore appears that even before its compilation the effectiveness of the Register, as a continuous source of viable information on the state of employment and manpower availability in the country, was deemed limited. And once created and put to use, its limitations were glaringly apparent, as Mrs Violet Carruthers, a member of the original National Register Committee, later admitted in a personal letter to Mr Vivien: 'I shall strictly charge my Secretaries that all reference to my connection with the National Register Committees is to be kept out of my tomb stone. I am most heavily ashamed of the whole business, which for futility and ineptitude has been hard to beat – even in this war.'[20]

Lack of organisation was patently to blame for such a situation, but lack of political will was also a key factor, since Liberal leaders still recoiled from the ideology of compulsion. Walter Long, President of the Local Government Board, claimed not to agree that 'compulsory registration means compulsory service, and I am strongly of opinion that the ultimate object in view can to a large extent be secured given compulsory registration, without resort to any further compulsion either for the army or for industrial purposes'.[21] This attitude was coupled with an insistent but not necessarily well-founded fear of popular revolt at such a measure. But in September 1915, after registration was completed, it was clear that a conscription bill of some kind was expected. Instead, events took another indecisive turn with the appointment of Lord Derby as Director of Recruiting. He was given the twofold task of generating sufficient troops for the army, within the confines of the voluntary system; and of doing so in a way which would ensure that young, single men would be taken before the older, married men.

What evolved was a personal canvass based upon the returns of the National Register, in which all British men available for military service between the ages of eighteen and forty-one were asked to attest their willingness to serve in the army (due to political tensions it was decided to exclude Ireland from this scheme, and from the later conscription Acts). Those who responded positively were attested and sent home, under the understanding that they could be summoned to the Colours with two weeks' notice. The returns of the canvass were divided into 46 groups, according to ascending age and marital status, so making it possible to summon single, younger men before married men. The results of the scheme were, however, disappointing: of the 2,179,231 single men noted in the Register, only 1.15 million attested their willingness, of whom 318,533 were actually available for service as both medically fit and in an unstarred occupation. Attestation among married men was much higher since they were publicly promised, by the prime minister, that single men would be taken first. Yet even this group produced only 403,921 fit and unstarred men, out of a total 2,832,210 available.[22] In other words, the Derby Scheme did not secure the voluntary services of the majority of British manhood, though it did introduce a degree of method and system yet unknown to the recruiting effort in Britain. And so, by Christmas 1915, it became clear that the introduction of conscription was unavoidable.

On 5 January 1916 the Liberal prime minister, Herbert Asquith, proposed a bill in the House of Commons, which eventually led to universal compulsory military service for all British men. This, the first Military Service Act, was to be applied only to unmarried men and widowers without children or dependants, between the ages of eighteen and forty-one. Unmarried men engaged in work of national importance, or those who were the sole supporters of a household, were to be excluded; as were men with medical disabilities and conscientious objectors – who could apply to military tribunals detailed by the Derby Scheme. Indeed, the entire bill was suggested as a consequence of the Derby Scheme, and within the terms of reference laid out by it, and not as a proposal for conscription. In his speech, Herbert Asquith claimed that 'in view of the results of Lord Derby's campaign, no case has been made out for general compulsion. . . . This Bill is confined to a specific purpose – the redemption of a promise [to enlist the unmarried men first] publicly given by me in this House in the early days of Lord Derby's campaign'.[23] The bill was passed in the Commons on 12 January 1916, and received the Royal Assent on the 27th. In principle, and despite Asquith's words, Parliament had, for the first time, enforced conscription upon a section of its male citizens.

From its inception this 'Bachelors' Bill', as it became known, proved to be inadequate in providing sufficient military manpower – and that was hardly surprising. By this time voluntary recruitment had diminished to an exceptionally low level, the numbers produced by unmarried Derbyites and conscripts were not very high, and married men in both latter categories were not being called up. By March 1916 it became clear that this intermediate measure was, in the words of Sir William Robertson, Chief of the Imperial General Staff, a 'farce and a failure'. In a memo to the Cabinet he claimed that 'Of the 193,891 men called up under the Military Service Act no fewer than 57,416 have failed to appear'.[24] A further problem was the inadequacy of the National Register, and keeping it updated for recruiting purposes, precisely as envisaged by Mr Vivien before its compilation. On 16 March 1916, for example, *The Times* reported that 'there have been nearly 100,000 removals since the Register was taken on August 15 last, and a large number of men of military age have not been traced'. By September 1916 'the military authorities began taking strong action against the supposedly large numbers of unexempted men who were evading the net. Parties of soldiers swooped on the exits from railway stations, parks, football fields, cinemas, theatres, and prize fights. All males who looked of military age and were not in uniform were apprehended.'[25] Few men were found in this manner, which greatly antagonised the public, and was ultimately abandoned.

Such a situation clearly reflected that the provisions of the Bachelors' Bill were unequal to the task of attaining enough men for military requirements. Extended debates, both in Cabinet and in the Commons, eventually led to a new bill being introduced on 3 May 1916, in which it was proposed that compulsion be applied to all men, regardless of marital status, between the ages of eighteen and forty-one. The bill, which was to be an extension of the existing Military Service Act, was passed on the following day, by a huge majority of 328 to 36, and received the Royal Assent on 25 May 1916. It was a watershed: universal conscription had become a fact in Britain. In the remaining months of 1916 and throughout 1917 the schedules of reserved occupations specified in the Act were revised four times. In July 1917 another Military Service Act (Conventions with Allied States) was passed, allowing for the conscription of British subjects residing abroad, and of Allied citizens residing in Britain, under the same terms specified in the original Act. In February 1918 an entirely new Military Service Act (II) was introduced. The age limit was raised to fifty, with a proviso for the conscription of men up to the age of fifty-six and the extension of compulsion to Ireland, if the need arose in either case. Once again the schedules of reserved occupations were completely redrawn, also giving the Ministry of National Service, formed in November 1917, the authority to cancel exemptions granted on occupational grounds. In July 1918 the Act was amended, with regard to this latter clause, whereby the schedule for the minimum age of exemption in most protected occupations was raised to twenty-three.

The aggregate result of all the legislative efforts from January 1916 was the conscription of 2,504,183 men into the British Army. In other words, over half of all the men recruited during the First World War were conscripts.

The bulk of this book is devoted to the works of the conscripts themselves, followed by an essay on their disappearance since the war and throughout the century. The main chapters are a presentation of their experiences in their own words, drawn from their diaries, letters and unpublished accounts, as a means of investigating their identity. This approach offers two advantages. The first is a focus on the final two years of the war, which is often ignored. Because of the overriding interest in the volunteers, much of the existing literature reflects the first part of the war, culminating in the battle of the Somme as the apex of their experiences. However, the writings of the conscripts reflect the grim reality of Flanders at a time in which the trench system had become established, but the BEF had become a loose framework within which soldiers existed, rather than a rigid and guided organisation. The second advantage is that this study re-creates the human experience of these men, rather than the military one. Instead of battles and shells it is a discussion of baths and food. The fact was that the conscripts arrived into a given situation of war, and it is against this background that they wrote of their experiences. Shooting, sniping, 'going over the top' and death were an integral part of their surroundings. Moreover, the war as a 'purely military event . . . is of strictly limited interest', as Eric J. Leed put it.[26] It was stagnant for long periods, with relatively few large battles; while the regular schedule of military activities occupied approximately one-third of the men's time – the rest was spent in a regular schedule of very human survival activities, such as building dug-outs, eating or sleeping. The conscripts' interpretation of battles would therefore add little to the body of knowledge about the war, beyond yet another personalised view of it; and such work could shed light only upon a small portion of their existence.

Then there is the matter of searching for the individual soldier at war. According to Tony Ashworth, the 'story of both large and small dimensions of the First World War is, to some extent, one of increasing bureaucratization: the conflict grew progressively more vast and specialized, as well as more and more centrally controlled and regulated by formal rules; whereas areas of personal and local discretion diminished.' This idea is complemented by Leed's claim that the 'experience of war was an experience of marginality', and the '"change of character" undergone by the combatant could adequately be summarized as marginalization.'[27] In other words, both agree that the individual became diminished in the war, either through bureaucracy or through experience. While agreeing with them, I would suggest that the one field in which the individual cannot become diminished is his personal existence – on its very human level. Regardless of his status, as cannon-fodder or general, a person is always aware of his bodily needs and his preservation. Focusing upon this aspect is therefore a means of coming closest to the person who became a soldier: the one who fought in battle, but also the one who searched for food, hunted lice, and dwelt in filth.

Finally, the myths of the war should be considered, and especially the one attributable to the non-existence of the conscripts. As reflected in the Epilogue, a major cause of this myth was prevailing concepts of heroism. When discussing this issue, battle tends to be the focal point, not only because it was so dramatic, but simply because it is more tangible in its results to the onlooker, even one of many years past. The Charge of the Light Brigade, catastrophic though it was, has sustained its image and appeal in the public mind not only because it was heroic, but also because it failed. The results of the charge gave an image to the act itself. The force, which was disproportionate to the undertaking, failed; yet the mere attempt has become enshrined in the national memory. 'The camp life of the Light Brigade', or 'The day the Light Brigade went hungry because supplies were unavailable', are not images that are appealing to the public mind, basically because they are not tragic. The critic Northrop Frye explains the appeal of tragedy to the onlooker as 'intelligible because its catastrophe is plausibly related to its situation. Irony isolates from the tragic situation the sense of arbitrariness, of the victims having been unlucky, selected at random or by lot, and no more deserving of what happens to him than anyone else would be'.[28] In other words, tragedy is a catastrophic event unique to those who experience it, largely removed from the sphere of regular life; yet understandable in that it occurred to other people – individuals such as the onlooker. Hunger, dirt or even camp routine are basically part of the daily experiences of everyday humanity. As such they are not usually equated with endeavour, which is what defines tragedy and heroism.

Yet a significant element of the mythology of the First World War is its tragic image, far removed from any accepted aspect of daily life. So one historian writes of it unrolling 'with the inevitability of a Greek tragedy', while another claims the battles had the structure and inevitability of 'mannered Jacobean tragedies'.[29] But in the public mind, conscripts did not belong to this tragedy. They had not rushed off to volunteer, only to have their ideas and bodies shattered by an horrific reality. They had not transformed themselves from civilians into soldiers. They were not heroes. At best, they may have been Kafkaesque heroes, propelled into a system that placed them within an horrific war, leaving them to cope with its reality, and their own thoughts, armed only with an instinct for survival. That said, investigating their military endeavours as counter-proof of their deserved heroic stature would be somewhat redundant, since it would simply raise them to the mythical level of the volunteers, without actually highlighting their singular attributes. By showing their bravery one would basically be applying an existing myth to a new population, rather than investigating the population itself. And it is the aim of this book to move away from tragic images to human horror, from public heroes to real people – even if they are but Unknown Soldiers.

A NOTE ON TERMS AND SOURCES

The term 'conscript' should be clarified, in two ways. The first is technical: for the purposes of this book it refers only to men enlisted in the British Army – not the Navy or the RFC – under the various Military Service Acts between January 1916 and November 1918, and who served on the Western Front. The second is more conceptual, and reflects upon the difference between volunteers and conscripts. As already suggested, in the public arena the divide was between patriotic and unpatriotic men. This is a harsh judgement upon a vast population of men, and as shown throughout the book, it is also incorrect. But there is another aspect to be considered, and that is motivation. Voluntarism denotes, by definition, a positive and accepting attitude to the military framework as a means to achieving an ideological goal of victory. A volunteer wants to be in the army, even if its organisation and his placement within it are alien and even repugnant to him. These considerations are not relevant to conscripts, since their personal opinion is not sought before the act of enlistment, which in their case is not a self-induced act. Therefore the motivation of conscripts, in accepting the military framework and in fighting, is unclear. Although conscription does not necessarily contradict a positive motive of participation, such as patriotism, it cannot be equated with that of a volunteer.

The opinion of the the army high command during the war was not so balanced: 'It must not be forgotten that under enlistment on a voluntary basis the Army was composed of men imbued with a spirit of self-sacrifice and patriotism, but under the Military Service Act a leaven of men whose desire to serve their country is negligible and has permeated the ranks.' This opinion was penned by General Haig, who along with Lord Kitchener and many other senior officers was opposed to conscription, and it was this prejudice which both led to the delay in introducing the measure in Britain, and which shines through in the above quote. And yet, since he was writing in 1917, Haig did not have to contend with the eventual victory of the British Army in 1918, which was largely composed of conscripts: a force with 'negligible' motivation cannot win a war, especially under the dire circumstances of 1918. And so, leaving prejudice aside, the issue of motivation of conscripts, especially in comparison to those who went before them, the volunteers, must be clarified.[30]

The medical writings of the period offer an interesting insight into the matter, because of the traumatic disorders suffered by many men as a result of their exposure to the army and especially the experience of war. These have become known as 'shell shock' or 'war neurosis', yet at the time the source of these disorders was unclear. The problem was not unique to the British Army, though it has been noted that it was the massive appearance of shell shock which transformed the entire field of psychological medicine in Britain.[31] However, Britain was the only power to enter the First World War with a volunteer army, and therefore, at least initially, medical opinion was loath to correlate between shell shock, conscription and motivation – though the possibility was admitted. In discussing such a theory by a German neurologist, two British doctors note that 'it is important to remind our readers that Gaupp is writing [in 1915] of a conscript army . . . further, that up to the time of writing the present chapter, all the "shock" patients in Great Britain have been men who voluntarily elected to serve their country, the majority of them having enlisted in the earliest stages of the war'.[32]

By the end of the war this situation was reversed; however, in order to understand the relevance of this correlation, a comparison with the continent may be enlightening. All the other major participants in the war conscripted large armies from the start, and the problem of conscripts' motivation was therefore immensely relevant to them. In Austria a dispute arose concerning the treatment of the afflicted men, who were initially diagnosed as suffering from 'an organic impairment of the nervous system', and were accordingly sent out to rest in rural areas. But as the war progressed and the number of mental casualties grew, opinion among psychiatrists changed, and the symptoms were explained as an unconscious 'malady of the will' – an escape into illness – and thus malingering. This shift was reflected in the treatment given to the men, which combined, among other measures, psychological inducement to patriotism and 'therapeutic shocks' of electricity – which were all also apparent in British treatment of war neurosis.[33]

After the war, because of the complaints of several men who had suffered the ailment and the attitude of the military authorities to it, an Austrian commission of inquiry was established, to which Freud was appointed expert witness on the electrical treatment of war neurosis. At a public hearing of the commission in October 1920, he attempted to explain the difference between malingering, which is impelled by a conscious motive, and neuroses, which form around an unconscious motive, and the connection between the two: 'All neurotics are malingerers; they simulate without knowing it, and this is their sickness.

We have to remember that there is a big difference between conscious refusal and unconscious refusal.' In explaining the cause of the unconscious refusal, the neurosis, of mentally wounded soldiers Freud singled out conscription as a crucial element. For many men 'it was dreadful to have to submit to military treatment, and poor treatment by their superiors had an influence on many in our army and that of Germany. . . . it is also true that we had a people's army, that men were forced into military service, that they were not asked whether they liked to go to war, and that is why one has to understand that people wanted to escape [into illness].' The effect of malingering was wrought since 'in war neuroses the intention to stay sick is much stronger – not for pleasure, but to escape military service'. Freud basically presented 'a conflict of motivation, i.e., the desire of the ego to preserve itself safely and comfortably versus the desire to do one's duty according to one's own or society's standards'.[34]

Without necessarily accepting the psychological distinctions made by Freud – distinctions which allow for a deeper understanding of conscripts' attitudes – a similar conclusion was reached in Britain by a War Office committee that investigated the phenomenon and treatment of shell shock. At the same time, the committee had to contend with the singular case of the British wartime army, as composed of volunteers and conscripts; and the existence of shell shock in both populations. As a result, conscription was not mentioned in the discussion of the symptoms of shell shock; however, the lengthy examination of the correlation between shell shock and recruitment was framed entirely within this context: 'In recruiting a voluntary army the candidate attempts to conceal or minimise any factor which he thinks will prejudice his chance of acceptance; conversely, in recruiting a conscript army he makes the most of any disqualifying defect and suggests, or even tries to prove the existence of, unexisting defects. The mental attitude of the recruit towards military service is therefore a cardinal factor to bear in mind.'[35]

Like Haig's opinion, this conclusion appears to assume categorically that the First World War conscripts necessarily had a negative attitude to the army, especially in comparison to the volunteers, and that their motivation was low, or even non-existent. Although it is impossible to apply such a condemning assessment to a population amounting to more than 2.5 million men, it remains a fact that the option of volunteering was open to British men aged over eighteen for sixteen months. If an individual wanted to express his accepting attitude to the war and the army through personal enlistment, he could have done so. After this date all eighteen-year-olds were conscripted, though some were returned to the labour force for munitions work; and as the Military Acts progressed, so were the older men. And while the eighteen-year-olds are a singular group within the conscripts, in that they did not have the prior option of volunteering, it is also quite possible that if voluntarism had continued the majority of enlistments would have been from within their age group – since that had been the case during the period of voluntarism, especially in the labour force.[36] In other words, the question of motivation in young conscripts in Britain was valid in the abstract sense; whereas for the older men, those who had the option of volunteering, the issue was much more real. These men could have volunteered, but did not – for whatever reason.

This is not to suggest that conscripts were either unmotivated or unpatriotic. Rather, it is to place them within the wider context of the process they experienced, as men, and as human beings. As reflected throughout the book, their overall attitude to fighting and winning the war was undoubtedly positive, but that does not mean that they viewed the army, or their placement within it, in the same light. However, this work makes no claim that the conscripts were badly treated by the army because they were conscripts, or that the volunteers were treated better. The bitter truth was that once any man reached the front, his status was irrelevant: the war dictated reality, and it was up to each person to survive.

One of the reasons for the lack of research into the conscripts is the lack of obvious sources. As Kenneth Boulding put it, the 'task of the historian is always to make bricks without straw, to make what he believes are correct images of the past from an extremely imperfect sample of recorded data'.[37] The conscripts have left an exceedingly imperfect sample: there are only five published memoirs known to have been written by such men, and these cannot be deemed representative – either in number or in social class.[38] The class issue, in fact, is a problem with most of the First World War literature, since much of it was penned by middle or upper class officers. However, given the very small published sample, this problem is especially prevalent with the conscripts.

Frederick Voigt, for example, claimed his book was 'no more than a rearrangement of his diary and his letters home', with the narrative divided between eloquently formulated reflections upon his ideological convictions; muted tirades against his existence; and lengthy paragraphs of speech and dialogue uttered by his 'common' comrades: 'Gorblimey – when's this bastard life goin' ter end! When I think o' Sunday mornin' at 'ome wi' breakfast in bed an' the *News o' the World* wi' a decent divorce or murder, I feel fit ter cry me eyes out.'[39] Given there are many such passages of reported speech in the book, often much longer, Voigt must either have had an extraordinary memory, or he noted down each word as it was spoken, or else he recreated it later within his own cognisance of the speech. In any case, this is a rather impersonal memoir, with an approach akin to that of Professor Higgins listening to Eliza – out of his own personal fascination with a species rather than out of empathy.

Alfred Hale's memoir, as a comparative example, is far more interesting simply because it is so personal and focused upon himself, even if he was an upper middle-class musician, and rather pampered at that; in other words, definitely not an ordinary, working everyman. But for all that, he recreated only his own experience, from his own distinctive stance; being aware of other people only as a reflection upon himself and his situation. As such his work offers a higher degree of integrity, and an immense insight into the man and the manner in which he tackled his conscription, and the enforced transition from civilian into soldier. And on a much wider scale that is the purpose of this book, based on unpublished primary sources akin to the spirit of Hale's writings: diaries, letters and accounts, all drawn from the collections of private papers in the Imperial War Museum. However, rather than using these as 'authentic' illuminations of an authoritative text, they have been analysed and constructed into a narrative that remains, as far as possible, that of the conscripts themselves, in their own words. And in order to understand this process, it is worth considering the nature of the sources.

Diary — Of the three types of sources diaries are the most personal, in that the writer commits to paper his life as he sees it at a certain point in time, for his own personal use in the future. Army orders forbade soldiers of Other Ranks from keeping diaries when serving overseas, in case these fell into enemy hands. Diaries were therefore not available for purchase in France or Belgium, which means that the decision to keep a journal must have been made by the soldier before he left British shores – unless he were to have one sent to him from home, but this may have been kept from him by the army authorities. None of the diaries in this study commence prior to a soldier's enlistment, the first entries being made either on the day of induction into the army or, more commonly, upon crossing to the war zone. A number of soldiers started a journal only once they were in France, and since diaries were not to be found, they kept their chronicles in notebooks, army books or even on sheets of paper.

Most of the diaries cover only certain periods within a soldier's career, usually ending with the last date in the diary, unless extended on to notebooks or sheets of paper, and are often missing days, weeks or even months of entries. The types of entries also range widely, from a slightly elaborated timetable – such as 'January 12 1917, parade 3 o'clock a.m., entrain 5.30. Reach Southampton 12 noon. Embark 6 o'clock p.m.' – to a full narrative involving events and characters: 'July 9, 1917. Major says we get no pay till he finds out who made a hole in a water trough which the officers pinched from the men, so there is a general opinion of "no pay, no work".'[40] This immense variety in the form and content of the diaries suggests they were written by men unused to keeping a diary in their civilian life, who also often lacked adequate time to do so while in action. However, it also reflects that they viewed their military service, especially overseas, as a unique experience, isolated from their normal course of life – and as such worthy of preservation for future reference.

Letter — As with diaries, here also there are infinite combinations of form and content. The external form of a letter was basically dependent on the availability of paper and time, the soldier's location, and his writing skills. Indeed, a letter in this collection may be a few words scribbled in a trench just before going into battle, on a torn scrap of paper; a note on a page out of an army book; a complete narrative written on the back of a printed army form; or just a letter in its accepted form of words put together on notepaper. The content of any given letter was influenced by three major factors: censorship, the intended audience and the abilities of the writing soldier. Censorship prohibited any explicit reference by the soldier to his location, expected movements (in the rare event he knew of them), or military actions. Therefore no letter could convey the exact military experiences of the writer to the reader. The audience, be it family or friends, was always known to the writer (as opposed to an anonymous bureaucrat, for example), which means that all the letters were created within the context of a relationship. In other words, the letters were a sharing experience.

The army authorities regularly distributed field postcards which all soldiers in the ranks had to fill in by order. These were multiple-choice postcards printed by the army, on which the soldier had merely to encircle the relevant information, such as 'I am well' or 'I received your last letter'. And so, unless a major upheaval such as the spring retreat or summer advance of 1918 made this impossible, most soldiers managed to assure their families of their existence. However, no extra message could be added in handwriting, and since a field postcard could not be sent to anyone outside a soldier's family, a letter was really an optional form of communication used by a soldier who wished to preserve a more personal contact with his civilian life. As a result, the content of a soldier's letter may be seen as a compilation of his two identities: a civilian and a soldier. In the first instance it may refer to people, places and events which formed the mental and physical landscape of the soldier as he was prior to his conscription. In this way, communication was established by the soldier crossing back into the civilian world of the reader. But if, in the second instance, the soldier wished to share his new identity with a civilian reader, he still had to do so in terms understood by the latter. In other words, military experiences in the war zone had to be transferred into civilian terms in order to be understood by a civilian reader. Since this was very difficult, most of the letters studied here dwell upon human experiences, such as hunger and cold, far more than military and combatting experiences.

Written Account — The written accounts used here vary between one handwritten page recounting a single episode or period within the military career of a conscript, to several typed volumes covering his life. There are three salient points to consider in defining this type of source. The first is that, unlike diaries and letters, accounts were written after the event, and not in its midst or shortly afterwards. The second is that these texts were written for a wide and mostly anonymous audience. Put together, these two issues reflect that the writer probably sat in repose, carefully selecting the experiences and opinions he wished to impart to subsequent but unknown readers. However, it is the third issue, concerning the motivation for creating an account, which is most influential in determining the form and content it may take, because it addresses a basic question: why did these men bother putting pen to paper, years after the war ended?

An account is really a combination of self-reckoning and a subjective attempt at setting the record straight. Through letters, and possibly diaries, many of these men had attempted to communicate and present an account of themselves during the event itself. But such documents often did not include the whole story, not only due to censorship, but because some of their experiences and activities were untenable in their own eyes, and so unpresentable to civilian society. In sociological terms, a job could not have been well done 'had not tasks been done which were physically unclean, semi-illegal, cruel, and degrading in other ways; but these disturbing facts are seldom expressed . . . we tend to conceal from our audience all evidence of "dirty work" '.[41] Writing an account is therefore a means of cleansing oneself; a confession of sorts. Michel Foucault claims that since the Middle Ages it has been ' . . . a ritual in which the expression alone, independently of its external consequences, produces intrinsic modifications in the person who articulates it: it exonerates, redeems, and purifies him; it unburdens him of his wrongs, liberates him, and promises him salvation'.[42]

In the case of the conscripts, the confession is to the 'sin' of participating in the First World War. In an essay written during the war, Freud claims that civilians recoiled from 'the brutality shown by individuals [soldiers] whom . . . one would not have thought capable of such behaviour'.[43] And after the event, soldiers were once more civilians who had to live with themselves within a society that basically rejected their actions, even though it imposed them upon these men through conscription. Writing an account could thus be a means of confessing their deeds to society, and of explaining them.

Given these clarifications of the nature of the writings, it is clear that a correct reading of them enables a search for the person behind each one – and their identity. For in each case, an individual had an image of himself that was continuously being synthesised with the experiences he gained in his military capacity – from training through to combat. And so, in order to compile a collective image, each text or personal collection was read separately, and documented as such. However, each text was also read from a collective perspective, and documented within sixty categories of shared expression and experience. In this way, each sentence of each document could be, and often was, of value in several ways. For example, the following paragraph was documented in four different categories of shared experience:

Sunday services behind the front line were 'conducted by a dreary man in officer's uniform, plus a white dog-collar. He would ask God to look after us and biff the enemy, while only a few miles away an equally worthy, or unworthy, German priest was no doubt asking God to do for them all the things that our man was requesting for us. We had, after all, been sent here by a responsible government to kill Germans and they had been sent likewise by their leaders. If we happened to be in the trenches on a Sunday the biffing went on just the same as on any other day. Surely we were putting God in an impossible situation.'[44]

These sentences provide information on the organisation, content and importance of religious services in the British Expeditionary Force in France (compulsory Church Parade every Sunday, with a 'war-inspiring' sermon); on this soldier's attitude to the Germans (a country similar to Britain, with soldiers placed in a situation identical to his own); on his attitude to the war (initiated by 'responsible governments' in order to kill people of identical stature on both sides; within the overall context of this collection, the words were probably meant as ironical — especially with the reference to putting God in an impossible situation); and finally language (sniping, shooting and daily trench warfare are 'biffing').

By reading and documenting each text in this way, every category of experience and attitude became a small database which, when arranged in a logical manner, evolved into a narrative told by these conscripts, in their own words. In this method of research, analysis and presentation the personal element of each narrative was preserved, which informed the collective image that began to emerge. At the point in which the image of experience was eventually established, the definition of an identity became possible. The conscripts were finally revealed.

If to comprehend is the same as forming an image, we will never form an image of a happening . . . whose protagonists are in their essence invisible.

Primo Levi, 'Carbon', *The Periodic Table*

PART ONE

Civilian into Soldier

Awful years – '16, '17, '18, '19 – the years when the damage was done. The years when the world lost its real manhood. Not for the lack of courage to face death. Plenty of superb courage to face death. But no courage in any man to face his own isolated soul, and abide by its decision. Easier to sacrifice oneself. So much easier!

D.H. Lawrence, *Kangaroo*

CHAPTER ONE

Enlistment

'. . . beyond the release from boredom
there is the joy in uniforms which stimulates
war. The instinct for fancy dress is hard to kill . . .'

Hans Zinsser, *Rats, Lice and History*

In every army, and for every individual, enlistment and basic training are the basic rites of passage, from the status of civilian to that of soldier. From forms to uniforms, drill to discipline, they are the introduction to the mysterious world of the military, instilling frameworks and friendships that will enable each person – volunteer, conscript or officer – to exist in the army, and in battle.[1] However, in wartime Britain, it was the *process* of enlistment that was different for volunteers and conscripts: for the volunteer, it was an act of free will; for the conscript, it was a bureaucratic maze, marked by the lack of choice or control of the individual over his own fate. Moreover, the volunteer experienced the entire process at the recruiting station; the conscript was within the process long before he arrived there.

For the volunteer, both the decision to join the army and his physical presence at a recruiting office were an expression of personal desire. A classic summary of such a self-motivated process was given by one who volunteered in September 1914: upon seeing ambulances full of wounded men, 'I determined to join up that same evening. I went home, had a hasty meal, smartened up and duly presented myself at the HQ of the 24th London regiment.'[2] In direct contrast, the inner deliberations or self-motivation of the individual conscript were irrelevant. It was a state dictate, and a formal, printed summons, sent through the mail, which brought him to the recruiting office on a given date, regardless of his own thoughts or inclinations. The Military Service Acts of the First World War, which were the legislative tool that enforced conscription, reflected this clearly. In each, the specified group of 'male British subjects' were 'deemed as from the appointed date to have been enlisted in His Majesty's regular forces for general service with the Colours or in the Reserve for the Period of the war, and have been forthwith transferred to the Reserve.'[3] In other words, both the decision to enlist and the act of attestation were revoked from the sphere of the individual.

The supremacy of a state system over individual free will was well summarised in the following account: 'I was a Post Office Sorter from 1906 and was called up under the Military Service Acts June 1916 after having previously volunteered for the Army Post Office and withdrawing my application in 1915.'[4] The writer had clearly debated the issue of enlistment, and decided against it; but the introduction of conscription made his personal decision irrelevant. Being 'called up' was the formal notification that he was 'deemed' to have attested his willingness to serve in the army, and as such he was already a member of the Reserve force. In fact, it was at this point that both terms passed into common usage in the language, and officialdom. Army forms slowly began to reflect this change with the introduction of conscription in 1916, and by 1918 it had become standard. For example, there was a version of the attestation form clearly defined for 'men deemed to be enlisted in H.M. Regular Forces for General Service with the Colours . . . under the provisions of the Military Service Acts, 1916'. Printed on the form were also the two crucial articles, left open to be filled in with the appropriate dates: 'Deemed to have been enlisted' and 'Called up for Service'.[5]

The conceptual shift from free will to a printed summons actually necessitated a huge expansion in the process of enlistment, which encompassed far more than forms. Before the introduction of conscription the pre-war, rather limited system used for the regular army had merely been expanded erratically to accommodate the volunteers. Conscription meant that the bureaucratic machine had to be set in action much before an individual actively enlisted. First, a man eligible for conscription had to be singled out from the civilian population. Second, he had to be transferred on paper to the army Reserve Corps, which in effect marked his transition from civilian to soldier. Third, the newly conscripted man had to be informed of his new status, through a summons to the local recruiting office. In technical terms, this process was administered through the local authorities, with the aid of the National Register of August 1915. Copies of the registration forms pertaining to men between the ages of eighteen and forty-one (and those who subsequently reached the age of eighteen) were given to local military authorities by the local civilian ones. 'From these forms cards were prepared, three for each man, for use by the Area Commanders (white), the Sub-Area Commanders (red), and by local Recruiting Committees (blue).' In this way military registers were also created in each area, and these were kept in parallel with the local registers, since the local authorities notified the Area Commanders of all deaths and changes of address of men of military age. 'By these means the military authorities were kept posted as to the men available for recruiting . . . so far as the National Register was complete and accurate.' For their part, the military authorities informed the civilian ones if a man was called up for enlistment, or killed in action. The system was far from watertight, and communication between the two branches was often inconsistent, largely due to the multiplicity of forms.[6] And so, with the establishment of the Ministry of National Service in November 1917, the military and local registers were revised, as were the methods of communication between the two authorities. Since the National Register had not proven itself for industrial needs, all local registers were rearranged strictly on an alphabetical basis, regardless of occupation; and serial numbers, identical for both authorities, were given to the men's forms. These measures all made revisions and corrections of the two registers, military and civilian, easier. However, the actual system of calling men up through the local recruiting committees remained essentially the same.

It was undoubtedly a bureaucratic maze, which began with a registration form and ended with a call-up notice. More significantly, it was one which a conscript had been shunted through – without his consent and without his knowledge. In other words, he was completely passive. This may be seen, for example, in a diary entry for 14 February 1917: 'Received calling up notice from Croydon Recruiting Office.'[7] The diarist was a civil servant, probably in his late twenties when he was summoned. As such he was comparable to the volunteers who went before him, who disrupted their personal and professional life in order to enlist. In his case, however, his life was disrupted for him by the external force of an army summons while he remained passive.

The eighteen-year-old recruits, who usually joined up when they were eighteen-and-a-half, comprised another large section of the conscript population. Their enlistment was best typified by the following summary: 'In the December of the year 1916 I reached the age of 18. In the following March I was duly enlisted.'[8] In this case the conscript's professional life was not disrupted, since he had not yet created one. This was also true of the man who recalled that 'During the period 1914–1918 I was a quiet youth of a working-class family until the 5th May 1916, when at the age of 18 . . . I joined the 2/4th Battalion East Lancs Regiment'.[9] Passivity is apparent in both cases: the authors' age initiated a bureau-cratic process, yet as the focus of this process they were required only to comply with the orders sent to them. There was nothing personal, they were statistics: their age, gender and nationality fulfilled the prerequisites laid down by the state for the enactment of the bureaucratic process of conscription.

One option, open to young men who wished not to be identified as conscripts, was volunteering for a unit prior to their eighteenth birthday, then awaiting this date for actually joining up. For example, one young man, who wanted 'the pride of being a volunteer', found out that 'certain regiments were permitted to accept men who offered themselves at eighteen if they were physically fit. . . . Consequently, two days before my eighteenth birthday . . . I was enrolled as a member of the London Rifle Brigade.'[10] Another youth used this method as a means of controlling his placement in the army, and therefore volunteered for the Royal Flying Corps: 'It was 1917, and as I had no desire to be conscripted into the infantry when I was eighteen, having a strong desire to be an airman. . . . Just after my eighteenth birthday and while waiting for my call-up, I went over to Leeds to stay with my parents until that fateful day in early September [1917].'[11] The men who enlisted under the Derby Scheme may be seen as a combination of voluntarism and conscription: when canvassed in their own homes or offices the Derbyites attested their willingness to join up. In other words, they attested themselves, and were not deemed to have done so by the state; yet their free will was expressed as an answer to a question, and not as a self-motivated act. As a contemporary satirist put it, the issue was 'whether the necessary men are to be compelled to volunteer or persuaded to be compulsorily enrolled'.[12] However, once attested, they were treated exactly as conscripts in that they became the passive subjects of the bureaucratic process. This is well exemplified in the case of a man who attested under the scheme in November 1915. Being single, he was placed in Group 5, which was called up within two weeks of the first Military Service Act being passed. His employer appealed at the local tribunal established under the scheme, and he was moved to Group 10. But 'this availed me very little as the next ten Groups were called up together'.[13] A further appeal postponed his eventual enlistment to April 1916. It is thus clear that once an individual came into contact with the bureaucracy that eventually controlled conscription, his identity as either Derbyite or conscript was irrelevant.

There were, however, advantages to the Derby Scheme. Lt Edward Allfree, a solicitor with four children, happily attested his willingness to enlist under the scheme, precisely because it combined the act of free attestation with an externally imposed schedule. Allfree had not volunteered because he thought his familial duty superseded his patriotic one, yet he felt some guilt over the matter. The scheme allowed him to pay lip-service to his sense of duty to King and Country, in that he attested his willingness to join. Yet it also forcibly removed him from his family, without him actually having to initiate this action: '. . . the burden of deciding when one ought to enlist was removed from the individual'.[14] Thus in contrast to the conscripts, who were passive throughout the entire process of enlistment, Allfree and all Derbyites became so only after their attestation: 'There was now nothing to do or to worry about but wait until one should be called up. In due course I received notice that my group was called up, and that I was to join at Canterbury Barracks on 10th June, 1916.'[15]

The second stage of enlistment under conscription started when the individual attended the local recruiting office. In effect, it was this part of the proceedings that reflected equally upon volunteers and conscripts, since both were filtered through an identical system, comprised of four stages: completing an attestation form; undergoing a medical examination and classification; taking the oath of allegiance and the King's shilling, which was a day's basic pay for a private soldier; and placement in a military unit. At the end of the day, both also emerged from the recruiting office either as classified soldiers or as men officially and certifiably exempted due to incompatibility with military requirements. But the similarity is misleading, because in terms of status the two groups were totally distinct: the volunteer arrived at the recruiting office as a free man, who took the oath only if he 'accepted the conditions of service'.[16] As such he could actually depart the premises at any time, up to the point at which he was sworn in as a soldier. W. Cobb, the post office sorter discussed above, exercised this privilege when he withdrew his voluntary application form in 1915. In another case a group of men wishing to volunteer in August 1914 waited for three days in the crowds before Great Scotland Yard, the Central London Recruiting Depot, before deciding to leave and go in search of a less crowded recruiting depot.[17]

In contrast, the conscripts did not decide when to present themselves at the recruiting office nor when to leave it. Upon arriving at the office they were already attested soldiers whose time and movements were no longer under their own control. They were subject to the demands of the military authorities. The immediate implication of this situation was that from the moment they entered the recruiting office they could be

31

treated as new recruits, the lowest form of life in the army. An eighteen-year-old who enlisted in Worcester in December 1916 noted that 'the first bloke as I met on the parade ground was the old Sergeant-Major–the recruiting officer. "What the hell do you want?" he said. "Oh, I've come to join the Army, sir," I said.'[18] Another conscript recalls having 'my new khaki uniform more or less thrown at me and . . . told to report again in the morning'.[19] But at base, and in many cases, reporting to the recruiting station was merely another stage in the business of bureaucracy, extended much beyond anything experienced by the volunteers. Alfred M. Hale, a minor composer who was conscripted in 1917 after previously being exempted by the Navy, noted that 'my "calling-up notice" required my attendance at the Ealing recruiting office at 9 a.m. sharp on the morning of 1 May'. Hale did indeed present himself at the prescribed time and date, only to be interviewed by a recruiting officer who suggested he procure a rejection certificate from the naval authorities. He thus went across London to the appropriate office but failed to get the certificate. Thereupon his solicitor despatched a clerk to 'worry the Naval authorities' who sent him 'from pillar to post before he got an answer', which was still negative. This was the start of Hale's 'ordeal', in which dealings with bureaucrats played an immense part, as did the external constraints put upon his freedom. His eventual enlistment on 4 May led him to compare his experiences with 'a certain compartment full of convicts bound for Dartmoor I had once seen at North Road Station, Plymouth'.[20]

Alfred Hale was a patently unmilitary individual, and his descriptions may therefore be slightly exaggerated. However, all the descriptions of conscript enlistment portray the movements of the individual as a process of response to bureaucratic orders revolving around a series of papers procured from military clerks and doctors. For example:[21]

14 February 1917	Received calling up notice from Croydon Recruiting Office.
15 February 1917	Asked for permit from Croydon Recruiting Office to allow me to be medically examined in London.
16 February 1917	Obtained paper from Civil Service Rifles saying they are willing to accept me.

17 February 1917   Heard officially that I was to be released if fit physically for general service.

21 February 1917   Received permit and was examined and passed. Resigned from Specials.

28 February 1917   Joined up.

Each of these entries refers to some form of contact with bureaucracy – and this is the complete record as it was originally written, not an abbreviated version. It was the diarist who saw his enlistment as a bureaucratic process, initiated by the summons sent to him. And while he undoubtedly made an attempt to exercise some control over his fate by requesting a specific unit, the Civil Service Rifles, this was still done within the confines of a set procedure, governed by permits and forms.

The physical act of enlistment in the recruiting station began with the attestation form, which was composed of questions concerning the personal particulars of the individual conscript. This was probably the most important document created for each soldier, since it became the basis of his military service file: any information or forms pertaining to his life or career in the army were added to it throughout his service. There was no standard attestation form among the different branches of the Army, which tended to differ in both form and content. However, all recorded age, place of birth and/or address (parish/town/county), nationality, occupation, marital status, next of kin, religion, residential status and prison record. In the case of conscripts many of these details were already known and recorded because of the National Register of August 1915: the first summons they received was based upon the returns of the register; the completion of the attestation form therefore served more as a confirmation of their particulars. Within the military service file, it was this form which was most regularly updated with regard to matters such as promotions, transfers, health, wounds, participation in campaigns, subsequent decorations, and a summation of periods served 'abroad'. Personal particulars were also regularly updated, from changes in marital status and family composition (births and deaths), to the next of kin's address. The last entry on the form would always be the date and administrative reasons for discharge.[22]

Once all the particulars were confirmed, recruits passed on to the second and most crucial stage of the enlistment process at the recruiting station: the medical examination. Upon it rested the decision as to whether an individual would become a soldier, and if so what would be his classification for service. As they had already been attested, many conscripts viewed the entire process of enlistment as no more than the medical examination and its results: 'Examined and passed. Class A,' or 'Had a medical was passed A1'.[23] Given this emphasis, it is ironic that the medical examinations were notoriously superficial throughout the war. In the period of voluntarism the medical examiners were civilian doctors who were paid one shilling for every man they passed, and nothing for men they rejected. It is therefore hardly surprising that the examinations were rapid and cursory, especially in light of the urgent and permanent need for more recruits. During the conscript era the examiners were initially conscripts themselves and subsequently civilian GPs who were paid a flat rate of £2 per session, for the examination of thirty to forty men; but 2s 6d per man for the examination of fewer per session. Yet the pressures of time, the heavy influx of men and the need for soldiers still rendered many of the examinations inadequate.[24] The following testimony was entirely typical of the medical examinations and examiners, and the public perception of both: 'I went down [to the recruiting office] on Friday and passed the doctor who hardly looked at me.' Much also depended on the personality and attitude of the examiner: 'There was another doctor in the room whom I saw . . . [socially] today who says he would have rejected me at once: most unfortunate.'[25]

Before January 1916 the medical examiner classified a man as either 'fit' or 'unfit' for military service. In this way D.H. Lawrence, who had been called up early in 1916, was immediately exempted from service due to tuberculosis. In his novel *Kangaroo*, he summed up the process simply: 'He was summoned to join the army: and went. . . . Was medically examined in the morning by two doctors, both gentlemen, who knew the sacredness of another naked man: and was rejected.'[26]

But conscription and the ensuing reorganisation of manpower both within and outside the army brought in its wake a more detailed scale of fitness for service. The Department of Recruiting in the War Office issued new instructions that created an A, B, C system of classification, in which 'A' men were fit for general service, 'B' men were fit for service abroad in a support capacity and 'C' men were fit for service at home only. Each category was then graded in a scale of 1 to 3, the latter representing the weakest element.[27] Alfred Hale, for example, who had a nervous disposition and became flustered by the directives shouted at him in the eye-test, was initially classified as C2 and thus unfit for active service overseas. As the war progressed and the military classification standards deteriorated, he was upgraded and eventually sent to France.

Upgrading was very common, often reflecting the constant need for combat men at the front. Yet in some cases it was undertaken against army orders, and with little regard to the suitability and fitness of the soldier for active service. For example, in the summer of 1918 Brigadier-General Crozier specifically disregarded an order that B grade men should not be employed in 'offensive action', since he considered it absurd. In so doing, he effectively upgraded all those B men he placed in action to A1. In general, the lower-graded men did not respond well to the sweeping acts of upgrading. An officer of the Royal Welch Fusiliers who served on the Western Front throughout the war claimed that 'it was characteristic of men transferred from category units and subsidiary services to resent re-posting to front-line service, and to scheme to get away from it'.[28] In many cases it was the army authorities that instigated a mass upgrading due to sudden heavy losses at the front, or some other unforeseen circumstance. This also affected the youngest conscripts, who should have had some measure of protection through the Military Service Acts, in which it was stated that 'steps shall be taken to prevent so far as possible the sending of men to serve abroad before they attain the age of nineteen'.[29] In this way, the young A.J. Abraham enlisted late in 1917, yet in March 1918 he suddenly found himself in France: 'My Battalion was composed entirely of eighteen-year-olds, known as A4 boys . . . [who were by law] regarded as being suitable only for home defence until we reached the age of 19. A few days after the German breakthrough became obvious we were reclassified overnight as A1 and a draft list of about two hundred names went up on the Battalion Orders Board.' F.A.J. Taylor also claimed that this attack resulted in men being 'upgraded from C3 to A1, recently wounded men had their convalescent period cut short, leave was cancelled and from all parts of Britain men were hurriedly collected together and shipped across the Channel to fill the gaps'.[30]

The introduction of conscription did not really solve the problem of military manpower, and the standards of medical examinations fell even further in an attempt to get more recruits into the combat zone. The basic problem was that these questionable selection procedures produced an extremely inadequate class of soldier, a result which was ultimately useless to the army. The Royal Welch Fusiliers suffered heavy casualties in the first days of the battle of the Somme, and sent urgent requests for replacements. The condition of the recruits who arrived late in July 1916 reflects the cursory medical inspection they had undergone: 'Whether Volunteers, Derbyites or Conscripts, the average physique was good enough, but the total included an astonishing number of men whose narrow or misshapen chests, and other deformities or defects, unfitted them to stay the more exacting requirements of service in the field. Permission to send back a very few was accompanied by a peremptory intimation that a complaint of any future draft passed by the Base would not be listened to. Route marching, not routine tours of trench duty, made recurring casualties of these men.'[31]

Before conscription was introduced, men who were clearly unfit usually did not attest and were therefore not medically examined and exempted. Conscription made this process necessary, thereby putting even greater pressure upon the medical boards who were obliged to examine all men summoned through the bureaucratic machinery, even those who presented disability certificates from civilian doctors. This procedure is well illustrated in the correspondence between Captain Edward Gleave, an officer in the regular army serving on the Western Front, and his brother Humphrey, a medical student who suffered from colitis. In February 1916 the latter, who lived in Leeds, suddenly found himself enmeshed in the bureaucracy of conscription due to the January Military Service Act: 'I went down to the recruiting office again today. I saw the doctor. . . . He said he could not reject me on [Dr] Roberts' certificate because he did not reject anyone. I must attest and then if I had colitis I must apply to a board of 5 Leeds doctors, and they would probably exempt me. . . . If not the recruiting man declared they would give me light duties and peptonised milk and anything in fact: In which case I should be very glad to go but I am afraid we know the contrary. They are accepting almost anybody now: cripples, men with hernia etc., etc.'[32]

By mid-1917 the truth of Gleave's last remark had become apparent in all quarters. The pressing need for recruits had reduced selectivity to the exceedingly low point at which disabled and unfit men were enlisted and often also unrealistically graded. This was reflected in an autobiographical novel written by a teacher from Glasgow, in which the hero, Stephen Lethbridge, was summoned to a medical board in mid-1917. He had been exempted on medical grounds the previous year, yet due to the 1917 Military Service Act he was called up for re-examination. He was interviewed by a civilian doctor who 'asked the stereotyped questions. "Have you ever had fits? Have you ever been in a sanitorium? Have you ever been in an asylum?"' Based upon this interview, a brief medical examination and a certificate from Lethbridge's own physician, he was classified C3. Since teachers were only taken if they were B1 or above, Lethbridge was sent to the president of the medical board, a young military doctor. He glanced at the civilian certificate and asked if Lethbridge was in constant pain. Since he admitted to being in constant discomfort and only some pain the RAMC man recategorised him as B1.[33]

By the end of 1916 only 6.5 per cent of new recruits were rejected, while approximately 50 per cent of those taken were placed in grade A.[34] Both the army and the public felt outraged by these figures, which appeared to benefit neither the individuals examined nor the army. The standards of classification were therefore revised yet again in autumn 1917, after being reviewed by a select committee, which 'observed with disquiet the lack of public confidence in the medical boards'.[35] As a result it was decided to fundamentally restructure the procedure for the medical inspection of recruits, with the aforementioned reintroduction of civilian GPs working under civilian supervision. In turn the classification system was also changed from the A, B, C grades and inner categories to four single grades: Grade I incorporated all the previous A men; grade II had the B1 and C1 men, with all the remaining B and C men grouped together in grade III. Grade IV was for the rejected men who suffered from severe disabilities such as valvular diseases of the heart and epilepsy. This was undoubtedly a far greater degree of thoroughness, which was also reflected in the letter of a recruit from late 1917 who had suffered from measles and was passed on for a second medical examination in a hospital: 'I had a sort of double quarto white sheet filled up with my name, address, illnesses . . . and habits (including horse-riding and jumping, good cyclist and OTC work). Also were [*sic*] very keen about drinking (wine or spirit etc.) and smoking. . . [I saw a] 'Johnny' who examined me . . . I then went with some dozen other men . . . and was X-rayed and had an electrocardiogram taken . . . I was then tested for blood pressure etc. — had to whizz up and down stairs and then had my pulse felt.'[36] These new measures did much to ensure that obviously unfit men were not placed in Grade I and sent out to fight. Yet ultimately, fitness remained a relative term: such were the demands of war that military considerations nearly always overrode medical ones.

Once the attestation form had been completed, and the conscript had been medically examined and classified, he passed on to the third stage of enlistment in the recruiting office: taking the oath and accepting the King's shilling. After the lengthy bureaucratic stages of enlistment experienced by the conscripts – and in the case of the medical examination, often embarrassing too – the oath was an important mental focus. A solemn, personal moment of consideration, that gave the proceedings a considerable moral authority.[37] From that moment the conscript was officially a soldier on active service, as opposed to being in the Reserve Corps – but he had to be placed in a different unit: the fourth and final stage of enlistment in the recruiting office. This procedure should have been based upon the conscript's medical classification and, as far as possible, his own preferences. However, in the vast majority of cases, military requirements were the only true measure, given the need to despatch most available men to the front, either in a fighting capacity or as auxiliaries. Due to the evolving nature of the war and the rapid expansion of the British Army over such a relatively short period of time, this was the case throughout the war. Even in the period of voluntarism, a recruit's personal wishes were usually considered only if a lull in the fighting had temporarily reduced the urgent need for replacements at the front. In light of the limited choices open to the volunteers, it is clear that the conscripts' options would be narrower still. Indeed, part of the propaganda of the 1915 Derby Scheme was that if men attested freely they would be given a greater opportunity to express their own preferences regarding placement. Yet even this option was severely qualified: 'Although every endeavour will be made to allot them when called out to whatever unit in the service they may wish to join, no pledge will be given that their request will be gratified; and they will have to be allotted to whatever is in most need of their services.'[38] Overall, it seems that this was actually the policy applied to recruits throughout the war, including the conscripts.

As noted, the medical classification of a recruit decided his placement, in the broad terms of suitability for a combat unit. And so, given his grading was A or I, and he was willing to narrow his selection to fighting regiments, a conscript did have a few options: '[I] was given the choice of three infantry regiments. I chose the Rifle Brigade having a chum in that unit.'[39] The need for a familiar face was very often an influential factor in choosing a unit, and was also the logic behind the Pals Battalions which were created throughout the country at the beginning of the war, in an attempt to counter the anonymous and off-putting military framework with a familiar human landscape. At base, they offered a recruit slightly more options on service with friends. This was true also of local regiments, where similarity of background replaced personal friendship as an incentive for choosing them. Professional affiliation was another important factor, as in the case of the civil servant who requested permission to join the Civil Service Rifles.[40] This element, however, was viable for fit men only within the confines of combat units. An eighteen-year-old apprentice grocer, conscripted in 1916 and classified A1, asked to be placed in the Royal Army Service Corps, since he felt his experience would be useful there. But the army based their decision on other considerations: 'He [the recruiting clerk] frowned and said "full up", he then went on to say that drivers were wanted in the Royal Field Artillery, and as I looked a nice light weight, and came from a town full of horses it would be just the job for me. Without more to-do he produced a form, [and] took my name and other particulars.'[41]

In some cases a conscript was placed only some days after he had completed the enlistment process at the local recruiting station, especially if he had requested a specific unit for which he was fit and needed. Often this required a bureaucratic process beyond the capabilities of the local recruiting station, in which case the conscript had to pursue his case for some days:

20 February 1917   Examined and passed. Class A.

26 February 1917   Reported at Birkenhead. . . . Sent to Chester and passed for Civil Service Rifles. O.K. Went home for the evening.

27 February 1917   [Went to London early in the morning, to Somerset House.] Papers not arrived from Chester, so nothing done.

28 February 1917   Papers arrived am fitted out.[42]

The process of enlistment was at an end once the conscript was placed in a unit. The commencement of his military basic training marked his assimilation into the army as a private, much the same as a regular or volunteer soldier before him. But he had arrived at that point in a different way, through a new and extended process. The conscript experience, both before and within the local recruiting office, was basically a series of responses to the bureaucratic process. Conscription was meant to be the great social equaliser, in that all men were selected according to criteria of age and nationality, regardless of income or class. It was also meant to be more efficient. But ironically, the apparent lack of selectivity only served as a premise for yet further expansion of the bureaucratic machinery, since all men, be they fit and suitable for military service or not, had to be processed through it. The detailed schedules of exemption attached to each Military Service Act, for men either medically unfit or required in a reserved occupation, could release an individual from military service only after he had undergone the process of attestation and enlistment. In other words, the sheer volume of processing work increased several-fold, simply in order to fulfil the requirements of the Military Service Acts. But ultimately, it reflected little upon the efficiency of the system: this massive attempt at bureaucratic organisation for the benefit of the army and the nation was mocked by the very organism both were serving – the war. By its erratic and changing nature it often made nonsense of any attempts at method. For example, in the first day of the Somme campaign some 60,000 British soldiers were killed or wounded. This resulted in an overwhelming need for replacements in the field, regardless of the training, capability and suitability of those men available. They could have been volunteers or conscripts, athletes or cripples: at the front they were needed in the trenches, and that was the sole relevant criterion.

Two conclusions may therefore be drawn from the conscripts' enlistment experiences. The first is that their lack of choice was really limited to their initial transition from civilians to soldiers. Once within the army system they had very few options simply because the system itself often had none. Attempts at planning could be easily countermanded by the events of the war – mostly huge battles, including those initiated by the Allies, that cost much and gained close to nothing. In fact, as Norman Dixon put it, the British Army in the First World War resembled 'the saurians of a bygone age, huge in strength, massive in body, but controlled by a nervous system so sluggish and extended that the organism could suffer fearful damage before the tiny distant brain could think of, let alone initiate, an adequate response'.[43] This situation had affected the volunteers only once they had taken the oath and signed away their civilian identity. The conscript experience was different largely because the dictates affected them long before they donned uniform. In other words, the second conclusion is that the conscript's lot was worse than any of his predecessors simply because he started his army career as a name on a piece of paper, and was so treated throughout.

CHAPTER TWO

Basic Training

There's an isolated, devastated spot I like to mention
Where all you hear is 'stand at ease'
'quick march' 'slope arms' 'attention'
It's miles away from anywhere, by god it is a rumen
A chap lived there for fifty years and never saw a woman.[1]

The bureaucracy of enlistment wrought a technical transition in the status of the individual, from civilian to recruit. Basic training was designed to complete this process by advancing the recruit to the status of soldier. It was here that the civilian started to acquire a military image, if not stance. It is very difficult to establish a coherent pattern of the induction and training experiences of all the conscripts discussed here, largely because coherency was no longer a marked characteristic of the British Army by this point. In August 1916 it was decided to dispense with separate training schemes for each part of the BEF – the regular army, the Territorials and the New Armies – from which soldiers were despatched to them in a 'strand feed' system. Instead, a single, overall training scheme was created, organised in sequentially numbered units which fed the entire army. Within this framework, the general trend of transformation from civilian to soldier, first in base depots and then training camps, was the same for all – in the broadest terms of allocation of equipment, inoculation and military training of various types. However, the time and locations in which these took place, as indeed the length of the entire process of training, was extremely erratic. While one conscript spent three days at a base depot followed by three months in a training camp before being sent out to France, another passed through a depot in two days and then spent five months training.[2] However, as in the process of enlistment, this lack of uniformity reflected more upon the army as an organisation in constant mobility and subject to sudden dictates, rather than upon the conscripts themselves. That said, many of their writings offer little detail on training, possibly because it was a period of adjustment or else because it may have faded into insignificance in comparison to the vivid and harsh experiences of trench life. Some men totally ignored it, whereas others summed it up succinctly and blandly: 'I will pass over the months of training. What with physical "jerks", route marches, bayonet practice, firing, bombing and drilling I became much harder, both in body and soul and further I learned to swear with the worst of them.'[3]

The process of enlistment was completed once the conscript was placed in a military unit. In some cases he would immediately be marched away to the railway station and taken to a depot camp, where he would be kitted out for the start of his basic training. In others, conscripts were sent home after enlistment and told to report the next day, or days, for the commencement of training. Some recruiting offices were part of a military camp, in which case conscripts were given uniforms on the premises, and then sent home. Whatever the lapse of time, however, the army world became absolute to the conscript once he approached the train which would transport him to a training camp: 'The sergeant said "cheerio and the best of luck", we bundled onto the train and soon were off. I sat back and wondered what the future held, little did I realise then, that it held days which seemed like years and years that seemed like days and a nightmare.'[4]

For most conscripts the first days of training served as a period of double initiation: into the army as an organisation, and into the company of the fellow recruits with whom they would spend the following months, sometimes even years. Undoubtedly the two were interconnected, in that part of the 'culture shock' of joining the army was the novel human landscape. An easy process of socialisation could alleviate the disorientating and uncomfortable aspects of the unknown military experience, as in the case of a clerk who trained with the Civil Service Rifles: 'Am thankful am with a decent lot or it would be unbearable. As it is, don't find it too bad.' A young Scotsman who travelled with three friends was welcomed to the camp by a ferocious kinsman: 'Arriving at Dunbar . . . [we were] met in the squadron office by a sergeant major; I was greeted with "Whaur the hell do you come frae?" He was a Jamieson too.'[5]

Unfortunately, the inverse could also be true, with socialisation made harder by unsavoury company. An eighteen-year-old recruit from a genteel home in Harrow-on-the-Hill wrote his mother: 'I came up in company with 20 other weird blighters whose native haunts seem to be Stratford and Bow! . . . poor me, amongst twenty East-enders!' He felt his position worsen some days later when 'four new recruits [arrived] in our hut to-night – one of which is said to have just come out of prison for theft! Nice!!' Alfred Hale also found himself sleeping next to 'obvious jailbirds', and complained that the public were unaware of 'the emptying of the jails of the country and the mingling of decent men in labour camps with thieves and possible murderers'. One exceedingly religious conscript noted in revulsion: 'Many of my associates were unable to march to the station being under the influence of England's greatest curse: Strong drink, and so had to be taken to the station in conveyances.' To confirm his doubts regarding his new associates, it appeared that when this group eventually arrived at Stoughton Barracks 'we were described as the mysterious eighteen, as this number of the company had been lost'.[6]

The first stop for new recruits was at the permanent depot of the corps or regiment in which they had been placed. Here they would undergo an outward transformation into soldiers, and sample the rudiments of army life such as eating in mess halls, sleeping in huts or tents and squadron drill. Sometimes these camps were inadequate for the huge waves of new recruits sent there. 'During the War all regimental depots were like transit camps, men were coming and going all the time, meals were being served at all hours.'[7] One recruit recalled extra tents and huts hastily erected outside Fort Burgoyne, a large RGA depot, with men sleeping on the ground due to a shortage of beds or mattresses. Another man noted that 'we slept in an old barn for the first night with rats for company'. The eating arrangements were equally inadequate, forcing men 'to feed at tables set up outside the tents or in the huts, or to retire with one's food into one's tent and eat it there'.[8]

The first days in the army were the most difficult for any recruit, basically because they lacked any code of normality. Civilian life, and all its implications of home, society and occupation no longer applied, but the norms of military life had not yet been acquired. For the conscript this period may have seemed even more alienating since his reason for being there was not self-induced. Even a Derbyite like Allfree, who had willingly attested, felt himself to be a 'victim' by the end of his first day in the army. The eighteen-year-olds appeared to be most affected, since many had never left home before, regardless of their class or background. And even those who had been making their own way in the world from a younger age were unaccustomed to the rigid and impersonal framework within which they suddenly found themselves.

Their experience is best summed up by one who wrote that 'somehow, the prevalent feeling is – that I'm dreaming and everything is unreal!'[9] In fact, 'surreal' would be a more fitting description of the conscript experience at the regimental depots. The army world revealed itself to be total and self-sufficient, functioning according to codes that appeared similar to those accepted in a civilian society, while they were actually dissimilar. A name as a means of identifying an individual was replaced by a regimental number, each subsequent transfer to another regiment entailing a new number, and therefore a new identity. Clothing became a uniform, composed of unfamiliar garments such as tight breeches and puttees. Overcoats were rolled when unused, not hung up. Boots were intended for marching, not walking. Food was identified by a familiar name, yet tasted unlike any dish sampled in a civilian environment. A basin was used for drinking tea and not mixing food in. In short, much of the cognitive knowledge and comprehension of daily existence acquired by an individual throughout a civilian lifetime had to abandoned in one fell swoop. In its stead the conscript had to rapidly absorb the alien language of military life, if he were to survive in the army.

It appears the military authorities were aware of the problems of alienation, even if they were not necessarily defined as such. In some training camps there were 'Old Soldiers' who filled the role of mentor and guide to new recruits, by showing them the technicalities of military life, such as making up army beds and rolling on puttees. These men had usually been wounded on active service at the front, and were placed as room orderlies in training camps while recuperating. There were also defaults in the system that were helpful. Where names remained applicable, such as in the weekly pay parade, it was always in alphabetical order – a fact which often had more far-reaching social implications than envisaged, since it meant that men of a certain draft were always placed together in the same order. As a result, deep friendships were struck up: 'The chap in the bed next to me seemed quiet and reserved, but eventually we started to talk, his name started with "C" like mine, and as everything was done in alphabetical order in the army we always were able to keep together.'[10]

Despite the long and detailed process of enlistment at the local recruiting office, a large portion of the conscripts' experiences at the depot camp involved various bureaucratic and medical procedures. The individual's personal particulars were noted once again, after which he was allotted a regimental number.

Then came our medical inspection, and after stripping we carried our documents with us in the nude, queuing in the long hut. Here were several doctors and orderlies and clerks, as well as other victims like myself. One had to strip to be measured, weighed and sounded, and to hop across the room in a nude state, first on one leg then on the other. Your sight was tested, and all the various particulars about you were called out to a clerk, who wrote them on a buff form. I was eventually passed as A.1 and fit for active service abroad.[11]

Another conscript underwent his examination on the morning after his arrival in the depot. The corporal charged with his draft was anxious to be efficient, and thus ordered men to strip in readiness some minutes before they actually entered the examination room: 'When I eventually went into the MO I was all goose flesh . . . the stethoscope was soon on the back and chest, the limbs were tapped and pulled, the eyes and ears tested, the teeth examined and the Medical sergeant who was writing it all down on a form was told A1, will need attention to some teeth. . . . I do not think he held my testicles and told me to cough . . . perhaps it did happen to some men who complained or were suspected of having a rupture, it was of course a standing joke in the army'[12] The thoroughness of these descriptions reflects upon the poor esteem in which the medical examinations administered at the recruiting offices were held: all these men had already been examined and classified before their arrival at the depot, yet obviously these medical findings were considered doubtful by the military authorities who were responsible for training.

The physical transformation of a recruit was simply achieved, first with a haircut and then by placing him in a uniform. The experience in the barber's tent was best defined by one conscript, who put it succinctly: 'I had my hair cut: it was a prison crop.'[13] The matter of uniform was far more complex, concerning not merely the external, visible layers of dress, but every item of clothing required for the daily existence of an individual as a human being and as a combat soldier. A basic kit was: 'two tunics. Two pairs of trousers, one overcoat, cap, 1 pair of boots, three pairs of socks, two pairs pants, 3 shirts, knife, fork & spoon etc etc.'[14] In addition, the recruit was given rudimentary cutlery and a mess-tin incorporating a plate and a bowl, used for all forms of food and drink. The lack of a drinking utensil could be easily overcome by buying a tin mug in a local store, or having one sent from home. In either case it was important that the mug be a bright colour that would stand out and deter theft, which was very common.[15] A razor, toothbrush, shaving brush, button brushes and shoe brush were also supplied, and 'even a needle, cotton and wool to mend and darn, all in a canvas holder they called a housewife'. One rather pedantic conscript noted that the shirts and braces he was given were 'quite okay', but the pants were secondhand, as were the button brushes which were also 'rotten'. The socks were 'fair' and the cardigan was 'passable'. The razor, toothbrush and shaving-brush were all 'atrocious'.[16]

The kit was distributed and signed for by each conscript in the Quartermaster's Store, then the men were marched back to their barrack room or tent where their external transformation took place: 'We were told to take off all our civilian clothing and put on the things we had been issued with, and soon we were pulling on camphor smelling underclothes, and being artillerymen, breeches, puttees and tunics . . . it was confusing.' The conscripts' outward civilian identity was then literally packed away, when brown paper and string were distributed and the men were told to make parcels of all their clothes, apart from their boots. These were then mailed to the conscripts' homes. In some cases the paper and string were not produced unless paid for. Alfred Hale recorded the remarks of the postman who brought the package he had sent home: 'Come from Hounslow I reckon, I have delivered a few in this district and I know the brand. They make the recruit pay for paper and string and they make the Government – that's the public – pay too, but paper and string ain't forthcoming when the time comes. How the shoes and socks isn't dropped out and lost beats me.' Some men kept their own underclothes for use as pyjamas, which were not provided by the army, and as a comfort against the roughness of army issue clothing.[17]

The issue of belts was a problem encountered by some conscripts. They were an integral part of the official uniform, yet were often not distributed with the basic kit. Despite the triviality of this accessory, its absence was a great hindrance to a soldier due to army orders: 'I cannot go out of camp till I get a belt.'[18] This letter was written two days after the conscript joined up, yet he got a belt only three weeks later, which meant that throughout this period he could not leave the confines of the training camp. This may have been a military measure for imposing discipline upon new conscripts, by denying them access to civilian life. But another possibility was the presence of 'barrack rats' who absconded with equipment, or corrupt quartermasters who sold the belts to recruits who wanted to leave the camp, instead of distributing them with the basic kit. The Quartermaster at Dover Castle was one such individual, who blatantly demanded a bribe in exchange for a belt. The conscripts eventually organised a stampede on the Quartermaster's Stores and everyone got a belt without leaving a 'tip'.[19]

The conscripts still had to be issued with further kit and equipment, but this could be done either at the depot or at a subsequent training camp, in accordance with the variations of their training schedules and the fluctuating ability of the army. For example, one conscript got his uniform in the depot on the day he joined up, yet his boots were issued only twelve days later, at a training camp. At this time he was also issued with a 'second-hand tunic and trousers for use on fatigues and other dirty work'. A week later he got his 'equipment': 'belt, haversack, pack, ammunition pouches and braces, bayonet prop, rifle sling, entrenching tool and handle etc.'[20] Another conscript claimed he got his entire kit of uniform and equipment during the three days he spent at a depot in Chichester, whereas a third recalled getting his uniform only after three weeks, while at a permanent training camp, and at last 'felt like a real soldier'. Lt Allfree spent his first ten days in the army wearing the civilian suit in which he enlisted, since no uniform was forthcoming; while his boots 'wore out with continually marching about on rough gravel.'[21]

A conscript remained at the depot only for a period of days, two weeks at the most. Once he was in uniform, the medical examination completed and a regimental number allocated, the main function of this station in his training had been completed. One man recalled spending just a few hours in a depot, being kitted out on the spot and then moving on. Very few regretted leaving these camps, which were exceedingly anonymous and alienating: 'You were nobody's child here – you belonged to no particular unit and no one took much interest in you.' And so, following the system established by the training of Kitchener's New Armies, recruits would be sent on to the training centres from the depot in groups, where they would be organised into battalions and other units.[22] Once arrived in these centres, accommodation and food became the focal point of the conscripts' experiences, largely because they were basic to their life, not just to their military existence. Both issues were also crucial in forming the conscripts' attitude to training and army life in general. If the sleeping accommodation was comfortable, and the food good, or at least palatable, the attitude would be far more favourable than if the reverse were the case. Moreover, an individual expected to find solace in food and sleep, and felt himself to be cognisant with these issues from an early age. If he was faced with unknown elements of both, his feelings of disorientation might be much increased.

Due to the difficulties in creating enough training camps for the huge influx of recruits throughout the war, accommodation often posed a problem for the army and therefore for the conscripts. The most common form of army housing was in huts, specially erected for this purpose, and bell tents. The latter, however, were inadequate as long-term accommodation under harsh weather conditions. In camps in which no other solution could be found, men were sometimes billeted with local families during the winter. Army policy was against this solution as it was deemed expensive in comparison to hiring buildings or constructing camps.[23] The conscripts, however, usually enjoyed the experience since it ensured home cooking, a clean bed, and a warm attitude: 'we were very kindly treated.' Housing in proper buildings was also considered a stroke of exceptional luck by many who had lived in huts or tents. These, in turn, appeared luxurious to the conscripts who were housed in a closet pan factory while training in Queensborough. When in production, the factory moulded the pans, which were then left to dry on racks made of battens and wooden uprights:

> The uprights were about 6 feet apart, the shelves were about 4 feet wide between the aisles and about 2 feet above each other. There were four or five tiers. . . . Each of two large sheds held about 250 men. . . . We were given one section of rack each to stow kit and sleep in. This worked out to a space 5'9' × 2' × 2' so it was close packing. We were baked in summer and frozen in winter as in the latter case no heat was provided . . . a convict prison would have been preferable as regards accommodation. It was a vile place. Huts or tents would have been paradise but anything was good enough for common line troops.[24]

Even if one was not housed in a factory, lack of space was a prevalent problem. In August 1914 the army had accommodation in barracks for 174,800 men. This meant that with the first wave of volunteers 'the cubic space allowed per man was reduced from 600 cubic feet to 400 cubic feet',[25] and often far less. In a Machine Gun Corps training camp in Grantham one conscript noted: 'Slept four in three beds.' The beds themselves usually comprised some kind of straw mattress placed on a wooden board: '[My bed] consists of 3 horse-rugs I should call them, and a sort of straw filled sack for a mattress, lying on three boards raised about 6 inches from the ground. Also a sort of bolster stuffed with rotten straw.' Training camps that dated to pre-war days also had iron bedsteads: '[These] were in two parts and the bottom half was pulled out until it met a slot which secured it to make a six foot length bed with six legs. There were three small air mattresses which fitted the bed and a paillasse [*sic*] stuffed with straw for a pillow, two blankets one to hold the mattresses in position and one for cover. These blankets stunk of sweat and camphor.'[26]

Food and meals were the best documented issues in the writings of these conscripts, since natural appetites were much enhanced by the physical rigours of training. The army provided its recruits with three meals a day. Breakfast was usually bacon or kippers with bread, either on its own or with margarine or dripping, and tea. Lunch, or 'dinner', comprised meat in some form, such as pie, stew or boiled beef, which was always accompanied by potatoes and often also another vegetable. If a pudding was served it was 'watery boiled rice with currants or raisins floating about in it . . . one sometimes got bread pudding or a slab of jam tart'.[27] Tea, served at the end of a day's training, which was usually in the late afternoon, was always a slab of bread with jam and margarine, accompanied by tea.

In absolute terms the quantity and quality of army food was probably questionable, but put in the context of civilian expectations it became an interesting class indicator. A somewhat privileged young conscript wrote: 'This morning we had for breakfast a concoction which was described to me by my neighbour as 'troipe and onions' — none use [*sic*], *I COULD NOT*, so went on bread and margarine.'[28] Another eighteen-year-old conscript of a lower middle-class background claimed: 'With regards to grub it is very good considering we are in the Army, we have pudding of some description nearly every day for dinner besides some sort of meat & vegetables so it is not bad is it? it is better than I thought for.'[29] With the passing of time most conscripts got used to army provisions, yet food remained crucial in determining a conscript's attitude to his training experience. For example, a conscript who had apparently quite adapted to camp life was moved to another training camp after two months in the army, whereupon he noted: 'Absolutely fed up . . . grub awful, served in the hut. Milk pudding more like soap.'[30]

The quantity of food available was a much more serious issue. In his book, F.A.J. Taylor recalled that as an eighteen-year-old recruit he was permanently starving, a situation which was worsened by all the physical exercise in training. He often assuaged his hunger by scrounging from canteens and shops, and slipping into two sittings of dinner. In most camps the rations were sufficient, at least as a basis that could be supplemented by food parcels from home or the offerings of the YMCA hut. But this was not always the case. Taylor noted that late in 1917 'all hell broke loose . . . [with] the stamping of hundreds of hobnailed boots on the wooden floor' when the daily ration of a slice and a half of bread was cut to one, and then replaced by two biscuits. The next day bread appeared once more on the tables.[31] Another man wrote of

> a riot on Wednesday over the food question. They have been cutting it down, it was bad enough on the march but its been getting worse & on Wednesday a lot of chaps broke out & we had to get a lot of fellows . . . with fixed bayonets to go & break up the rioters. They raided all the canteens of the different regiments . . . until the bayonets came on the scene & that ended the trouble without bloodshed . . . & *incidentally* the food has increased so it has done no harm in one way, but it was rotten while it was on.[32]

The writer was an instructor in a training camp, and later an NCO, who was conscripted in 1916. His observations, written in mid-1917, actually reflected upon the basic problem of feeding the conscripts in training, since men who were already in the battlefield had first priority in the allocation of food, and even they did not always receive sufficient supplies. For at base, the real problem was the food shortage in Britain by this stage of the war. Potatoes, sugar and butter were commodities in short supply, while the price of meat rose dramatically. By April 1917 the purchasing power of 10s was the equivalent of 3s 6d. before the war; and early in 1918 food rationing was introduced. And the situation was not aided by conscription, through which 20 per cent of agricultural labourers were removed from the field into the army – in addition to the 15 per cent who had joined as volunteers – thereby further diminishing food production.[33]

Even in camps in which the meals served were satisfying, the problem faced by all conscripts was that no food was provided after tea. Throughout the evening men had to supply themselves or go hungry: 'I soon learnt what Army grub was like, and the whole of my money went in food to make up for the wretched grub we received.' Three main solutions to the problem were available: food parcels from home, teashops in local villages, or the resident charitable hut, such as the

Salvation Army or the YMCA. Most men appeared to have received parcels, and it was the habit to share these with one's room-mates: '[I] have had one half [of an apple pastry sent by his mother] for tea today – of course I had to share it with those near at hand.' The parcels represented a much needed link with home, while village life and the tea-shops offered a comforting glimpse back into civilian life. One conscript recalled that 'Mrs Watson's wee sweetie shop alongside the billet did good business from the frugal earnings of the troops'.[34] Alfred Hale wrote of a cottage near his camp in Thetford, where suppers for the troops were provided at a reasonable price: 'There I had a good meal of eggs and bacon with a cup of coffee, the whole not badly cooked or served by any means. I had supper at this cottage most evenings while at Thetford.' Another conscript, who had been in the army for some weeks, wrote to his family of a 'novelty' in restaurants in Mansfield: '. . . hot meat pies and peas . . . and a very nice dish it is for 4*d*. I sampled two plates last night. . . . We have not had very large meals today yet, but two previous days, our food has been alright, but we can't rely on it and ten to one it's short when we are hungry.'[35]

This latter comment made the recreation huts provided by a church or charitable institution an indispensable fixture in all army camps, including those overseas. A cup of tea and a bun for a penny a piece, besides much else – such as twelve or fourteen stewed prunes for 2*d* – could be purchased there. Soldiers of all classes considered them a solace: 'I should like here to pay tribute to and express my appreciation of the Y.M.C.A. who provided . . . large recreation huts where food and refreshments, and one might say all the necessaries of a soldier's life could be purchased at the most moderate prices . . . They provided a need for soldiers that the government made no attempt to supply.' The final option for obtaining supper after hours was not always open to all soldiers: '. . . after I have written this [letter] . . . I'm going to adjourn for my supper at fourpence ha'penny per pint.'[36]

Purchases were made possible due to the weekly pay parade, which was another focal point of the conscripts' existence. The basic rate for a private soldier was one shilling per day. For many this was the only source of funds to which they had recourse, which made the cheap rates of the YMCA hut most appealing. Others, who were luckier, had supplementary funds sent from home – often as 'enclosures' to letters – while older men of professional or social standing, such as Hale, had an independent income: 'How I recollect procuring pen and ink and sitting at a table trying to write a cheque, as I wanted some money from the bank, or to pay a bill perhaps. Fancy a private like me with a cheque book! Why, only officers had banking accounts and cheque books.'[37]

At first sight, especially to those unused to earning a wage due to their age or social class, the system of payment appeared confusing: '[it] is very complicated. Apparently one never gets one's exact amount of pay, it is sort of debit and credit idea.' The writer was an eighteen-year-old, from a genteel family, who had suffered poor health prior to his conscription and throughout his training, a matter which caused him even further worry regarding his pay: ' I hear that I *do* get paid for hospital – so there will be about 4/- due to me – *when I get it*, which will probably not be for two or three weeks.'[38] In fact the pay parade, which took place every Friday, was very simple and methodical:

> When we draw our pay, the Company lines up in platoons and each platoon sorts itself out into alphabetical order. Some weeks one platoon is paid first and the following week a different one . . . Some weeks the A's go first and others the Z's, so it is always a bagatelle as to whether you will get finished early or not. When your turn comes you file up to a table where an officer and a sergeant are sitting. You remove your hat, and shout your name and regtl. no. [*sic*] (in a loud voice). The sergeant looks at a list and says 'seven shillings' to the officer. You present the flat part of your hat to the officer and he places thereon the named amount. You say 'thank you Sir' and hop it. We march through pretty rapidly when the marching gets oiled.[39]

Lt Creek, a young conscript who joined the regular army after the war, claimed the alphabetical system was not so egalitarian: 'Being a "C" was a big advantage as one was always near the front for pay . . . during the whole of my service I only knew the "W"s to start first once.' Pay day was also the occasion in which deductions owed the army by a soldier were made. One conscript had a pair of boots stolen in his first week in the army, while they were displayed for parade. 'Although I had carried out orders I was compelled to pay 27/6*d* for a new pair, at a rate of 2/6*d* per week, and as the officer changed from one pay parade to another during the eleven weeks an explanation had to be given as to why I was restricted to one shilling, the obligatory minimum which any soldier had to be paid.'[40]

A medical experience common to all conscripts was vaccination and inoculation. The anti-tetanus vaccination was given within days of joining up, usually even in the depot camp; the anti-typhoid inoculation was administered in the following weeks, but no longer than a month later, in a training camp, with a second one, if needed, some weeks afterwards. A typical schedule for these injections was noted by one conscript in his diary: 'Enlistment, 7.8.1916; vaccination, 21.8.1916; first inoculation, 8.9.1916; second inoculation 6.10.1916.' Not all recruits needed both vaccination and inoculation, since childhood vaccination was sometimes adequate in later life; indeed, only two conscripts record receiving both. And, as ever in the army at that time, military requirements could also decide the medical schedule, as in the case of the conscript whose draft was suddenly rushed to the front: 'Were to have been vaccinated on the left and inoculated on the right arm. Only the latter was done.'[41] Though it is clear none of the men knew what they were being inoculated against, the event was singled out in the minds of most conscripts. This is probably due to the feeling of physical discomfort the procedure evoked, especially after the inoculation, and the accompanying rest period. Most men 'suffered in varying degrees some painful but temporary after effects'. the most common affliction being a stiff arm. For this reason drafts were left to rest, given sick leave or put on light fatigues for the following forty-eight hours. One man even noted going on a furlough after inoculation.[42]

The need for inoculation alongside other measures for the preservation of public health in the army, and especially the training camps in England, was clear in light of the many references to epidemics of various kinds. One conscript noted that 'Ripon [training camp] was many times placed out of bounds owing to outbreaks of contagious disease'; whereas another recalled his hut being in isolation, because one of the men was a disease carrier. After two weeks the original forty men were reduced to twenty, but rations were still supplied for the original number: 'That fortnight was probably the only time I spent in the British army when I was full to repletion.'[43] Men were conscripted from the entire spectrum of British society, regardless of the cleanliness of their homes or the history of disease in their area. This meant that despite the various medical examinations described above, it was clearly not always possible to isolate a man carrying an infectious disease such as measles or spotted fever (also known as spinal meningitis, a highly infectious and deadly illness). Moreover, due to the clause providing for conscientious objection in the 1907 Vaccination Act, and its application to the army, it was not possible to enforce inoculation upon every individual soldier.

From the start of the war questions were raised on this issue in Parliament; and Lord Kitchener put out an appeal for inoculation to all men who enlisted, quoting the casualty statistics from typhoid during the Boer War (from 57,684 cases 33 per cent (19,454 men) were invalided, and 13.9 per cent (8,022 men) died). The debate continued throughout 1915, and even after conscription was introduced the House was assured that 'a soldier who is deemed to have been enlisted under the Military Service Bill will not be deemed to have consented to vaccination'.[44]

Given the crowded conditions of the training camps, the danger of epidemics was much increased. And so the need to isolate those afflicted by a disease was coupled with the need to preserve the health of the remaining men: 'There are a few cases of measles in the camp and there is some talk of isolating the camp. If so we may not be allowed to send letters. They take great care of us and we gargle our throats night and morning and snuff disinfectant up our noses at the same time to kill the germs.' Another conscript claimed 'we gargle with Condy's Fluid twice a day' as a precaution against spotted fever, since several men afflicted with it had been isolated in the camp. In these cases the measures were effective and the fear of an epidemic passed. Another conscript recalled being less lucky: a week after his draft arrived at a training camp in Dover, an epidemic of spotted fever broke out. All the men were confined to the barracks for three months, at the end of which time eighty men had died. A week later the entire camp was put under confinement for a further two weeks due to an outbreak of scarlet fever.[45]

The interaction, both social and sexual, between the conscripts and the civilian population in England posed further possibilities for the spread of disease – and therefore also epidemics within camps. Besides visits to shops and tea-rooms in local villages or towns, men also went on home leave or furloughs, so making contamination from a distant location possible. The nature of these writings means there were very few references to sexual activity by the conscripts, which is to be expected: it would not be deemed acceptable to write to one's mother about sexual experiences, nor to recall them in a memoir written for an audience of strangers. The only explicit reference to the issue is made by Alfred Hale, who wrote that many men in his camp were 'carrying on . . . to the extreme point of sexual intercourse . . . [with] girls of the prostitute class'. Another man claimed more coyly that next to the factory building in which his unit was billeted was the house 'of a notorious female "the Black Diamond" [who] was so attractive to one eighteen-year-old, that . . .

he married her, who was old enough to be his mother'. The two other references to sexual activity found in these texts were written by men conscripted at the age of eighteen, who found the matter shocking: '. . . to be a "real" soldier I was told that I must get syphilis or some such disease . . . I was determined never to become a "real" soldier.' Much the same sentiment was expressed by the young man who was sent on guard duty in a VD camp, where the inmates exposed themselves in order to shock him.[46]

The army was clearly aware of the problems of disease, whether sexual or otherwise, and besides precautionary measures also imposed severe confinement upon men who were carriers:

> One night after being allowed home on evening leave, I was found to be a carrier of Spotted Fever. For a week I was incarcerated in a cell beneath the Tower Bridge Road, and at the end of that week I was found to be a victim of German Measles, and was taken to a fever hospital in Homerton. When I recovered I was allowed home on sick leave . . . [that same evening] I received a telegram informing me that I was to report at once to a Military Hospital in Mitcham . . . I was one amongst about 200 other men from all regiments, and at last after six weeks I was returned to my regiment . . . as a clean patient.[47]

'Clean' may also be taken in its literal sense, as a measure for the preservation of public health in training camps. One conscript, who was exceedingly worried about cleanliness due to a bad skin rash, noted that all new arrivals in his training camp had to have a bath, and that 'it is ABSOLUTELY COMPULSORY for everyone to have at least one bath per week'. But neither of these claims are repeated in any other writing examined here. Moreover, when this conscript moved to another training camp he complained about not having a bath for over a week: 'Apparently we have to wait till we are told to have one – and they do not seem to care much when you have one.'[48] Yet the army did appear to provide bathing facilities in the camps: 'There are little baths about 3 ft square and about one and a half ft deep. Then there is a shower above and you can have hot or cold water. It seems an awfully easy way to bath. You just soap yourself over and let yourself get under the rain.'[49]

In general, there were relatively few references to bathing or related activities in these writings, beyond the daily habit of washing and shaving – and the latter was an army regulation: 'They're fearfully keen on your being quite hairless about the chin!' In fact, shaving proved to be a problematic issue for some men. Those with foresight, and money, brought a safety razor with them upon enlisting, or had one sent to them, since the army issue razor 'could cut fast enough, and no mistake'.[50] Some men were used to being shaved in a barber's shop, and so had to learn how to shave themselves. For them an afternoon break in a local village brought great respite, since it offered a visit to the barber and a shave, rather than a struggle with the razor.

Laundry was a further aspect of cleanliness which was little referred to in the writings of these conscripts. As with bathing, awareness of this subject appeared to be linked to a class-related civilian habit. Men, and especially the younger ones, who were accustomed to bathing and a regular change of clothing prior to their conscription, made a point of trying to preserve these habits as soldiers. As a result, most of the references to washing in these writings were mostly from young men who wished to impress upon their mothers that they are still looking after themselves properly, in the manner in which they had been brought up: 'You ask me about the under flannel, I have given the one I had to come down in to one of the corporals along with my other washing . . . [he] takes the washing home to his wife.' The army made provision for the laundering of five military garments per soldier. Men who required more items washed, usually their own underwear, often mailed them home for this purpose, or paid for them to be laundered by local women.[51] Indeed, it is most likely that the conscripts' lack of documentation of their laundry arrangements reflects upon its being 'women's work' in which they had little interest.

Uniform, food and laundry were not the purpose of basic training – though they ultimately interested the men far more – but rather the framework within which they spent their days in various forms of drill, route marches, lectures and fatigues. In essence, the military training experienced by the conscripts differed little from that received by the volunteers before them, or in any professional army at that time, which meant that the first weeks were devoted to squadron drill. This was in order to instil the basic cohesion and obedience needed to activate various and complicated paradigms of behaviour, with the aid of short and simple instructions.[52] In addition, drill also helped in the external transformation of civilians into soldiers, giving them a military bearing and often also the feeling of belonging to an army. And for an army charged with creating combat soldiers in the shortest possible time, this was undoubtedly an important priority.

On the whole drill was considered 'a most tedious occupation, and when you were breaking in new Army boots it was a most painful one also'. However, given the uneven and often poor physical condition of many conscripts, great emphasis was laid upon it, as preparation for a much increased and varied training schedule: 'We have been on musketry to-day, gas drill, bayonet fighting etc.' 'Route march 12 miles, afternoon, physical drill.' One conscript summarised five months of training in one sentence: 'We had grenade throwing, firing rifle grenades, night ops, gas drill, bayonet fighting and firing on the range.'[53] However, it appeared that the conscripts' physical condition improved at a slower rate than the ever-increasing rigours of the training schedule: 'I think what made me feel queer was a route march which we went for yesterday morning we started about 8 & got back about half past eleven, we marched nearly 9 miles altogether so you can guess with drill again all afternoon, & gas drill for an hour in the evening that it was enough to knock me up.' The writer was John Thompson, an eighteen-year-old, and thus supposedly one of the fitter conscripts. Yet he had enlisted just over three weeks before writing that letter, clearly an inadequate period of time in which to improve his physique. But one week later the training load was increased further: 'We have been doing some skirmishing to-day, one side attacking the other in other words a sham battle, & it does take it out of you rushing up & down hills falling down etc etc . . . they do rush us through our training & no mistake.' For an older man, such as Frank Gray who was conscripted in 1917, these physical exertions were even harder for a 'man of forty, or approaching that age, who has turned soldier probably after six years of sedentary life and little exercise, when he falls over three strands of barbed wire in twenty yards is very far from laughing when he picks himself up'.[54]

Skirmishing, as Thompson relates, incorporated within it another important aspect of training: 'We were in two tanks facing one another, and were strictly enjoined by the instructor to look as fierce as possible!! Can't say I am particularly in love with basic training at present – it's too much like the real thing!'[55] Thompson's dislike of the fierceness which brought him closer to the 'real thing' probably stemmed from two major human impulses: aggression and the fear of death. The endless and repetitive drills in an environment similar to a battlefield were designed to increase the former and diminish the latter. And to this extent, a soldier who received insufficient training actually suffered mental inadequacies in battle, alongside physical ones. Aggression is an inherent instinct which is suppressed within the individual throughout his upbringing. An order to show aggression is therefore basically an entreatment to discard a lifetime of inhibitive conditioning.[56] But once released, aggression must also be trained in order to be of use to an organised armed force – especially if its supposed target is in a trench many yards away, since it is quite difficult to create feelings of hostility to an unseen enemy. At the same time, aggression is of an exceedingly individual nature, and its training must also be directed towards group cohesiveness, while ensuring it is focused only upon the enemy. This explains why in the exercise described above the men were first organised into groups and then enjoined to be aggressive. But at base, drill is about instilling discipline, which is a tenet of military life: to induce the hierarchical acceptance of orders, and to ensure that the exposed aggression is not turned upon the individuals within the hierarchy. In other words, this part of military training rests upon a paradox: half the time is spent exposing and refining the instincts of aggression within the recruit, whereas the other half is spent drilling severe obedience, and the repression of aggression, into him.

Work fatigues, apart from being a source of labour within the camps, were another intrinsic part of military discipline that did much to instil a sense of hierarchy, and especially the private soldier's place within it. A cookhouse fatigue, which was a 'rotten dirty job', or days spent moving 20,000 blankets,[57] left an individual in little doubt as to his standing. All soldiers also suffered from that part of army discipline known as 'bull', and the conscripts were no different:

6 May 1917   Realise what army discipline really is. Wind up properly.

7 May 1917   Another day of strict discipline. 3 hours squad drill, slow march . . . Officers and N.C.O.s proper terrors.

14 May 1917   Particular grievance today. Sergt. Roper made us double round for quarter of an-hour. Result everyone up in arms. What's the use though.[58]

Within this description of discipline it is interesting to note the opposing emotions of 'wind up' and 'what's the use'. That these were expressed within the space of a week may point to the effectiveness of that element within discipline which imposes fear of punishment. It may also reflect a slow adaptation to military codes. However, taking the last comment in the entry of 14 May, there is also a possibility that in the case of the conscripts the imposition of a military identity was much more difficult to establish.

Basic military training lasted for approximately six weeks. At the end of this period recruits went on to receive professional training within a particular branch of the army. As noted in the previous chapter, the corps within which a conscript would serve was usually decided upon in the recruiting office. In some cases this could be a military specialisation, such as artillery, which meant the entire process of training would take place within one camp. In others, the selection of an exact profession would be decided upon during training. Here also choice was sometimes possible: One conscript, who had enlisted in the Civil Service Rifles, 'went to Avington Park [during first weeks of training] for examination for Machine Gun Corps. Decided to join.' Yet in most cases military considerations, of some sort, ruled the day: 'I was posted to the 9th Battery & being just over 5 feet 6 ins [*sic*] became a gunner. Those below 5 ft 6 ins were drivers.'[59]

The training period laid down for Kitchener's New Armies was six months, yet according to the writings examined here in which the length of training was noted, five months was the average.[60] But as with the entire process of enlistment and training, the rule became but a vague guideline in the face of developments in the battlefield: some men enjoyed a complete course of training which 'lasted for nearly 5 months . . . [at the end of which] I was regarded as a fully trained gun layer'. Others, like H.L. Adams, were sent out to France with just three months' training: he was conscripted on 6 November 1916, and departed on 9 February 1917. In some cases professional courses would be completed, but essential training in trench warfare would be hurriedly sped through because of an imposed date of departure: 'Went through gas and threw bombs in the morning, thus compressing our 8 weeks course into half a day.' If the state of war permitted, supplementary training would sometimes be given in the base camps surrounding Etaples in France. The issue was probably best summarised by a Derbyite who enlisted in mid-1916: 'I was fortunate in getting full training – later in the war over-young conscripts were being sent to the front with criminally little training and experience.'[61]

The final two weeks of training were spent preparing for the imminent, though unspecified departure for France: 'They tell us that we shan't go across till Friday now, but it is like everything else in the army, we don't know until we wait & see . . . [today we were] making wills & doing other pleasant jobs.'[62] Spare kit was also handed in, and combat kit issued: a gas helmet with box respirator, caps, goggles, vests, body belts, field dressings and steel helmets. War kit inspection would follow, and often also a ceremonial parade before a high-ranking officer. This last was obviously meant to inspire the men by making them appear important in the eyes of a dignitary. Yet conscripts were often not impressed: 'A general came to inspect the brigade but I saw nothing of him.' Or: 'The whole battalion was inspected by two Field-Marshalls [sic] from the War Office – I suppose to see whether we are fit or not.' In the eyes of some, the conscripts were still seen as volunteers, as a Derbyite recalled when King George V inspected his unit: '. . . he stopped by me and asked my age. I said I was nineteen and he smiled – I was slim built and looked young and I suppose he thought I had lied to get into the army.'[63]

The last activity of training, common to all soldiers, was embarkation leave. Alongside a preoccupation with food, the desire for leave was a theme that ran throughout the writings of all these conscripts – in training, and throughout their entire military careers. In this way one diarist charted his training experiences practically as an element of his expectations for leave:

1 May 1917	Notified to go to M.G.C. on the 3rd. Great disappointment as we were going on draft leave on the 7th. Jolly hard lines.
6 May 1917	Great improvement in grub . . . Leave definitely off.
29 June 1917	New O.C. Course. Hopes of leave very bright, but after last week's disappointment afraid to hope.
30 June 1917	Went on leave.
2 July 1917	Back to camp. Don't feel too bad in anticipation of more leave at end of course.[64]

Even conscripts who reduced their training experiences to a few lines always mentioned leave: 'I had several leaves from here [a training camp] and finally seven days draft leave.' Letters home were always full of discussions of the issue, either as a heartfelt sentiment: '[I] hope now it won't be long before I can get leave', or as a reply to a family query: '[Christmas leave is] VERY IMPROBABLE . . . If Pa could concoct a reasonable excuse – someone coming home from the front or something – I would apply for weekend leave soon, but it's *hopeless* without some excuse I'm afraid.'[65]

These references to home, which are but few among many others not mentioned here, point to the strong ties the conscripts felt to the lives they left behind. That is to be expected: basic training was a new, harsh experience, in unfamiliar surroundings. And it had changed these men, at least physically. In their own summaries of the training experiences, there appeared to be a general agreement that all the drilling and exercise raised their standard of fitness. 'My girl and the folks at home were surprised how I had filled out, put on weight and looked disgustingly fit and well.' That this sentiment was expressed in all the types of writings examined here reflects both upon its importance to the conscripts themselves and on their general physical condition as a population. A former clerk noted in his memoirs: 'This time of training had been on the whole an enjoyable period of fresh air exercise which had benefited us all.' Another conscript wrote to his family: 'I am keeping fit so far and that's a big item I suppose'; while a diarist made several entries such as: 'Feeling much better for the changed life and developed voracious appetite.' His family also detected a physical change in him, when he went on leave: 'Everyone surprised at how well I looked. I suppose 5 months in the army has made a difference.'[66]

One eighteen-year-old conscript summed up the entire period by noting that 'I became much harder, both in body and soul'.[67] Yet it may be asked whether his soul, hardened though it was, belonged to the army in any way. In other words had he, and his fellow conscripts, established a military identity at the end of the training period? Overall, this does not appear to be the case: the external appearances of uniform and physical fitness, alongside the professional skills of fighting, existed within each individual's pre-conscription civilian identity. And this was apparent in all age groups. An eighteen-year-old conscript wrote after five and a half months of training: 'I am simply longing for the time to come when we are all together again, what an absolute treat it will be when that time comes.' Lt Allfree was glad to be posted to Dover Castle, since it enabled him to get weekend passes to visit his family who lived close by. Another married man noted explicitly that 'I fear all I enjoyed was evenings at Sheerness where my wife later came to stay'. While he was on leave one diarist noted that he 'spent . . . [the] six days making the best of my time giving no thought to returning'. Lt Creek probably summed up this attitude best when describing his feelings upon departing for embarkation leave after five months of training: '. . . but best of all we were individuals again'.[68]

There are two main functions to basic training, according Richard Holmes. First, to instil 'an adequate level of training in such things as weapon handling and minor tactics'. Second, it tries 'to ensure that the individual values which prevail in most civilian societies are replaced by the group spirit'.[69] As for the first, it is clear from this chapter that all these conscripts became trained and equipped soldiers of some kind, even if the process which brought about their transformation was not uniform. The fact that they did become soldiers, with a degree of shared experiences, points to the existence of some system, but differences in terms of length, location and content basically reflect that the army into which they were conscripted was an organisation with a rigid, intentionalist structure, that had suddenly become functionalist.[70] In other words, as a pre-war professional organisation it had processed a relatively small number of recruits – slightly less than 250,000 regulars – through a fixed and detailed training programme, from which they emerged as soldiers. Throughout the war this organisation had to apply the same, or slightly modified, process of training to a much greater number of troops. The volunteers had already strained the system excessively, and the conscripts probably brought it to a point of near-collapse, if only in terms of numbers: 1,138,070 men were conscripted in the first full year of compulsory service, many of whom were quite unsuited to military life. And as is apparent in their writings, adequate equipment, or even time, were not always available for the task. The accomplishment of any training in these circumstances was therefore an incredible feat. But it could only have been achieved by adapting the strict structure of the pre-war army, and its training programme, to the new situation; to respond functionally to reality.

It was this paradoxical combination of rigidity and functionality within the wartime army that most affected the identity of the conscripts. On the one hand, they had to become rapidly accustomed to military hierarchy and discipline; on the other, they had to learn how to fend for themselves. Taken from a civilian existence governed by relatively clear and accepted codes, they were thrown into a system which put severe physical and spiritual demands upon them. While drill instructors instilled a physical transformation, the army did not provide the tools for a mental or emotional process of adaptation. This was left to the individual himself, who fell back upon the only support known to him, which was civilian. Whether it was the tea-shops in a village, letters to and from home, or a permanent yearning for leave, the conscript comforted himself by evoking images from civilian life, with which he identified strongly. As a result, at the end of basic training the conscript was still a civilian in uniform, and not a soldier.

The absence of a military identity in the individual did not, however, preclude the existence of a group spirit of some kind – as apparent from the writings of the conscripts who returned to the training camps from embarkation leave, and awaited their departure overseas. In this period of waiting they were effectively in a state of limbo: no longer fresh recruits who had to be drilled into the semblance of soldiers, yet, having never experienced battle, not quite fully fledged combat soldiers. And regardless of their attitude to, or enthusiasm for, this vocation, it is obvious that these men were now very familiar with the military framework and their position within it. A comparison of the two main journeys made by the conscripts to the training camps – as new recruits, and as soldiers on the verge of departure to the battlefield – confirms this. Whereas the first, as shown at the start of this chapter, is often described in terms of alienation, isolation and fright, the second presents images of men adjusted to each other and their circumstances: 'I met a dozen of our fellows on Waterloo & we all came down together [from embarkation leave] . . . We had a fine journey down. Everyone packed his troubles in his old kit bag & we were very cheerful.'[71] The period of training had obviously instilled a manner of camaraderie and sharing within these men, that was clearly appropriate to a sense of common destiny – or fear. This, in turn, may be viewed as a group spirit of sorts, though perhaps not one that replaced the 'individual values', of Holmes's definition. It was a military group by circumstance, composed of men in uniform who still essentially saw themselves as civilians. It now remains to be seen whether the passage abroad, and the demands of trench warfare, would redefine the identities of the individual or the group.

CHAPTER THREE

To France

The wet wind is so cold,
And the lurching men so careless,
That, should you drop to a doze,
Winds' fumble or men's feet
Are on your face.

Isaac Rosenberg, *The Troop Ship*

The departure from Britain was very significant to the conscript experience, for two reasons. First, the event itself was unique, since most conscripts would never have set foot on foreign soil in the normal course of their lives. Second, the change in geographical location also heralded the final shift in their status: from men enlisted for military service to combat soldiers on Active Service. The 'real thing' was about to commence.

The end of the official training period was probably best marked in the minds of most conscripts by their embarkation leave. Yet once returned from it their departure to France was often postponed for some days, even weeks. As already noted, troops rarely knew the exact date of movement, despite its being expected: since the career progress of an A category soldier was from training to the combat zone, the termination of the first could only signify the commencement of the second. And to a great extent, in comparison to his knowledge of future movements at the front, here the conscript was actually in command of some information regarding his fate, albeit unspecific. This was probably yet another aspect of the army's imposed functional nature, since many such decisions were often taken at short notice, alongside a general policy of keeping recruits uninformed of their whereabouts and future movements. However, a description of the experiences of a regular battalion that crossed to France on 10 August 1914 clearly emphasised that from the start of the war exact schedules and troop movements were indeterminate. On 6 August the battalion moved to Dorchester, and the officers were told that 'our stay was indefinite', yet on 9 August they were told that 'we would start again to-morrow'. The situation was not very different in 1917: 'We were all ready last night to start away this morning, & just as we turned in one of the Sergeants came into the hut & told us all we weren't going to-day, for some reason or other . . . & now we don't know whether it will be to-morrow or Thursday, but anyway I expect it will be some time this week; don't the Army like to unsettle you?'[1]

Despite the delays, the day of departure was still special, even shocking for most men: 'One suddenly realizes that the time of training is at an end, that one is at last on Active Service.' The conscripts appear to have attached a near-mystical significance to this title, as if their new status emanated from the words themselves and not from the physical activity of departure. One conscript, who numbered all his letters home, even commenced a new serial upon embarking for France, i.e. 'First letter on Active Service.' In the same way another man marked every Saturday in his diary as the number of weeks in which he was on Active Service.[2] In addition, army regulation ensured that all future correspondence from overseas would be marked with the phrase, thereby giving an official seal to the distinct status of combat soldiers, both in the eyes of the men and from the civilian perspective.

The schedule of departure on the day itself also contributed to its uniqueness. The days of uncertainty would come to an abrupt end with the call for a draft that was to leave within hours. One conscript claimed his draft was given six hours to prepare, while in another case the call came late in the evening, in preparation for the following morning: 'Draft consisted of about 90 men and owing to early hour of departure all sober and comparatively quiet. . . . Great fun, exchanging goodbyes with everyone.'[3] The last comment highlights the emotional aspect attached to any act of leaving, which in this case was also compounded by the knowledge that the parting was in order to go to war. In this way, one conscript recalled being 'deeply moved' by 'a special tea and an address from the colonel' given just prior to the draft departing. Another man noted that 'quite a fuss made of us this morning as we are "on draft"'. The 'fuss' was really an extended round of farewells, from pals and superiors alike. This moment of informality with the latter undoubtedly added another overtone of novelty to the day, especially as it appears to have been structured into a procedure approaching a 'ceremony of informality': 'The Roll was called, & then the Regimental Sergeant Major came & shook hands with each one & wished us all 'good luck'. . . Our old platoon sergeant shook hands as we came on to the parade ground . . . Sergeant Bates – we all autographed his 2 photographs this morning.'[4]

The formal ceremony of departure constructed by the army was also designed to induce emotion. The men on draft usually marched to the railway station through the streets of the nearest town, often preceded by a brass band playing familiar tunes. One conscript recalled singing a popular song 'that had caught the fancy of the Army – as, indeed, of the whole population of the country – with its silly chorus: "Good-bye-ee / Don't cry-ee"'. Emotion was difficult to withstand under these circumstances, which were specifically designed to emphasise the warrior status of these men in comparison to the civilian bystanders who often cheered them on, or gave them 'a rousing send-off'. Hence the surprise of one conscript 'at the apathy of passers-by who were going to business. Thought they might have given us a cheer as we were going out to fight.'[5] The pride of the soldier as warrior was actually very much dependent on the civilian admirers he left behind: 'No end of girls came on the platform and said goodbye to the boys, some crying. It made me think – I won't say what . . . one thought seemed uppermost in my mind. I was at least doing my duty, and with the band playing our "march past" and the cheers from the crowd on the platform outside the train, it made one feel proud to go.'[6]

The men themselves also sometimes contributed to the ceremonial aspects of departure, so also probably acknowledging the importance of the day. One eighteen-year-old conscript recalled the populace of Sheffield lining the streets and cheering on his draft as they marched to the railway station: 'Many of us had bought small union jacks with which to brighten our march through the streets. . . . When we paraded that day, ready to march off, we had attached these little flags to our rifles.'[7]

Once on the train bound for an unknown port of departure, usually Folkestone or Southampton, the conscripts started a new stage of socialisation. A draft was often composed of an entire group that trained together, but it was almost always amalgamated with other units from the same training camp. On the train, or at the quayside, they were joined by units from other camps and 'old soldiers' who were returning to the front after recovering from wounds or being on leave. One conscript, who crossed to France in March 1918, noted that he knew only three of the six men with him in the train carriage that took them to Portsmouth. His description, which was that of a typical draft, also reflected upon the state of the army at this time and the necessities imposed upon it by the war:

> Three of the men I did not know. The corporal and one of the privates I knew slightly. They were old caterpillar drivers, [who] had been invalided home on two separate occasions on account of illness caused by exposure and were now going out for the third time. The Lance-corporal, newly promoted, had been training in this country for over three years but owing to defective eyesight had never been sent abroad. Chance had thrown us together a little at Avonmouth, and we had found a few common interests and experiences.[8]

Another aspect of this interaction between units in unconfined spaces such as stations, trains and ports was the possibility of desertion. Despite men being in uniform, the above description makes it obvious that units intermingled, so making supervision much more difficult. One conscript recalled 'the voice of the Sergeant-Major calling out that no one was to leave the train under threat of dire penalties'. Once arrived in a port more delays were probable, sometimes necessitating an overnight stay in a transit camp. In this instance another conscript noted in his diary: 'Am now warned not to leave barracks as absence from roll call means liable to be tried by District Court Martial.'[9]

Overall, the day of departure was exceedingly long, a typical schedule for it being: 'Parade [in the training camp] 3 o'clock AM. entrain 5.30. Reach Southampton 12 noon. Embark 6 o'clock PM. Leave 10 o'clock PM. Reach Le Havre 7 AM.' There was very little for the men to do in these hours of waiting, other than talk among themselves, walk around the docks, read or play card games. This pattern often also repeated itself once the troops were on board. One conscript recalls spending thirty-six hours on the boat, 'though only a very small part of that time was actually spent in motion'.[10] Another summed up the hours before the journey thus: 'We went aboard at 5 o'clock and lay in dock till dark. Making tea and Housy Housy seemed to be all there was to do. A great crowd of fellows was on board the ship which was the Manx packet boat "Ben-my-Chree".'

Housey Housey, also known as 'House', was a card game very similar to bingo and

> was the only game allowed . . . which could be played for money as all other gambling games were strictly forbidden. . . . Each one has a card

with numbers on & the man who is running the game has a bag of numbered counters which correspond to the numbers on the cards. He pulls out a number from the bag & shouts out the number. Each player will scan his card & should such number appear He will put a small stone on it. The winners are those who get all their numbers covered first, or else a line covered. . . . Vast numbers played this game.[11]

Upon embarking each man 'was issued with a life belt which had to be worn until our arrival at Le Havre in the early hours of Monday morning. Each party on the ship (about 100 to a party) were issued rations which had to be served out by the sergeant or officer in charge.'[12] Most of the writings examined here describe the crossing in terms of the origin and quality of the vessel, and the overcrowded conditions. One conscript noted in his diary that it was a 'rotten little paddle boat'; whereas another estimated that he had crossed with 1,200 men 'in a small transport boat which in better times had been a pleasure steamer'. In a letter to his parents one eighteen-year-old claimed to have 'thoroughly enjoyed the trip', while also noting that 'the boat was very crowded – I saw soldiers of practically all the Allied armies on board – most of them returning from leave. It was one of the old cross-channel boats that we've watched coming over dozens of times.'[13] In his case the duration of the crossing was just two hours, but for most it was much longer, often lasting the entire night. One man recalled that the men on his ship reached France in 'none too pleasant a temper' since the boat proceeded in a 'ghostly manner' due to many stops along the way. In addition, smoking was prohibited as a precaution against light, and talking was limited to whispers. Under these conditions sleep was the only possible option, yet the crowded conditions made this exceedingly difficult: It was necessary to lie curled up for one's feet were close to another man's head and on each side they were wedged in tightly. In other words it was 'a case of "sardines in a box" ', as one conscript put it. Another found sleep impossible under such circumstances and went up on deck, where an officer sent him down for guard duty in the horse deck, which was densely populated with men: '. . . my duty being to walk up and down to see that no one struck a match. Found this by no means an easy task as fellows were laying about all over the place & being pitch dark found myself walking on one or two & now & again getting roundly cursed.'[14]

The troop ships sailed across the channel under cover of darkness, escorted by battleships and destroyers. The necessity of all these precautions became clear to one conscript who took a walk around the docks in the hours before embarkation: '[I saw] Two large ships in dry dock that had been torpedoed. They had terrible gashes in their sides in the neighbourhood of the engine room. . . . Not a pleasant sight to see as we were going on board ship later on.'[15] This man was to describe many more unpleasant sights once he arrived in the battlefield, most of them far worse than merely unpleasant. Yet this was his initial contact with the consequences of war, and as such it gave him pause to consider his future circumstances. Most conscripts, however, did not witness such tangible evidence of the war before reaching France, and their impressions of what lay ahead were based mainly upon the stories imparted by the 'old soldiers' with whom they were travelling: 'It's a good thing for you fellows that you have two old hands going out with you. We'll soon show you what can be done with a sheet. We'll rig up a cosy little shack. Of course it isn't all bad life out there. There are always the "staminays" [estaminets] and the "vinn blank".'[16] In some cases the army authorities also saw fit to provide some vision of their expectations from the men they were sending abroad: '[We heard] A stirring harangue by the O.C. [Officer in Command] supported by sleek S.M.'s [Sergeant Majors] and sergeants of the Training Group. We were urged to go in and win. Give Jerry all the results of Bayonet, Grenade and Rifle training we had so well (?) [sic] absorbed. Give Jerry Hell! – and we went off to do it.[17]

Overall, however, the conscripts' process of adjustment to the circumstances of being on Active Service was influenced mainly by intimate experiences of overcrowding, boredom, uncertainty and iron rations. Since these were to be the prominent elements of their daily existence in the trenches, the cross-channel journey was very informing as a preparatory experience. However, as in the case of basic training, they were not provided with any mental vision or framework that would prepare them for the non-physical implications of war. Therefore their thoughts during the crossing dwelt upon the element of departure from England, with which they were familiar, rather than upon the unknown that lay ahead in France. The issue, and the journey, are best summed up by a conscript who crossed to France late in August 1916: 'Few of us had ever before left our native land, and certainly none upon an errand such as this. And the War, after raging for a couple of years, had lost its original glamour. Moreover, we were only amateur soldiers, so for most of us our state was not a happy one; yet we were not miserable, having no idea what was in store for us on the other side of the Channel.'[18]

Once a troop ship reached the shores of France more delays were probable. Alfred Hale recalled arriving outside Le Havre at 7 a.m., yet disembarking only at 11 p.m. 'owing to accident to propeller'. Another conscript noted that after a long and turbulent crossing disembarkation was delayed for four hours due to an unknown reason, after which the men were kept waiting on the quayside for a further hour. As a result 'many gave way to cursing and swearing'. The most common reason for delays in entering a port was bad timing. Since the crossings had to be undertaken at night, the army could only schedule departures according to favourable tides on the British side of the Channel. Ships therefore often reached the French side at low tide, making it necessary for them to wait for the tide to come in. In one very detailed account of a crossing the author claimed his ship anchored off Le Havre at 5 a.m. but only entered the port at 2 p.m.: 'We were eventually towed into the dock by a tug & were loudly cheered by the French people on the quay.'[19]

Aside from cheering crowds, that were not always in evidence, the docks served as an initial introduction to France, and as such were often a disappointment: 'It was almost impossible to believe that I was in France at all. The docks of —— [sic] so very like the docks of London or Liverpool or Glasgow that if it had not been for occasional notices in French I could easily have imagined myself in England or Scotland.' Indeed, the dock workers were mostly English, and once disembarkation began the quayside became 'packed with Tommies – every Regiment, every uniform – a never ending stream pouring from Britain to France, Scotties mixing with Colonials & even coloured troops'.[20] It was only upon leaving the docks that the conscripts became acquainted with France as a foreign land.

Boulogne and Le Havre were the two ports in which the troop ships usually docked. Etaples was the large base camp close to the first, and a camp near the town of Harfleur served the latter. One young conscript who passed through it on his march to the camp wrote to his parents that 'my impressions of the town were awful smells & general dirtiness & dustiness! Millions of French kidlets in blouses – you know – running all over the place.' These children were a stock feature in many initial descriptions of France. For example, Robert Graves, who arrived in Le Havre in 1915, was accosted by 'numerous little boys . . . pimping for their alleged sisters'.[21] Dust and dirtiness were also frequently mentioned, yet these were often simply a reflection of the men themselves, as they marched for miles heavily laden: 'It was a good 4 mile march along a dusty road on a hot day & as we had to carry all our equipment we had quite enough by the time we reached camp . . ... Along the road we were besieged by French children asking for 'biskeet' & as they seemed to appreciate them more than we did they got all they wanted.' Army biscuits were notoriously hard and difficult to eat. This same conscript had first encountered them on the troop ship, noting then that 'it was impossible to bite them through until you had worried them with your teeth for a long time & by that time all your jam or jelly had either dropped off or got all over your hands & clothes'.[22]

Many conscripts arrived at Etaples, which was a huge camp that could accommodate approximately 100,000 troops at any given time during the period 1916–18. A conscript who arrived there early in 1918 'got the impression of bees swarming in and out of hives'. Men would spend up to three weeks in this camp, depending upon the latest war developments, and the corresponding reinforcements and replacements needed in the front line units. Soldiers arriving at a time of relative calm would receive much needed extra drilling on the infamous 'Bullring', 'a large dreary expanse used by Napoleon as a parade ground'[23] alongside lectures and practical training in trench warfare. At other times men would spend no more than a night at the camp, before being divided off into smaller groups and thence sent up the line. Indeed, upon arrival men were 'regrouped' or 'paraded alphabetically & were then allotted to our tents. Letters G H I & J going to "B" lines. This had the effect of splitting up the various little groups of friends that had chummed up coming over & one found oneself again amongst strange faces.'[24] In other words, alienation was strongly felt in this camp, since, like the base depots in which the conscripts started their training in England, it was intended for processing huge influxes of men over short periods of time.

The only form of accommodation in the Etaples camp was bell tents with wooden floors, pitched in long lines: 'At the top end was the sergeant's tent who was in charge of that particular line. The tents were crowded out. In mine there were 18 men & we had a rare job to put out kit & find room for ourselves. At night when all were in there were more feet to the pole than there was room for so that the feet had to pile on each other. It was a good job it was summertime as the door was left open & gave more air. I am sorry for the troops who came there in winter.'[25]

A young conscript who spent three weeks in Etaples in February 1917 proved him right on this point. He was allotted two blankets, which were inadequate for warmth, and because there was ground-frost the inhabitants of his tent awoke to find their water bottles and boots frozen. They had severe problems in getting the latter on, 'and owing to the absence of water were denied the luxury of a wash for that day'.[26] In Harfleur, which was also a large camp, the accommodation was more varied: 'On either side of the highway were endless rows of wooden or iron huts, many surrounded by gay little flower gardens planted and tended by the men; there were innumerable white tents in long straight lines as far as the eye could see along the valley.' But here also conditions could be unpleasant in colder weather: 'Got served out with two blankets, one of which was quite wet'.[27]

The base camps emerge from these writings as well-organised and strict establishments, perhaps surprisingly so in view of the overall functionalist state of the army: 'This place was like a huge machine turning out finished troops by the tens of thousands every day & everything was done strictly to time table & with very few intervals. In fact had they not done so there would have been a terrible confusion as the whole valley was full of troops as it could possibly be.'[28] In Harfleur the daily regime started with reveille at 4.30 a.m., whereupon the men rose, washed in a pail of water, polished their brass buttons and boots, and ate a hasty breakfast. By 7 a.m. they were ready for the day's exercises, complete with full pack (weighing 65 lb in the case of infantrymen) and rifle. In summer men frequently fainted from the heat and weight upon them, since the training ground, 'a big plateau', was at the end of an uphill march. All the elements of basic training with which the conscripts were acquainted from England were practised here again, in addition to more practical preparation for the front: 'We . . . marched off about 8 to some trenches about a half an hours march from here, & we were in same till about 10 o'clock last night, we had to do it just for practice you see, & had our dinner & tea in them.'[29]

In Etaples the routine was practically identical, except that the daily training was held on the Bullring. This name was derived from the word 'bullshit', which was military terminology for drill and other forms of repetitive training.[30] In addition, the instructors on this training ground were notoriously obnoxious, treating the troops rather like cattle, and putting them through 'violent exercises of all kinds, including bayonet drill, gas drill, climbing, jumping etc'. There was 'a S.M. [Sergeant Major] there called Black Jack who was a 'holy terror'. . . . He thought nothing of running a man for the most trivial offence & giving him pack drill so that he became cordially hated by all artillerymen who passed through the base. It was said afterwards that he was killed in a row with some Australians who refused to put up with his bullying way.'[31] Trench digging and building positions with sandbags were also practised; and, in addition, each corps exercised its professional military skills such as wiring and bombing. A gunner recalled being marched to the gun park for a test in gunnery: 'Certain marks of proficiency were awarded which had a bearing on your ultimate destination. A good 'layer' for instance being sent right up to the guns while the less efficient went either to the wagon lines or DAC.'[32]

In general, the training regime in the base camps presented these conscripts with very little innovation, beyond the degree of violence to which they were exposed. Discipline was clearly strict, as were certain elements of the routine. 'Lights out' was at 9 p.m. in both camps, and passes for the neighbouring towns were restricted to those men who were in residence for longer than eight days, due to quarantine regulations. As one of them put it to his brother: 'It is much the same as at Minster as regards training, only of course we are under canvas instead of in huts.'[33] The exception to this general statement was the gas training given in the base camps, and especially the gas tests. Gas warfare commenced with a German attack on the British line in Ypres, in April 1915. However, since this form of warfare progressed with the war, there were constant innovations both in the respirators supplied, and in the instructions about their use. Most conscripts received rudimentary instruction on gas warfare and respirators during their training in England, but Lt Allfree noted that 'recruits coming out to France were always very nervous of gas, and their ignorance with regard to it was appalling'.[34] More intensive practical instruction was meant to take place in the short period men spent in the base camps in France. However, this meant that those who simply passed through a base camp for one night were actually being sent to the front with insufficient gas training.

According to army regulation, every soldier in a base camp in France was meant to be processed through a standard course 'which included an hour immersed in a cloud of gas (to give him "confidence in his respirator") and half a minute exposed to tear gas (to give him a fright and teach him to take anti-gas precautions seriously). Masks had to be put on in a regulation six seconds – but before being allowed to do so, and while still exposed to the tear gas, men had to repeat their name, number and battalion.'[35] Not one of the conscripts describes such a precise experience, or even one closely resembling it. There are more general references to gas training, and the reactions they evoked. More specifically, it seems the poison gas test was sometimes held in a sealed tent, but more usually in a wooden hut, 'with notices up at either end warning one to have one's mask properly fitted on after passing a certain point, and the word "dangerous" in large letters on a notice board close to the entrance. . . . We approached the hut in single file, and entering, passed through one by one, and so out into the open air outside. It was nothing but one long passage with windows on one side only.' Alfred Hale was not very affected by this experience, but another conscript noted in his diary that 'we were all nearly choked so don't know what a real gas attack can be like'. The tear gas test was usually held in a tent or a trench, at the end of which the men 'were like so many children all crying, the tears rolling down our faces'.[36]

Another feature of life in these camps was a medical inspection:

This took place in a large hut & a batch of men marched in & told to strip naked. Rather a shock for a sensitive person but it had to be done. We then passed in a line in front of the MO [Medical Officer]. The following questions were then fired at you. 'Eyes alright? teeth alright? quite alright? jump over that chair!' This was the time for any imperfections to be noticed. Fellows with bad feet such as hammer toe bunions or flat feet were given a ticket to see the chiropodist. Those with bad teeth one for the dentist & those with eye trouble the optician. There seemed to be a department for every possible complaint.[37]

This gunner had his civilian spectacles exchanged for army issue within two days. Another conscript claimed he was passed as A1 after his medical examination in Etaples.[38] Since the conscripts had been medically examined in the recruiting office and in the training camps, this third examination points to serious deficiencies in the physical standard of the conscripts that had been sent to the front – and in the medical examinations in Britain. It was clearly as a response to this problem that this extra examination was introduced in 1917.

Food and meals appear to have been an issue in which the two central base camps were unequal. Undoubtedly the task of feeding such huge numbers of men in one location was immense, and its implementation in both cases was quite remarkable. Yet it appears that in Etaples the camp was better organised in this respect: 'The meals were all taken in large mess-rooms of which there were several & large queues formed up in front of each about 5 deep & regulated by Military Police for all the world like lining up for the pictures or the theatre & each room had two sittings so that if you were not well to the fore you had a long wait for your meal. The food was good here and fairly served out.[39]

But the quantity of food allotted each soldier in Etaples was less satisfactory: 'On many occasions after finishing my first meal I would come out and again take my place in the queue for a further meal. On some occasions it was necessary to do this three times in order to get a decent meal.'[40] In Harfleur the food was 'not as good as when we were at Minster & we don't get as much either but must put up with it eh?' In both camps breakfast was eaten early, before the day's drilling began. But in Etaples the men were marched back to camp for a large meal in mid afternoon, whereas in Harfleur this occurred later in the day. And so in this location the local French peasants set up barrows on the edge of the training ground from which the troops bought snacks such as oranges, chocolates, 'and the eternal Spearmint. They seem to think we can't win without [it] and that it is the staple article of sweet in the English army.' Only in the late afternoon were the men marched back to the camp for a meal, which was both dinner and tea. This was set out on the end of long trestle tables, and as a result 'it was the noisiest and the greediest who seized most of the rations'.[41]

As in the training camps in England, the men had to provide for themselves after tea, or whatever was the last official meal of the day. Due to the size and organisation of the camp in Etaples, this was not difficult: 'There were all kinds of places for the troops to spend their evenings such as the YMCA, Salvation Army, Church Army etc. & in all these places you get a mug of tea coffee or cocoa & cakes of various kinds & even a fair meal at very low charges.'[42] Descriptions of the facilities in Harfleur are similar, and in both cases parcels from home provided a welcome source of food and home cooking. This option, however, was open only to those men who spent longer than a few days in either of the camps, since their families had to be informed of their new address.

The conscript's departure from the base camps was as sudden as their previous departure from the training camps in England: 'We didn't know ourselves till about 9.30 last night, after we had all turned in the Orderly Sergeant came round & told us we were all to be prepared to go up the line to-morrow night which is to-night.' Another conscript recalled being awoken at 1 a.m. in preparation for leaving two and a half hours later.

The men returned the small amount of kit which they had received upon arrival, such as blankets, and were then issued with line kit: 'This consisted of 2 blankets, a ground sheet, 50 rounds of small arm ammunition & emergency rations viz 1 tin bully, a tin containing tea & sugar, & a small quantity of small oval biscuits. These all tied up in a white calico bag & instructions given us that these were not to be touched until ordered to do so by an officer. An order that was obeyed by very few, the tea & sugar being too much of a temptation to the chaps when nothing could be obtained at nights.'[43] Departing drafts were usually composed of men who had crossed to France together, though not necessarily of men who had trained together: 'About 100 of us promiscuously picked out to go up to the front but neither Adams nor myself although most of our friends have gone. . . . No system of picking out these men at all. Sub just walked down the ranks and picked out a man here and there.' The men were divided off into groups, according to the needs of the various units to which they were being sent. A typical summary of this situation was given by a gunner: 'I was among the group of the 31st Division & of all those who had come over with me, only 2 were with me for this division so of course we 3 stuck together.' In W.V. Tilsley's autobiographical novel *Other Ranks*, the Derbyite hero Dick Bradshaw felt 'Rotten that he, Platt and Wilson should have been parted and sent to three different units after being so long together at Codford and Witley; and all three afraid to approach that big bull-necked Sergeant-Major to see if he could arrange for them to go up together. Were all drafts split up indiscriminately now, all nominal rolls so strictly adhered to?'[44] A march to the nearest railway station was again preceded by a short ceremony, in which 'the C.O. came out and addressed us about duty, and the chaplain said a few words'. One diarist noted that the chaplain in his camp delivered 'a rather bloodthirsty speech . . . telling us to kill as many Germans as possible and show no mercy'.[45] And then the men were sent off to the front.

In general, most conscripts appeared to have viewed their stay in the base camps quite favourably: 'grub good, & fags duty free! Haven't quite got into relation between French & English money.'[46] Despite the strict schedule, the conscripts had been in the army long enough to be familiar with the overall appearance and regime of a training camp. Problems of adjustment therefore stemmed from their presence in a foreign country, surrounded by unknown faces. For within a period of weeks the conscripts experienced three complete changes of landscape, both human and physical: from the training camp in England to the troop train and ship, then to the base camp and finally to the departing draft. A fourth change would be experienced upon their arrival at the front line unit to which they were despatched. Since this was to be a recurring problem throughout the conscript's army career in France, their experiences in the base camps were actually a suitable form of introduction. One conscript summed up the situation aptly as 'very strange, but expect we shall get used to it'.[47] This young conscript did indeed stay in Harfleur for two weeks, and ultimately adjusted to it. Yet many conscripts moved up the line within days of their arrival. Their acceptance of the transitory nature of these camps may show that for them normality had already become a relative notion, within which the known existed alongside the unexpected.

The journey from the base camps to the front line combined the two major systems of British troop movement in France: marching and French troop trains. The conscripts already had wide experience of marching, not only on the parade ground but also cross-country; they had also become familiar with long periods of confinement in British trains and ships. In other words, they had already learnt much about endurance and discomfort, yet the initial contact with French trains was still a surprise: 'Long before this we had learned that the soldier must not expect luxuries and on this journey we were not permitted to travel in first class carriages, but found our accommodation in cattle trucks, there being 30 men in each truck.'[48] This conscript's overall account is not imbued with irony, yet it is interesting to note that the introduction to cattle trains moved a number of men to similar turns of ironic phrase: 'first class carriages not supplied, satisfied with cattle trucks . . .' These also had the words '40 Hommes 8 Cheveaux' inscribed upon them, though men and horses did not travel together in the same truck; one soldier was posted on guard duty in each truck of horses. The inscription was remarked upon by most conscripts, and as one of them later wrote: 'we thought [this] was an estimate of how we were regarded by the staff (mostly old cavalry men although it was an infantry war) . . . We thought one man with common sense was worth fifty horses.'[49]

Once the men were in the wagons, 'we settled ourselves as best we could on the bare wooden floor, those knowing ones who ranged themselves around the sides were able to lean back & were the best off while those in the middle had to lean against each other.[50] Since the journeys were both very slow and extended, the discomfort was immense, even if fewer than forty men were accommodated in each truck. One conscript claims there were thirty-six in his, yet it 'was a tight-enough fit that we were to endure for the next forty-eight hours'. Another recalled there being 'no adequate ventilation; the truck had not been thoroughly cleaned since it had last been occupied; a faint sickening smell was mixed with the heavy air discharged from the lungs of thirty sleeping men.' One man spent most of his journey sitting in the open doorway of the truck 'with feet dangling out . . . 41 men & equipment in one truck. . . . Realizing what endurance means. Gee whiz feel about done up.' It was clearly an appalling journey; an inhuman one. And in the late twentieth century, a journey evokes somewhat stronger feelings than 'gee whiz'. As Denis Winter put it: 'To a generation with visual memories of the railway lines running into Hitler's death camps, tense faces peering from cattle trucks, there is something disconcerting about the imagery of this journey from base camp.'[51]

The trains themselves proceeded with 'plenty of creaks, groans and shrieks – bumping & clattering', which usually led to 'frequent stops for no apparent reason'. In all, these trains were 'slow but not sure, rickety and decidedly not comfortable; in other words beyond description; . . . a veritable picture or pattern of steam-snails.' Indeed, 'some idea will be given of the speed at which we went when I say that the distance [between Boulogne and Etaples] is less than 20 miles and the time taken was 3 hours'.[52] Comments on the slow pace of the trains are to be found in most of the writings examined here: 'Train still very slow', 'progress was always slow', 'had a 27 hour journey, could have walked quicker'. Indeed, one conscript noted that 'at intervals some of the boys get down from the train and run by the side as the rate we are travelling allows of this being done with ease'.[53]

This slow, halting progression was remarkable to the conscripts mainly for two reasons. First, the cramped conditions in which they travelled became even less endurable with the passing hours. There 'was no heating apparatus of any description but we found a brazier and some wood and cinders and made a fire but it was nevertheless very cold'. The trains were also not equipped with any facilities: 'Whenever we came to a halt men would jump down from the train and scramble up or down the embankments or snake for bushes behind which to relieve themselves.

Without any warning the train would start to move and heads would pop up from bushes or long grass and men hurriedly pulling up trousers, would come scrambling back into the train.'[54] These frequent stops were also used for making tea with hot water obtained from the waste-pipe of the engine's boiler. When the train suddenly began to move men dashed back to their trucks 'with the consequence that the best part of the water was spilled, sometimes over the men inside the truck'. Second, the conscripts found the French railway system itself a culture shock. Whatever their social background, all were acquainted with the British railway system as a model upon which to base their expectations – and these were obviously higher than those offered by the railway system in France. In this way Lt Allfree claimed the French trains were 'one of the slowest things imaginable', and another recalled arriving 'at some little tin pot station somewhere about Nieuport'. One conscript summed up his entire journey comparatively: 'The French trains are very different to our English ones and appear to travel at the rate of 1 mile per hour.'[55] It is interesting to note that whereas the discomfort of overcrowding was remarked upon with irony, it did not really surprise these men. After some months in the army, they had come to recognise physical discomfort as an integral element of their military life. But railways were another matter: they belonged to their civilian existence, as a normative feature of British life. There is a sense of disorientation in their descriptions of the relative deficiencies of the French system – as if something familiar had become strange. But there is also a degree of glee in finding an objective factor to blame for their uncomfortable journey. In other words, it was the French railway system, rather than the situation or the military organisation, that was to blame for the extended hours of discomfort.

The lot of the volunteer soldier was identical to that of the conscript in this case. Cattle trucks for the transportation of troops were used from the start of the war as a functional solution to the problem of mass movement – though there are very occasional references to men travelling in regular train carriages, and even first-class coaches. Once again these were compared unfavourably to British trains: '[The third class carriages were] narrower than ever I had seen . . . and with hard wooden seats. Seven of us squeezed into one compartment with all our equipment and when once we had fitted our knees into each other it seemed as if we were immovably fixed for the night.'[56] The slow progress of the trains was also apparent throughout the war. Robert Graves claimed the journey from Harfleur to Bethune, a railhead very close to the front line which should have been 'a short journey', took 24 hours in the summer of 1915.[57] At the same time he also noted that the train was composed of forty-seven coaches, though he made no reference to the majority being cattle trucks in which the men he commanded sat. As such, the most true comparison to the journey experienced by the conscript soldier, made by one of them, was to that of the officer, who 'had much less cramped and more comfortable accommodation in orthodox carriages, albeit with hard wooden seats'. Lt Allfree, who arrived in France as an officer, travelled up the line in a first-class carriage. He also made reference to the use of cars and motor-cycles which were at his disposal once he was in the line.[58] In other words, as an officer, his freedom of movement was enhanced not only by his rank but also, and as a result of it, by the modes of transportation open to him. In contrast, apart from marching and trains, the only other option known to men in the ranks was motor lorries – which were rarely used, and liked even less. One conscript recalled that 'this mode of conveyance was new to us, and the surprising thing about it was the great quantity of dust and dirt that flew up from the wheels and into the backs of the lorries'. Another man claimed that there 'are many more comfortable methods of travelling than by motor lorrie [sic] especially when on bad roads as these were. . . . The vans seem to suck in the dust off the roads & by the time we finished our journey we were like millers.'[59]

The journey to the front line, or movement between different sections of the line itself, often lasted two days, and culminated in a long march from the final station at which the troops were deposited. And by then, the conscripts had learnt that marching was a thread of consistency that ran throughout their military life. Their first experience as soldiers in Britain was being marched to the station that took them to the training camp: 'I will not dwell on the march to the station, the uncomfortable underclothes, the overcoat, the kit bag, the tight breeches and puttees, the heavy boots all made me feel that I was doing purgatory for past sins I had never committed.'[60] Many miles were marched away on the parade ground, and henceforth, under all circumstances and at all times as soldiers, the men proceeded in formation. It was integral to practically every activity in the military schedule, regardless of time, place, weather or fatigue. It became the bane of their existence.

In Britain the conscripts were taken on route marches with a full pack on their backs in preparation for the extended mileage they would cover in France. Once they had crossed the Channel this form of training continued at the base camps, where the men were 'marched to the spot [the training ground] in "full pack" every day, a distance of between 3 and 4 miles'. Another conscript recorded a 'march of about 8 miles with full pack under a blazing sun; just about done'. The physical exertion of marching was heightened by the 'additional kit which we have received here [at Etaples, that] has made a considerable difference in the weight of our packs which now hang heavy'. Packs of different units were not equal in weight, however; 'the artilleryman suffered when he had to march with full kit and rifle, his kit was not packed as conveniently as an infantryman, and his rifle was carried on the gun limber or ammunition wagon, as was his overcoat and spare blanket'.[61]

The basic weight of a pack was 55 lb 2½ oz. It comprised: clothing, 11 lb 14¾ oz; rifle, 10 lb 11¼ oz; 100 rounds of ammunition, 6 lb 4 oz; trench tools, 2 lb 9¼ oz; webbing, 8 lb 4¾ oz; pack, 9 lb 12¼ oz; rations/water, 5 lb 10 oz. However, in reality a pack was never less than 60 lb once the soldier had added the minimum of personal accessories, such as a muffler, a sweater or a notebook.[62] One conscript gunner recalled marching out of the line in October 1916 with a pack weighing over 100 lb. By night 'we felt that either we must drop our loads or else collapse ourselves; choosing the former course we deposited the joints amid the debris on the roadside, going thereby a little short of rations the next day'. Another unit of gunners chose a different option in their long march into the trenches: 'A lot of the fellows at the first opportunity dumped their ammunition which was the heaviest part of our kit & which as we had no rifles was no earthly use to us but which we were supposed always to have on us; each pocket of our bandolier held 2 clips of cartridges & in order that the loss should not be noticed the plan adopted was to keep the top pocket full & the remaining ones stuffed with paper.'[63]

The roads themselves, or rather the lack of them, were often another major hindrance to the marching men. The first march in France, from the dock to a base camp, usually alerted men to this difficulty: 'We here have our first experience of the cobbled paved roads for marching. It is not a happy one.' Marching under a hot sun in summer was very difficult, but in winter the situation was much worse. When it rained, 'the mud was simply awful. Got on the road but it wasn't much better than the fields as it was easily 6 inches deep in mud in places and got right over our boot tops.' At other times conditions were even worse with roads 'ankle deep in snow & mud'. In turn, this could often lead to ice upon the road, with strong winds cutting across the way.[64] Any protracted march under these conditions of heavy packs, unremitting weather and bad roads would have been exceedingly difficult; yet the circumstance of war made the situation far worse. One conscript noted 'the all-night march that followed our relief [which] almost exhausted us. The captain lost his way, and we kept scrambling through prickly hedges, going hither and thither, crossing and recrossing the same line of railway in efforts to locate our position . . . the difficulty of night movement can be imagined.' Long marches were usually punctuated by short stops for rest and drinking, yet water supply was often a problem. One conscript claimed 'men [were] crying for water' after 'a terrible night march.' Another described an 'extra long march and stopped in a place miles from anywhere and about 2 miles to go for water. It poured with rain, we were wet to the skin. Never so fed up in my life.'[65]

The physical discomfort at these times was immense, especially since many men suffered minor ailments which were intensified by the continuous movement. One young conscript recalled the pain of marching an entire night with his pack pressing upon a boil on his back. On arrival at the camp it had grown to such dimensions that he was excused seven days' duty.[66] But the most common afflictions were those caused by ill-fitting boots, as in a sudden retreat in October 1917: 'We went with full pack and equipment, blankets etc. . . . my feet got slightly blistered, with small boots and chafing of dirt, but carried on . . . with 'skeleton marching order' & could not go any father [sic] so fell out, so did Jack Moore & Taffy Jones to look after me, caught a lorry to the 5 crossroads at Bethune, from there Taffy carried me two thirds of the way to the hospital, & dumped me in the bath house, had a bath & was detained in hospital.'[67]

The most difficult marches were those for men coming out of the trenches, after a period in the front line: 'I have conceived the utmost respect for the infantry since I came out here. It's really one of the few stirring sights of the war to witness a remnant battalion of silent tommies plodding back laden like Atlas.' In some cases men fainted on these extended marches, or simply dropped by the wayside until their strength returned to them. The descriptions of the massive spring retreat of 1918 are most touching in this context, simply because everyone had to go on, all support systems having been destroyed, and 'everyone having seeming lost their direction'.[68] 'Barely room to march on the roads, since so many retreating, marched all day, part of the night . . . Soon we found ourselves surrounded by green fields . . . but we could not feel happy with feet in their present condition, and both officers and men were equally afflicted. The captain shared his horse with other officers, and stronger men carried weaker men's rifles; so we crawled along.'[69] But in some units there were no stronger men: '. . . we passed a Labour Battalion composed mostly of old men. They were being made to march as fast as possible in order not to be captured and every man carried big heavy kit bags in addition to heavy bundles of blankets, also their picks or shovels. To see these old men struggling along under their heavy burdens with sweat pouring from them as they trudged along was a sight enough to bring tears into a man's eyes.'[70]

And yet the march always went on, usually for days and miles at a time. A march between sectors: 'The first day's march was a short one only doing just under 5 kilometres, and off again next day, this time doing 16 kilometres . . . the next day we done [*sic*] 15 kilometres . . . [next day] another 16 kilometres . . . then off to Habareq 16 kilometres, thus arriving at our new sector, ARRAS.' The army's expectations of mileage per day may be estimated by the following comment: '. . . they treated us very gently, allowing three days to cover a distance of thirty-three miles.' One young conscript, a category B man who was sent out to France in the final months of the war, wrote to his parents of frequent marches. In one letter he described a 10-mile march, which he claimed the 'fellows stood splendidly. . . . If we go on like this we shall all be losing our categories and be A.1.'[71] Low-ranking officers sometimes joined the march, albeit without the weight of a pack on their backs; but the high-ranking officers were far removed from the men and the march: 'Once a glittering batch of generals passed us all dressed up. . . . They flashed past like a savage's idea of god – all angry and omnipotent and expensive – and a cloud of dust.'[72]

Under calm circumstances marching sometimes offered the men some mental respite. One conscript, whose unit was in a rest camp after an extended tour of duty in the trenches, noted 'a nice long route march'. Another wrote home of a three-day march in which he 'enjoyed the country and villages very much'. Yet overall, marching remained a constant horror of the conscripts' life. As one of them summed it up in a letter: cattle trucks on troop trains were awful, 'but still, it was better than marching'.[73]

Upon reaching the front line, or a camp close to it, for the first time, these conscripts had effectively completed their transformation into combat soldiers. It had been a long process, initiated, unbeknown to them, by their names appearing on a local register as liable for conscription. The subsequent notification of the local military authorities had led to a 'call-up' notice being sent to each man, and his eventual enlistment. The bureaucratic transition was completed after an individual had filled in an attestation form and been allotted a regimental number. The physical transition was completed once training in England, and later France, was at an end. The geographical transition removed the conscript from his home to a training camp, then to France, and ultimately to the front line – his sole habitat, for the most part, until the end of his military career. All of these brought about the external transformation of a civilian into a soldier. Mentally, it is clear that most men had adjusted to their new status by the time they reached the front line. And yet, this does not signify a transformation in their consciousness or identity, from that of civilians to that of soldiers. Conscripts arriving at the front for the first time viewed their surroundings through the eyes of the uninitiated civilian soldier, and not as military men:

> He tried to imagine . . . [his first] attack, but after the snippets of conversation he had picked up he knew that all his notions were far from reality. If these men were to be believed, hand-to-hand encounters were rare. You didn't run or charge across No Man's Land, but simply walked. Also, you saved your breath and went silently. No attempt made to intimidate the enemy with blood-curdling yells as at Witely Camp; you offered yourself as a target. If you came out all right, you grinned, and agreed that Old Fritz had put up a good show. If you got a Blighty wound – 'tres bon!'[74]

Months and often years at the front lay ahead of them, mostly isolated from civilian contact. Perhaps these were the circumstances that would cause a transformation in these conscripts' consciousness, bestowing upon them an inner identity of soldiers.

PART TWO

Actualities of War

If I had time . . . to study war, I think I should concentrate almost
entirely on the 'actualities of war' – the effects of tiredness, hunger,
fear, lack of sleep, weather . . . it is the actualities that make war so
complicated and so difficult, and are usually so neglected by
historians.

Field-Marshal Lord Wavell to Basil Liddell Hart

CHAPTER FOUR

Mud and War

. . . my father used
to become hoarse talking about how it was
a privilege and if only he
could meanwhile my

self etcetera lay quietly
in the deep mud et

cetera . . .

e.e. cummings, *my sweet old etcetera*

The Western Front was a foreign country. Not only was it *in* the foreign land of Flanders, it was also unlike anything the conscripts had ever encountered, even after months of training in the army. The long and arduous journey to the front may have given them an inkling of the desolation and discomfort to come, but in truth no uninitiated person could really have imagined the sights, sounds and smells of the trenches, nor that men lived in such appalling circumstances for weeks at a time, year in and year out. It says much about human nature that within a very short period of time – usually weeks – trench life seemed quite normal to these men. It is even more remarkable when the appearance and surroundings of the front line are considered: from the awful weather to the permanent presence of rats, from wading in the sludge to building bivouacs in it. It was a gruesome stage for a gruesome theatre of war, and these men set it in intricate detail.

The conscripts started arriving at the front in the autumn of 1916 – into an environment which was the product of two years of war. They did not see the process of desecration, but rather accepted as given the barren quagmire of a landscape, not knowing that it had once been an endless patchwork of well-tended fields and pretty copses and woods. On the other hand, they also had not watched the tortuous process of war construction: the trenches, initially a temporary measure in 1914, had become a well-established network of tunnels, sandbags and fire steps. It was an environment dominated by grey and brown, for the skies were usually heavy with rain, and the ground was largely mud.

Mud is indispensable to the imagery of the First World War. Most of the best-known literary works are full of references to the weather, but most especially to the liquid, brown substance. Every soldier in every poem or book is splattered by mud and sludge, stuck in an oozing trench. A figurative and literal entrenchment; a total environment. Take, for example, the opening lines of Owen's 'Dulce Et Decorum Est':

> Bent double, like old beggars under sacks,
> Knock-kneed, coughing like hags, we cursed through sludge,
> Till on the haunting flares we turned our backs
> And towards our distant rest began to trudge.

But the poets were not alone. Officers and other ranks, volunteers and conscripts – any human being who graced the trenches of Flanders for the shortest time, wrote of the weather. This is not really surprising, since Flanders and Picardy are highly affected by the Atlantic currents, which bring on rain at all times of the year – the annual rainfall often approaching 50 inches.[1] Digging trenches in this region was therefore an awful, indeed a bizarre, endeavour, since the ground was constantly damp and shifting, and any impression in the earth filled with water at remarkable speed. Moreover, the ice and snow typical to the area in the winter months, and inhibiting in itself, quickly turned to water under heavy shelling. Mud and water were therefore really prevalent in the trenches: one of the few mythologised images actually rooted in fact, and one shared by men on all sides. It is an issue that appears in many German writings, not least in Ernst Junger's highly influential *Storm of Steel*: 'Owing to heavy rain in the night the trench fell in many places, and the soil mixing with rain to a sticky soup turned the trench into an almost impassable swamp. The only comfort was that the English were no better off, for they could be seen busily scooping the water out of their trench. As we were on higher ground, they had the benefit of the superfluous water we pumped out as well. The collapse of the trench walls brought to light a number of those who fell in the last autumn's fighting.'[2]

The writings of the conscripts discussed here contain over one hundred and fifty references – of at least one full sentence – to the rain, wind, snow and sun which produced ice, mud, sludge and dust. It is a fascination verging on an obsession, yet one which points to the immense twofold importance of the weather in the lives of these men: both a backdrop to life at war, and an event of war. There are many observations such as 'Weather very hot', or 'next day was very snowy'; and narratives in which it plays an integral part: 'Lay down in six inches of mud & ice during a snowstorm for about two hours. Go back by the road and dig in at the side[;] wet through and feet frozen, can't get boots off to dry socks.'[3] The first two quotes establish the environment of life and action, while in the third the weather is a crucial part of the action. This leads to a further distinction, between the conscripts as men and as soldiers. As men their primary concern was human: 'The weather out here has been very cold I can hardly keep myself warm.' However, as soldiers the climatic conditions also had a functional aspect: 'Them guns [9.2 Howitzers] were 23 ton when they were fully put together and firing. . . . They would bring the guns in at night and you had to keep out of sight. Oh Christ it was a job. And, of course, it was all done in water – shell-holes and water.'[4]

Beyond these conceptual divisions, most references to the weather revolved around the awful mud within and around the trenches, which was apparent at all times of the year – and had already become a fixture of the landscape by the time the conscripts were fielded. In October 1916 one of them claimed 'everything is one slimy mass of mud'; by August 1917 the 'mud was appalling, and the ground was pitted all over with shell holes . . . and all the holes were half full of water'; and in October 1918, Flanders was 'a miserable place – undulating country – pitted with shell-holes full of water – & shell shattered trees everywhere. The mud is – well – best left unmentioned.'[5]

Given that many British men were used to rain and snow, the circumstances in Flanders obviously surpassed any normative concept of mud. Before considering its effects, many of the conscripts were therefore moved to simply comment upon its existence, which was clearly unique to the English eye: 'oh! the mud! You people in England have not seen mud!' Diary entries also reflected this unknown quantity: 'Arrived at about the muddiest place I have ever seen', or 'Mud something chronic'. In other words, the 'prevalent discomfort . . . is the mud which clings like poor relations and breeds twice as fast. It's burlesque simply. The roads are a swirling batter of filth which splashes the tree tops and the moon.'[6]

It is interesting to note that discussions of the weather caused many of these men to frame their descriptions in nearly identical terms. When referring to the watery consistency of the mud, one conscript claimed to be 'stuck in the sea of mud', while another noted 'everything a sea of mud'.[7] These conditions were constantly worsened since 'it rained without ceasing the whole day', or 'Rained fast every bit of the day'; and as a result, 'mud and water knee deep', or 'trenches knee deep in places'.[8] Such examples, of which there are many, highlight the uniformity of the conditions and the impact they had upon the conscripts. They also point to the fact that they were actually fighting two wars – with the Germans and with the weather, without it always being clear which was considered the worse:

> It wasn't the foe we feared,
> It wasn't the bullets that whined,
> It wasn't the business career
> Of a shell, or the burst of a mine.
> It wasn't the sniper who sought
> To nip our young hope in the bud.
> No It wasn't the guns
> And it wasn't the Huns
> It was the MUD – MUD – MUD.[9]

Mud appeared to permeate every aspect of these men's existence, since 'it rained the whole time we were in the front line and when we came out you could hardly see us for mud, it was simply caked on us'. '[It] made our dugouts almost intenable [*sic*], for we entered them through openings only two feet high. When crawling into them on hands and knees over the threshold of wet mud, our overcoats soon became so thickly coated that some of us cut wide strips from the bottom, to lighten the load, roughly hemming round the new edge at our later leisure.'[10] Even in camps behind the lines simple tasks, such as eating, became a struggle:

The rain has made this camp very muddy & it is very difficult to get about the mud being well over the ankles & very slippery & sticky. Our cook house was pitched in a very awkward position being in a sunken road & after drawing our rations if we wished to have our meals in our 'bivvy' we had to climb up the steep sides of the road bank & then wade through the mud past the mule lines before we reached our hut. This was a very difficult job when one was carrying a mess tin full of tea in one hand & a chunk of bread & jam in the other & many a meal went 'west' in the struggle without any chance of getting another.[11]

The basic problem of living 'up to our eyes in mud', was that it 'made movement very slow & difficult': it 'was an exceedingly trying business to extricate ones feet at each step and the progress likewise slow. We were all wearing gum boots which reached to our knees, otherwise it would have been impossible to walk.'[12] Some situations were indeed impossible, as in the case of a conscript who got stuck in the morass, and found himself exposed to the Germans for several hours. One man claimed it took nearly six hours for stretcher bearers to bring in a wounded man from the mud of No Man's Land, whilst another wrote of a blizzard which lasted for two and half days in April 1917, during which his dug-out 'became a quagmire. Several men buried in the wet clay.' Sometimes it was possible to help a man who was stuck, by forming a human 'chain to the nearest firm bit of ground and haul[ing] him out, leaving the trench boots behind'.[13]

Human beings were not the only ones afflicted: 'To give some idea of the mud, I need only mention that I saw a horse, harnessed to a French wagon, with its hind legs so deeply sunk in the mud, that it could not move. Its hind legs were buried right up to its haunches, so that its stomach was level with, and lying on the ground, with its front legs stretched straight out in front of it along the ground. It had to be dug out.'[14] Other horses were not so fortunate. One conscript recalled 'taking two horses down to the village trough to water, [when] two of another battery's horses became stuck and could not move, fell down and had to be shot'. Even if they did not get stuck, such conditions made the daily round of care for horses was exceedingly difficult: 'the captain sent us out to take the blasted horses for a walk in the rain and the mud.'[15] Worse still,

Watering is some job now as our way lies across a plain & the water lays here like a pond so that if you lead your mules you get splashed from head to foot & soaked, while if you ride, their backs are soaking wet & you get wet that way.

Still riding is best, but when you get to the troughs it is simply awful, you are almost up to your knees in mud as you are forced to dismount it being against orders to sit on a mules back while they are watering. Then the job of mounting again is very difficult seeing you are stuck in the mud & woe betide you if an officer should see you put your foot on the trough. So it often happened that the officer would give the order to move off before you were up & then you have to wade through the mud & get soaked through.[16]

The mud was caused by constant downpours of rain, which also brought periodic floods. As a result, being soaked was also a fixture of the conscripts' lives, with many diary entries such as 'It poured with rain, we were wet to the skin.' The rain was also a favourite topic in letters, being a point of eternal fascination to the British mind and easy to communicate to both civilian and soldier: 'We are getting very wet weather now, yesterday we had thunder and lightning and the rain simply came down in torrents, we all got soaked through and its a bit rotten when you can't get your clothes dried and have to put them on wet. It is pouring rain again today so we get another ducking . . . the rain is coming through [the tent] and that accounts for the blots.[17]

Men who lived in tents were actually 'flooded out', a situation familiar to those who were without any artificial shelter: 'Raining hard. No sleeping place, crept in a hole and had a rough night. Rain coming through.'[18] But even those who managed to find shelter in more substantial accommodation were not immune from water. A conscript who was in a concrete dug-out wrote home that it was 'fairly comfortable . . . [but] during the night the river Steenbeek (which runs close by) rises and floods us out and we have some difficulty in saving our kits.' Sometimes respite was found with a 'pump to pump water away . . . [since] trenches something awful'; but overall, there was very little that could be done in the face of these torrents. As one conscript put it: 'Storm & flood. My word when it rains in France it comes down in buckets full & continues for hours. Suppose it is the firing [that] does it.'[19]

The permanent presence of rain and mud were the background against which the seasons of the year presented themselves to these men. Both as British men used to a gentle summer, and as soldiers clothed in heavy uniform, days of extreme heat were very uncomfortable: 'It has been hotter than ever to-day, & as you can imagine we feel the heat very much indeed, it is really too hot to be comfortable, especially in this life.' For the normal round of military and fighting duties had to be fulfilled, '& all the while under a broiling hot sun' with 'flies . . . an awful nuisance, swarming about on everything'.[20] And as a result of the 'sweltering heat' 'we drip & drip, & sweat & sweat, till we fairly run away in streams of grease.' But warm weather also had its positive aspects. Frederick Voigt, a category B man who worked behind the lines, noted that 'for several months we had been working in a wood-yard and saw-mills. Our lives had become unspeakably monotonous, but the coming of warm days banished much of our dreariness.' Sunbathing was also possible between duties behind the lines, and sometimes 'it was so warm most of us kipped in the field instead of a billet'.[21]

The option of sleeping out in the open air or under tents became far less pleasant during the long cold months of winter, when strong winds and ice were common, and the monotonous drudgery of the front line made them seem even longer and colder. The winter of 1916 was especially bad: 'Terribly cold weather. Coldest winter ever known in France.' Late in the year a conscript noted 'snow again', while a man newly arrived in France wrote to his wife: 'Yes dear I should love some wool gloves, we get some severe frosts now, they would be better than mittens I think for our job dear.'[22] The new year brought little relief, with the extreme frosts of January 1917 emphasised by many of the conscripts. A diligent diarist kept a record of the weather, noting on the 21st that 'frost since 14th Jan', and 'Still freezing hard' on the 29th. Conditions on the latter date were in fact appalling: 'The winter is combining with the normal discomforts of war to some effect: This morning 16 degrees of frost were discovered by the authorities who take the trouble to issue the results of such research on pink paper each day. Anyway I awoke to find my sponge anchored like a coral reef while my outer blanket simply flew up like a sheet of roofing when I mobilised for ablutions.'[23]

There was little other mobility at the time, with men digging 'new trenches at night for many weeks but sometimes the ground was so frozen that we could not make any progress'. The appalling conditions of this month, and their demoralising effect, were best summed up as 'a sort of firm snow falling all the time. It is no use looking forward to any fine weather for this next three months . . . getting too cold to write and Bed [*sic*] is the best place.'[24]

Other periods were also harsh. In April 1917 there was 'hail, rain and snow', and in October that year the 'weather [was] very bad'. One conscript recalled a particularly heavy snow in January 1918, in which 'our already soaked overcoats had frozen stiff; the lowest parts like boards, only that portion near our body remaining pliable, but when removed, this instantly froze hard also, and could not be put on again'. Strong winds were also a severe handicap. In mid-winter they hardened the snow on the roads, and thus marching in and out of the trenches became extremely perilous. Men often slipped on to their backs 'and cursed the leading officer who was in such a hurry on his horse that we barely had time to regain our balance'.[25]

Yet even without the problem of icy roads, the combination of rain and wind made progress nearly impossible: 'To exercise this a.m. with wind nearly enough to blow a horse over and raining till I could hardly see where I was. Wind and rain all day; nearly frozen in stables.' The severe problem of cold, as also the ongoing battle for warmth, are a constant theme of many letters and diaries. One conscript recalled spending several hours each day jumping up and down upon the duckboards in the trenches, in order to warm up. Another wrote that he felt so 'cold I can scarcely hold this pencil that I am writing with, I wish I could have a little warm at the stove in the office it would be like paradise'.[26] Trench life, however, was far more earthly, with every spare moment between military duties devoted to 'scrounging around for wood',[27] chopping it, lighting a fire and sitting around it. Yet often even such simple tasks were confounded by the basic conditions. A flooded trench meant 'we were sitting around the fire with our feet in water'; and elsewhere a brazier was kept ablaze in a front bombing position 'where we continued to hang a ground sheet so as to obscure all light from it to the enemy. The smoke is rather troublesome until one gets used to it.'[28]

It was not merely the climate therefore, but the lack of protection from the elements which affected the men most. Life in the front line was especially bad, since the trenches were permanently wet and often also flooded out, while the nature of trench warfare often dictated lengthy periods of activity in which men could not remove their boots or dry their feet. As a result, the 'combined cold and damp underfoot brought on many foot troubles at this time, for the water gradually oozed through and soaked our heavy boots; feet turned numb and toes turned funny colours.'[29] This was a reference to the very common ailment of trench-foot, which was the general term attributed to a variety of symptoms, such as those described above, and also painful swelling or inflammation of the feet. In the worst cases, the inflammation spread to the knees or even the thighs, and hospitalisation was needed. Throughout the war 74,711 men, suffering either from trench-foot or frostbite, were admitted to hospitals in France. However, even in less severe cases trench-foot debilitated men for a number of days, in which they had to rest their feet in a dry place, such as the reserve line. In addition, men who had been afflicted once by the complaint were far more susceptible than others.[30]

Trench-foot resulted from wet feet being encased in wet socks and boots, often for sustained periods. One man noted that he had removed neither boots nor puttees for five consecutive days, another claimed that 'my feet have been wet now for three weeks, but it cannot be helped' and a third summed up wryly: 'My feet are incessantly wet through and "gawd 'ates me".'[31] To many, the basic problem was one of damp socks rather than wet boots: 'your socks were rotted and you never had a change of anything.' The latter comment was not always the case, since other men claimed that 'every day we were given a change of socks and made to rub our feet for ten minutes with whale-oil'.[32] 'Each day a man came from somewhere at the rear with a sandbags full of dried socks, hand over our wet socks, anoint our feet with the oil and put on two dried socks. Of course we never got pairs, or our own from the previous day, we just got the first two that came out of the bag, one might be a small brown one and the other a large grey one. As they were taken away and dried day after day they became stiffer and smellier and the stench in that dugout became indescribable.' Other men sought solace from home: 'Thank you so much for . . . [the] eight socks – all of which have come to make life exceedingly bearable.'[33]

Knee-high gum-boots, which are frequently mentioned in these writings, became standard issue for men in the trenches. But as with socks, the distribution of the boots was also not very well organised. One of these conscripts recalled being sent to a section of the front line in which the trenches were flooded, causing many men to complain of afflicted feet. Eventually gum-boots were issued, 'but, following a common army practice, they took them away after a few hours because someone else wanted them'.[34] Such boots also often proved inadequate, since the watery mud could be higher than the protection they offered. They were also 'not good for the feet', as in the case of a march out of the trenches which culminated in sitting around a fire in order to 'remove our "gum" boots. With me this is rather a painful business as owing to a tear in the boot the water has got in and caused my foot to become swollen and painful.' The affliction was treated and subsided within a week; however, this man went back into the trenches three weeks later, and was once again subjected to a bout of wet feet and boots. As a result, he developed a 'skin affectation [*sic*] which is causing much irritation', for which he had to be hospitalised.[35]

Casualties of the war were therefore also casualties of the weather, due to 'the ever prevalent problem out here: "What to do with your feet".' But in truth, all parts of the body – and the mind – were affected by the merciless Flanders weather. It was an event of war no less than shooting and sniping. As one conscript put it: 'Everlasting guns "popping off" day and night . . . rain, mud, wind and general desolation and misery.'[36]

The weather framed the environment, and often influenced it; but the trenches – in fact all military habitats – were decidedly man-made, and decidedly important to the quality of life. As a result, accommodation and billets, of any kind, are prominent topics in the writings of the conscripts. Since much of the First World War was fought within the confines of the trenches, it is often assumed that trenches were the only habitat known to its soldiers. There is no doubt 'dug-outs' in trenches were the major form of accommodation available to soldiers, especially infantrymen, in the front line. However, aside from one man who claimed to have spent thirteen consecutive months in one section of the trenches,[37] all these conscripts moved both in and out of the line, and around various sectors of it. And during marching and resting they resided within permanent and makeshift camps of huts, tents and bivouacs; derelict cottages and bombed cellars; barns, schools and any other structure that could be adapted to the needs of the army. Since the measures of adaptation were minimal, the most salient features of these dwellings were usually filth and lack of substance. But in accordance with the functional nature of the war and its developments, accommodation was basically an issue dependent upon availability, necessity and circumstances rather than planning.

The front-line trenches the conscripts occupied were very different from those known to the earlier soldiers of the war. Trench warfare evolved in September 1914, when both sides found themselves unable to break through the opposing line.[38] However, with the onset of winter and the shortage of supplies, ammunition and soldiers, what started out as a temporary situation of stagnant opposition developed into two permanent lines of stationary combat. As a result, the hastily dug trenches which marked the early line also had to be improved. In October 1914 a soldier wrote that in his sector the British 'trenches, engineer-planned, were good, and clean cut in straight bays and traverses, some of which had been

revetted with sandbags'.[39] Yet the communication trench, which facilitated
the movement of ammunition and rations, the evacuation of wounded
men and ultimately retreat, was not completed, which meant that despite
appearances the described trench was basically unsafe and required more
work upon it. As one captain explained to Robert Graves in the spring of
1915: 'When I came out here first, all we did in the trenches was to paddle
about like ducks and use our rifles. We didn't think of them as places to
live in, they were just temporary inconveniences. Now we work here all the
time, not only for safety but for health. Night and day. First, at fire steps,
then at building traverses, improving the communication trenches, and so
on; last comes our personal comfort – shelters and dug-outs.'[40]

By mid-1915 the process of consolidation was at its peak, and a more
institutionalised period began, effectively lasting till early 1918. At its
height, the front-line system was composed of three parallel lines of
trenches: the first or fire trench, then the communication trench, and
finally the support line, from which troops could still move rapidly to
the front in case of emergency. Trenches were dug to a depth of
approximately 4 feet, with another 2–3 feet of wall above ground
constructed out of sandbags; the floor was made out of slatted planks,
known as duckboards, which covered a drainage tunnel that ran
through each trench. Rather than straight, the forward side of all
three lines actually jutted in and out in dog-tooth shape, in order to
allow for guard posts. Even after construction, nightly working parties
laboured at these trenches, replacing safety buttresses and improving
their protection. Graves observed such a party at work in a typical
trench in 1915:

[They] were filling sandbags with earth, piling them up bricklayer
fashion, the headers and stretchers alternating, then patting them
flat with spades. The sentries stood on the fire-step at the corners of
the traverses. . . . Two parties, each of an N.C.O. and two men, were
out in the company listening posts, connected with the front trench
by a sap about fifty yards long. The German line stretched some
three hundred yards beyond. From berths hollowed in the sides of
the trench and curtained with sandbags came the grunt of sleeping
men.[41]

The German advance of spring 1918 shattered this system, making 'real
trench warfare . . . almost a thing of the past, and most of the fighting

was done in shell-holes and the open country'. In this last phase of the war, the trenches were 'merely shell-holes joined together. The sides were supported by brushwood to prevent them from collapsing. The huge shell craters were impossible to get out of if one should fall in as they were full of green water. The bridges were composed only of narrow duck-boards which were placed over the craters to make a track to the advanced trenches.'[42]

The writings examined here refer mostly to the trench dug-outs in which the men lived and slept between duties. A conscript newly arrived at the front line early in 1917 recorded his first impressions in stark yet encompassing terms: 'Look round. Chaps sleep in dug out which runs for over a mile in clifs [sic]. Plenty of rats, Dead bodies and bad smells.' 'Cliffs' were wide shelves hollowed out of the wall of the trench. Another man 'found the dugout leaking and a lot of water inside'; whereas a third recalled his initial experience in 'just an ordinary chalk trench. Its name was Fleet Street. Being in the Ficheux sector all trench names commenced with 'F'. Some dug-outs – some tin shelters in the parapet – duck boards all along.'[43] This latter was a description of a common solution to the problem of shelter in the trenches: an attempt to 'make ourselves as comfortable as possible under the circumstances. There is some sort of shelter formed by roofing an angle of the trench with corrugated iron.' But these improvised shelters often proved unsafe, as in the case of a dug-out covered with a 'piece of corrugated iron over the trench thus making a path over the trench. To our surprise a pack mule crossed over on this path one night but his weight proved rather too heavy for our simple structure and almost immediately after the animal attempted this route my comrade and myself found ourselves buried alive temporarily but managed to extricate ourselves.'[44]

Beyond structure, the conscripts' perception of the trenches and dug-outs was also coloured by less material factors, such as smells. A typical first impression of the trenches, as noted above, usually referred to 'Dead bodies and bad smells'. Another conscript noted that many dug-outs were 'really saps as they were right under the earth accessible by means of underground passages fitted up with electric light. These saps were rather evil-smelling with numerous rats about.' This evil trench smell was clearly pervasive and unique, resulting from a landscape dominated by death and rain: 'it was unwise to disturb the trench sides in any way because of the awful smell that came from the earth, upon which so many men had lost their lives'. The depth of a trench also meant that besides smells emanating from the ground, others, imposed from above, would remained trapped within for long periods. An authentic 'trench smell' incorporated that of death with 'a mixture of old gas, high explosive fumes and corruption'; whereas a dug-out 'smelt of damp chalk, candle smoke, fags, rat dung, and damp, dirty, sweaty, lousy humanity'.[45]

An interesting comparison with the British trenches, often made by the conscripts themselves, was with the German ones. In general, these were much deeper and more solid than those dug by the British. One conscript noted the German trenches he entered with his unit in December 1917 were the finest he had ever seen, with well constructed dug-outs 25 feet below ground, while another man recalled choosing new dug-outs in Vimy Ridge: 'There are German ones and were splendidly made, in many cases 15 feet to 20 feet deep with long corridors and recesses for sleeping in and all lined with boards.' Yet the hallmark of Flanders was apparent even in these well-protected structures. One conscript lived in a German trench 30 feet below ground, which was very damp and infested with rats; and another wrote home: 'Have seen some old German Dug-outs some are 50 foot deep and concreted, they make them very fine, but Oh they do smell of dead "bosche".'[46]

Rats were also integral to the trench experience. Most conscripts describe them in matter-of-fact terms, alongside sandbags, dead bodies, the acrid smell of earth, and the noises of combat: 'Mingled with these terrific crashes [of guns] were the screams of many rats, fighting and running about all over us.' But rats were most apparent in their search for food: 'Anything we could not pack into our mess tin was vulnerable if left in a dugout or even while we slept.' 'I had a surprise yesterday morning. When I went to my pack for my ration bag (in which I keep my bread and iron rations) I found a neat hole gnawed in it, & a big one right through the bag & half my bread & iron rations of biscuits gone! Rats of course – they are numerous and most bold at night time.' Boldness was a prominent feature of trench rats, since they often pursued their quest in full view of human beings: 'One morning, in preparing for breakfast, I placed my small dole of bread just above the trench, where we happened to be, and immediately a large rat appeared and made awkwardly off with it. By rattling my rifle . . . I made the rat drop the bread; after raking it in again and trimming the crust my meal was continued.'[47]

Food was not the only quarry in which rats found interest: 'in one of the dug outs the other night, 2 men sat smoking by the light of a candle very quiet – all at once the candle moved and flickered. Looking up, they saw that a rat was dragging it away – fast.' Though it appears the conscripts accepted the presence of rats alongside the other evils of trench life, they still made efforts to eliminate their existence: 'An amusing & effective half hour can be spent with an entrenching-tool after dark – slaying them!' Yet such an exercise could sometimes be detrimental to the soldier. One conscript recalled noticing a rat poised on the tip of his boot, cleaning its whiskers. Raising his bayonet, he was about to stab it when the rat ran off: 'It was just as well, for if I had missed him and stabbed my own foot I should almost certainly have been court martialled for 'self inflicted wound'.'[48] Isaac Rosenberg summed up this superiority of rat over man in the trenches, when he addressed his 'Break of Day in the Trenches' to

> A queer sardonic rat – . . .
> It seems you inwardly grin as you pass
> Strong eyes, fine limbs, haughty athletes
> Less chanced than you for life . . .

Dug-outs within the trenches were the shelter most commonly known to infantry soldiers. Yet even this term was applied to a variety of abodes hollowed out of the earth, within the close vicinity of the front line. Lt Allfree recalled relocating his battery into a new section of the line: 'I picked sites for the men's dugouts in a bit of copse to the right of the battery. These were to be just pits in ground, about five feet deep, which could be covered with corrugated iron and earth, and camouflaged.' Another conscript wrote of a 'big dug-out under slag heap – [with] electric light', but a dug-out could also be 'in [an] old gun pit', or any other ground formation which could be covered either with corrugated iron or canvas: 'we've had to get four posts and drag a sheet over the top, but really it's a jolly fine dug out.'[49]

The latter description was actually of a bivouac – a makeshift structure used by soldiers of every corps both in and out of the line. Civilians and soldiers uninitiated into the mysteries of British army life in France were unfamiliar with this form of shelter, as apparent from the above letter. Bivouacs were not passed on to succeeding soldiers occupying a post, but rather were created afresh by each man or small group upon their arrival at a new location: 'We immediately set to work, after having fed and fastened the horses, to make ourselves places of abode. Assailed with choppers, spades, spaces, bill hooks, and saws we ventured into a neighbouring wood and cut down suitable branches for making uprights and crossbars, over which we might fasten bivouac covers. These latter are large tarpaulin sheets very much after the style of a removal van cover.' However, bivouacs could also be 'a rude shelter made of sack on poles', 'a waterproof arrangement on sticks'.[50] or anything else that came to hand:

> Our camp was composed of all sorts of shanties rigged up of wood & canvas. It seems that the army authorities did not seem to think artillery men required any sort of housing while on active service so they supplied nothing. In consequence the men had to make shift the best way they could to provide shelter for themselves. This they managed to do by stealing or to use the army word 'scrounging' anything that may come in handy for the purpose. Those who were lucky had at sometime or another been able to annexe a sheet from a motor lorry or railway wagon & this would make a tidy bivouac for 4 or 5 men; others not so fortunate rigged up shelters about the size of a dog kennel which they had to creep into on their hands & knees.[51]

This conscript devoted many pages to descriptions of various bivouacs he constructed with other men, laying emphasis upon the major role of scrounging in everyday life. In one incident 'Holland found a dug out that had a front made to it of match boarding so we "pinched" this & cut it up with a saw as quickly as possible so that it should not be recognized. This made quite a good end to our tent. Soon after we had finished the Regimental SM came round looking for this wood. It appears that this dugout had been selected for the Colonel's quarters & there was a rare row when they found the front had gone.'[52] This account highlights the autonomous nature of the conscripts' daily existence behind the lines, noted above also by Lt Allfree, in that officers usually brought them to a suitable site on which accommodation could be constructed, then left them to exercise initiative and expertise in actually creating an abode. The issue is well explained by the following sequence of diary entries, written by a conscript whose unit had just entered a certain section of the line:

31 May 1917   Went searching for a kip. Baulk and Clark found a good one for 3 so I joined on invitation.

1 June 1917   Day spent in improving dugout.
[After five days the unit moves on to another sector.]

8 June 1917   We had to dig ourselves in for the night and it looks like rain. By 9.00 [*sic*] we had a nice dugout, and got down to it being very tired.

9 June 1917   Very nice rest, only the dirt kept falling in on us. We were in a nice mess this morning.

10 June 1917   Boarded up the sides and sandbags at the back to keep the dirt from falling in on us.[53]

Whatever their shape, bivouacs were basically exceedingly small shelters, not far removed from the ground. One conscript described building himself one that was 6 feet in length and 4 feet in height, with straw upon the floor. However, it was in 'terrible looking country – if you dig 1 ft touch water. . . . Looks like rheumatism for some of us.' Given their average size, men could rarely do anything but sleep in bivouacs, as in the case of one 'holding 9 people side by side and not many more than 8 feet long. . . . Slept fairly decently but couldn't move a muscle during the night and got very stiff before morning.'[54] Another man recalled a period in the front line in which eight men sat side by side in a cramped bivouac throughout the days, leaving the shelter only at night to go on duty. In a letter home, one conscript apologised for his lapse in communication due to the fact that 'four of us are squatting on the floor of a tiny dug-out, elbow to elbow, so that it is more than difficult to write'. In general, however, dug-outs were considered by most front-line soldiers as a relative haven of safety. Possibly the cramped conditions inspired a feeling of cosiness, or else a soldier's presence in a dug-out meant a short release from duties – for whatever reason 'there was always something warm and welcoming about a dugout'.[55]

Huts were a more substantial form of front-line shelter, but one usually allocated to officers. In some cases, however, permanent artillery camps in the support line, which fed ammunition and supplies to the front line, were constructed of corrugated iron Nissen huts:

Mine is like a barrel or a cheese cut vertically in half and the half then placed on the ground, flat side downwards. It is made of corrugated iron: there is a door in front and two windows, with panes of linen cloth, at each end. Round the hut is a low rampart of sand bags. The space between them and the sides is filled in with earth, and the whole forms a protection against bursting shells, at least against such shells as are not direct hits. On either side of the door some former occupant has arranged in the brown earth, small bits of chalk stone to make the words 'Caterpillar Section, A S C' and has planted little clumps of daffodils and a few violets.[56]

These images of homely permanence were in direct contrast to those evoked by tent encampments. Some of these were but temporary abodes which housed succeeding waves of men passing through en route, comprised of 'tents with neither straw nor floor boards'. The movement between these camps also 'caused us a lot of inconvenience and work as every camp, if only occupied for an hour, had to be left perfectly clean and tidy, and latrines etc. had to be dug in new camps where such did not exist. In addition there was the constant packing up of our belongings.'[57] Other camps were more permanent, offering tents of a more substantial nature: 'Drew and Ryan have wooden beds and these are placed along the sides of the tent to the right and left of the door. Butcher, Hartley and I lie on the tarpaulin sheets that form the floor. Our blankets and kit are piled at the back of the tent and when night comes we lay down our beds with our feet pointing to the door. On the centre pole are hung our gas masks ready for any emergency.' Despite this apparent cosiness, tents were insufficient protection against the elements: 'Terrific thunder storm in evening. Tent blown in and flooded out'; and in winter the situation was even worse: 'It is no joke camping out this time of the year . . . we are always flooded out.'[58]

Some sections of the front line were situated in close proximity to villages, and so cellars of houses abandoned by their civilian occupants would be used as dug-outs. Describing one such village, a conscript noted that 'many of the houses are in ruins. Many, though still inhabited, show gaping holes in their red roofs or white walls. British soldiers have made themselves shelters in the shattered cottages and have taken possession of empty cellars for dug-outs.' Besides a proliferation of rats, the basic drawback of this form of shelter was the lack of light, which posed further problems for letter writing.[59] But villages were still preferable to the trenches; and while marching between sectors and during periods of rest, empty schools and barns of various description were often used as shelter.

At best, these had an 'ample supply of hay for us to lay on spread over the barn floor. We noticed that all buildings had painted on the door posts their billet no. & the number of men it would accommodate.' At worst, men were billeted in 'barns with mud floors and no windows, the door and various cracks in the plaster being the only places for light to enter. Here and there upon the ground were slimy puddles, making it difficult to find a suitable spot to deposit one's baggage, the only alternative being a few old wire hammock-beds.'[60]

Most barns, stables and sheds were of an intermediate quality. As roofed structures they provided a refuge from the weather in a way no dug-out or bivouac could. In addition, some barns were 'fitted with bunks on the ship pattern with wirenetting mattresses'. But in most cases soldiers slept on straw strewn upon the floor, which often also housed 'plenty of mice & beetles. Umpteen earwigs.' A conscript billeted in a stable summed up the issue succinctly: 'Pigs and the calf have a far better house than we do. With all reverence, can begin to realise now the birth of Jesus in a stable. People cannot realise [this] until they have experienced . . . [end of entry]'[61] The most negative aspects of these barns centred upon the fact they were not constructed for human occupation, nor were they used exclusively to this end throughout the war. One conscript noted of a barn in which he was billeted that 'formerly this was an ammunition and food dump'; while another recalled one that 'had a row of brick posts 8 feet apart one side partly closed by a strip of canvas 6 feet high above which to the roof was nothing. It was really a large cart shed.' In disgust – and good weather – one man noted in his diary that 'I was billeted in a barn which had been used as a hen house, so bivouaced [sic] out with Hunter, had a good time'.[62]

Besides shelter, billets and trenches were also assessed according to the sleeping facilities they offered. Trench warfare dictated perpetual awareness in case of enemy snipers, interspersed with incoming and outgoing bombardments. This basically meant a constant and intense degree of noise and activity, which made sleep 'about as rare as strawberries'. The possibility of rest was often reduced still further by the lack of sleeping arrangements, as the man who noted 'poor trench shelters to sleep in, only about 6 hours sleep in 4 days'.[63] Such beds that were available were constructed of a wooden frame covered with wire netting. Sometimes men slept on the duck-boards on the floor of the trench, or directly upon the chalk soil.[64] Another option was 'funk holes holding one or two men [which] were dug to depths of up to 6 feet into the parapet side [of the trench] . . . and one got used to sleeping in these on waterproof sheets. Some were several feet off the ground; others perhaps only a foot from the trench bottom.' At other times men simply sat 'on the fire-step – wrapped up in your ground sheet & any spare sandbags or old lumps of canvas you can beg, borrow or pinch! And looking like an Egyptian mummy with a tin hat on – you just sit & smoke!' One conscript who slept on a fire-step recalled that 'out of the first four days and nights in the firing line, I only had about three hours sleep!'[65]

While in the front line, a soldier could be on a rota of two hours on and two hours off throughout a consecutive forty-eight hours, 'thus having little proper rest'. As a result, the men did not remove any articles of clothing, usually not even their boots, for the entire duration of their front-line duty.[66] Moreover, rats often clambered over sleeping men, 'so that we were obliged to cover our faces entirely with "cap comforters"'. But it was the noise of guns which most prohibited sleep for those men not on duty: 'One might as well be living in a huge drum on which a thousand savages are beating with different kinds of hammers.' Sleep therefore became 'impossible, although eventually as one gets used to the sound it is a matter of being awakened and then falling asleep while the noise is going on.' Due to these sporadic bouts of sleep within the perpetual din and constant duties, many men were exhausted and overwrought, as with a conscript who experienced a severe bombardment which lasted several days: 'As a result of the recent experiences my nerves were not normal and I was unable to compose myself sufficiently to sleep. . . . At night we were put on sentry duty but being so dead tired it was quite impossible to keep awake in spite of the fact that we could hear the enemy cutting the wire in front.'[67] The reserve line, the third line of trenches which men usually entered for four days after four days in the front line, offered more possibilities of sleep and rest. Since soldiers were not on an hourly rota of duty they could remove their jackets, trousers and boots. The supply of blankets in this line was also more plentiful, as one conscript noted of his first rotation experience: 'Had a blanket tonight for the first time since Etaples and turned in early to get good benefit from our blankets.' The various village billets were once again preferable from this perspective, since 'the bit of rest we did have was very comforting – in a stable'.[68]

The different kinds of shelter mentioned actually highlight an interesting issue: the mobility of these men. The image of the war, largely due to the static lines of trenches, is mostly one of stagnation. And in terms of battle or extensive military action, the image was absolutely true. Yet effectively, due to personnel and unit rotations, these men were often in movement – if only within and between the lines. But as a result, it is the functional and temporary nature of their accommodation which stands out:

> Our new camp is in a field near the village of —— [*sic*]. When we arrived there on Easter Sunday [1918] a feeling of hopelessness came over me. How could we ever make this place habitable? Was our time to be taken up with perpetual changes, taking down of huts and putting them up again, carrying about of timber and tents and corrugated iron? Were we no sooner to be settled on one spot and grown accustomed to it than we were to be moved to another? These thoughts came over me as I stood in the rain looking dismally and helplessly around me at the sodden grass field.[69]

Most front-line abodes disintegrated in 1918, when the structured lines of combat were abandoned, first in retreat and later in advance. The German attack in the spring caught the British army by surprise, causing most front-line units to flee: 'At 8 P.M. Fritz made a bombing raid which compelled us to retire. After a time there was a lull and we were able to get a sleep in a rather unconventional bed – the gutter of the road.'[70] The retreat continued for several weeks, dispersing units in all directions. One man recalled coming upon an abandoned, hastily dug trench into which he and two comrades jumped, 'immediately beginning to deepen it, for here we hoped to stay, not having slept a wink for forty-eight hours'. Yet after a few hours they had to evacuate this shelter:

> And now followed the saddest and most terrible part of the retreat, or so it impressed me. It was terrible not because of danger, for the enemy was following us within a half-mile's distance, but because of the utterly exhausted condition of the men, after half-a-week without sleep, moving, moving, digging, digging, and having very little to eat or drink . . . the men were so fatigued that order was impossible, for they dragged along as best suited their feelings. . . . At times, too, men fell out and sat on the ground, too exhausted, or without the spirit to continue.[71]

Another man recalled hearing an order to halt in the midst of this long march, whereupon he dug a hole together with another man, into which they both crawled with a ground sheet. 'We were very tired by now and dimly I heard someone say "Gas?" Someone else said "fuck the gas" and then I must have fallen asleep . . . I woke up just as the sky was beginning to lighten, feeling pretty rough. . . . Our eyes looked like oysters in buckets of blood and it was obvious that we had been gassed.'[72]

During the British counter-attack, the last of the war, in the summer of 1918, conditions were no better. The constant mobility of the retreat continued, simply in the opposite direction; and functionality, both as a response to events and in its basic form of simply existing, was supreme, with men snatching a few hours of sleep whenever possible. One man wrote of crawling under a desk in a school in a small Belgian town, while another recalled a night in which he lay down in exhaustion in the middle of a field. Upon awakening 'I looked down and saw I had been lying alongside a dead German, he was just a boy; maggots were crawling from him, the sergeant saw him too and exclaimed "Christ almighty, poor bugger", I turned away and vomited, I always had a squeamish stomach.'[73]

The conscripts existed in an environment of appalling weather and mostly uninhabitable abodes – and there can be no doubt that these factors greatly influenced their general attitude. While good weather did not necessarily make them glad to be soldiers, they accepted their situation more positively, if lack of complaint may be considered a measure. In other words, good weather reflected little upon these men simply because it did not make their existence substantially more difficult. Bad weather inhibited every task, human or military, and was therefore central to them, their writings, and their dire perspective. Much the same is true of their perceptions of billets and dug-outs, but in this case they were also guided by two basic principles: the protection offered by any abode, both from bombardments and from the weather; and the sleeping facilities it incorporated. One conscript summed up the issue in simple terms: 'I am quite accustomed [to] sleeping in queer places now and under strange conditions too'.[74]

But as ever, queer and strange were not absolute terms. Behind the lines men sought the cleanest and warmest form of shelter, when possible. In good weather the option of a bivouac shared among friends was deemed preferable to an inadequate barn or stable.[75] One conscript wrote of another solution: billeted in a shed 'not fit to sleep in . . . I & a couple of other fellows who have similar tastes as regards sleeping places, managed to sleep in an A.S.C. motor lorry.'[76] Yet these, and any other form of accommodation, were considered preferable to trenches and dug-outs in the front line – in which comfort and safety were merely relative to complete exposure to the elements and the enemy in the combat zone. Late in 1916, the period in which the trenches should have been at their relative best, one conscript wrote home that 'we are sleeping in some old broken down barns that will sound a bit queer to you, but they are a lot more comfortable than the trenches'.[77] Since these barns often gave scant shelter, the condition of the trenches must have been truly appalling. Another conscript, who also compared a filthy barn to the front line, noted: 'Apart from the actual trenches, we never again visited such filthy billets.'[78]

Before arriving at the front line the conscripts had no notion of the existence within it. Their expectations of shelter, comfort and accommodation were therefore still defined by their civilian identity, which had been processed through the military experiences of the training camps in England and France. This was apparent, for example, in a conversation between two 'old soldiers' and a group of conscripts crossing to France for the first time: 'But at least we have huts to sleep in,' we objected. 'Never a hut,' they answered us; 'just a waterproof sheet & a blanket unless you can pinch a blanket or two. It's a good thing for you fellows that you have two old hands going out with you. We'll soon show you what can be done with a sheet. We'll rig up a cosy little shack.'[79] Yet within weeks of experiencing trench life most of these men clearly placed survival over cultural considerations of propriety. The shape, size, quality of materials and appearance of an abode were irrelevant in the face of the need for sleep and shelter; filth and vermin were just a regular part of the environment. And while a miner or a farm labourer probably experienced a shorter period of adjustment than a bank clerk or a civil servant, the process in itself was the same for all conscripts. It was short, it was painful, and it did not make conscripts glad to be soldiers.

> Think of me crouching where the worms creep
> Waiting for someone to sing me to sleep
> Sing me to sleep in some old barn
> Where some old nag has laid his head
> Stretched out upon my water proof
> Dodging the rain's drops through the roof . . .[80]

CHAPTER 5

Living in War

It is unlucky for thirteen to sit down to a meal
when rations have been issued for only seven.
If sun rises in the East, it is a sure sign that
there will be stew for dinner.[1]

Certain people would not clean their buttons,
Nor polish buckles after latest fashions,
Preferred their hair long, putties comfortable . . .

Ivor Gurney, *The Bohemians*

The trenches and the rest camps were the environment in which the
conscripts went about the business of being soldiers at war. But while
military action was the purpose of their existence in mud and
rudimentary shelters, they still had to deal with the most basic elements
of existence: food, clothing and cleanliness. And it was these functions of
everyday life that often proved to be the most difficult to accomplish –
and the most crucial in determining their attitude to being conscripts.

A hungry man makes an inadequate soldier – which is why it is
generally accepted that an army marches on its stomach. In the First
World War it seems soldiers also sat in trenches according to a similar
axiom, since the writings examined here display an obsessive interest in
hunger, food and its pursuit. Lack of sleep, exposure to the elements,
mud, dirt and lice are undoubtedly awful, yet they are also clearly
endurable, since soldiers lived in such conditions throughout the war.
But men cannot function without food: it is a human, not a military
necessity. It is also a question of expectations, which may be modified but
never erased. The original expectation may be of a certain quality and
quantity of food, and over time this may be replaced with poorer samples
– yet the demand for nourishment will not disappear. A body expects to
be fed on a permanent basis. Moreover, in war it is also an issue of
danger: hungry men 'are very susceptible to cold, get bored easily, take
increasingly little interest in others, and can eventually assume a "don't

care" attitude which resembles the zombie-like trance of utter exhaustion'.[2] The essentially stationary nature of trench warfare made many soldiers doubly susceptible to these dangers. As C.M. Lloyd told Beatrice Webb, 'The terrible monotony of the trenches concentrates all the men's thoughts and desires on food and drink'.[3] And it was an intense concentration.

The official daily quota of food per soldier in 1916 was 1¼ lb of meat, 1¼ lb of bread, ¼ lb of bacon, 3 oz cheese, ½ lb fresh vegetables and small quantities of tea, jam, salt, butter, mustard, pepper, condensed milk and pickles. This list should have provided each man with 4,300 calories a day, as opposed to 3,859 consumed by the average British civilian.[4] All these are meant to be historical facts. However, perceptions differ from facts in that they incorporate attitudes and interpretations, often as facts. To this extent, the official record of a soldier's daily rations was largely irrelevant, since none of these conscripts was aware of it. In other words, it may be interesting to note that in 1916 a soldier should officially have received 1¼ lb of bread per day, which was approximately one quarter of a loaf. Yet it meant little to the conscript who wrote the following diary entry on 25 August 1916: '. . . never had such a rotten time . . . rations scarce, as many as 24 in a loaf sometimes, and never less than 8'. In fact, this disparity highlights the difficulties of supplying troops in time of combat, and the specific problems facing the British economy throughout the First World War. But to the hungry soldier these were of little interest: his perception was one of hunger, substantiated by his factual record of at least eight soldiers to one loaf of bread, and his expectation of a sufficient share in the rations provided. This perception was further coloured by the dire condition of being 'up to the knees in mud . . . and absolutely impossible to be without lice'.[5]

This small example shows that any discussion of food or hunger experienced by these men should not be in light of an official record, but rather in comparison to *their* perceptions of the regular fare of a combat soldier. In other words, in order to understand their obsession with food, it is necessary to establish what they knew to be their daily ration. The most comprehensive list of such found in these writings was noted by a caterpillar driver:

We have two menus, one for ordinary occasions when we are living a settled life, the other for times when we are moving about and when the bringing up of supplies is difficult.

The first one is something like this.

Breakfast.   Tea, Bread, Bacon.
Dinner.   Stew (or Roast Meat if there is a good cook)
                Potatoes (sometimes) Boiled Rice (occasionally).
Tea.   Tea, Bread, Butter, Jam or Cheese.
Biscuits and Cheese are generally to be had for supper by those who
wish them.

The second menu is after this style.

Breakfast.   Tea, Biscuits, Bully Beef.
Dinner.   'Macconochies' i.e. tinned meat and vegetables.
Tea.   Tea, Biscuits, Jam.[6]

The tins were manufactured by Maconochie Bros of London. The
'Analytic Report from the Lancet Laboratory' noted that 'each tin
contains ¾lb of fresh boneless beef together with potatoes, haricot beans,
onions, carrots, and gravy. . . . It provides a very palatable, attractive dish,
nourishing and stimulating. We found the contents of the tin sound, and
an examination for metal in the gravy gave a quite negative result.'[7]
At the start of the war a standard scale of rations for all troops was
fixed. This was revised in 1917, 'as the world shortage increased and
provision became more difficult. . . . [Thus] with the concurrence of the
medical authorities, two scales were introduced, viz., one for troops at the
front, and another, a smaller ration, for GHQ and troops on the line of
communication.'[8] In fact, the staple diet in the front-line trenches
differed only slightly from that described above: 'For breakfast we had a
slice of cold fried bacon with tea and a biscuit or small piece of bread; for
dinner a stew of bully beef and onions, or, if we were lucky, a
'Machonocie' [*sic*] ration – a tin of cooked meat and vegetables; for tea,
biscuits, jam, and tea; for supper, what was left over, usually only bully
beef.' Troops on the march breakfasted on a similar menu, 'a dinner of
Iron rations (Bully Beef and biscuits) which are partaken of as opportunity arised [*sic*] and the third meal of the day is prepared by the Cook
at the end of the day's journey and very often consists of a soup made of
Bully Beef and Pork and Beans.'[9]
Bully beef was clearly the backbone of the British culinary experience
in France. A tin of 'bully' was an integral component of fighting order,

alongside a shovel, flares and three bandoliers of ammunition. However, while it may have been nourishing, it was also monotonous, moving many to note 'bully beef again for dinner'; or 'we get so much "bully" that I loathe the sight of it'.[10] The tins themselves also presented some problems: 'Each tin has an opener which in most cases fails to open the tin properly & then one has to finish the job with the opener in your jackknife [*sic*]. You would then have great difficulty in getting the meat to come out of the tin whole so you would have to dig it out in chunks. . . . Further unless you were very careful you could get a very ugly wound from the jagged edges of the tin.' Bully beef was usually eaten directly from the tin, but it was also possible to fry 'it with an onion or two', or even to incorporate it into a stew, which was another staple dish of the British Army: 'Army stew is indescribable. It consists of many things, and is made according to the taste of the cook and the materials at his disposal. "Macconochies", rich in fat, form the basis, a few tins of pork and peas or beans are thrown in, a piece of fresh meat cut into small pieces and perhaps some potatoes are added: the whole is well boiled and the result is "stew". It is known popularly as "S.O.S." — Same Old Stew — though I have heard of other interpretations.' Another conscript 'made the interesting discovery that rice was sometimes added to the stew in order to camouflage the maggots in the meat'.[11]

In the later stages of the war jam was invariably lemon marmalade, which was also used for sticking pictures to the wall. Sometimes another jam was supplied, which was 'almost tasteless stuff from Australia, labelled "peach and melon".' Often it 'was not to the liking of the troops who heaved it over the trench parapet in bomb fashion.'[12] Army biscuits, another mainstay of the soldiers' diet, were 'of concrete consistency', 'just like dog biscuits'. One conscript claimed he 'broke one front tooth upon them before I had been in France a month'.[13] Bread was 'always in the form of a round Coburg loaf'. However, when 'the bread ration in France was reduced from 1¼ to 1 lb [in 1917], the medical authorities demanded an issue of 2 oz rice daily and 2 oz oatmeal three times a week. In due course of time it was ascertained, however, that the troops would not eat more than 1 oz rice a day, and the latter scale for rice and 6 oz oatmeal weekly was adopted.'[14]

Variations on these menus were not frequent, but they were possible. One conscript enjoyed 'Rice and figs for dinner for a change', and another wrote of stewed barley and prunes, or even a rabbit stew.[15] A further possibility was cooking upon stoves, mostly improvised: 'Drew has

1 A typical pre-conscription recruiting poster, shaming men into volunteering (Imperial War Museum, London).

2 Record of Service Paper, known as an Attestation Form: this is the version brought into circulation for conscripts from 1916. It makes provision for conscientious objectors, and is authorised by an Approving, rather than a Recruiting, Officer.

Army Form B. 103.

CATEGORY A.

Casualty Form—Active Service.

Regimental Number 83/67

Regiment or Corps 3rd N.F. for No. 23 O.C.B. Catterick

Rank Pte. Surname Woodcock Christian Name Henry

Religion C. of E. Age on Enlistment 18 years 6 months

Enlisted (a) 22.11.17 Terms of Service (a) D of W Service reckons from (a) 13.5.18

Date of promotion to present rank.............. Date of appointment to lance rank..............

Extended .... Re-engaged .... Qualification (b) ....

.... or Corps Trade and rate ....

.... Signature of Officer ....

Occupation Student

Report		Record of promotions, reductions, transfers, casualties, &c., during active service, as reported on Army Form B.213, Army Form A. 36, or in other official documents. The authority to be quoted in each case.	Place of Casualty	Date of Casualty	Remarks. Taken from Army Form B.213, Army Form A.36, or other official documents.
Date	From whom received				
		Embarked			
		Disembarked			
		Deemed to have been enlisted	Newcastle	22/11/17	
		Called for service	"	13/5/18	A2573
		Posted to Att. Depot Nth. Mid Bde	"	13/5/18	
		Post. 3rd N.F. for No. 23 O.C.B	Catterick	7/6/18	
			2nd Lieut for O/C		
		Reception Depot North Fus			

(a) In the case of a man who has re-enlisted, or enlisted into Section D, Army Reserve, particulars of such re-engagement or enlistment will be entered

(b) Signaller, Shoeing-Smith, &c.

W. 9635—M2733 2000m 9/17 (35611) C. F. & S., Ltd., Form B./2/1807. P.T.O.

3 Casualty Form – Active Service: a compulsory attachment to every Attestation Form. As of 1916 each one carried the three crucial dates in the conscription process: 'Deemed to have been enlisted', 'Called for service' and 'Attendance at depot'.

4 A recruiting station, 1917: a queue of men called up (Imperial War Museum, London).

5 *Being sworn in: an emotional point in the conscription process (Imperial War Museum, London).*

6 *An eye test: just one part of the medical examination. Because of the demand for soldiers at the front, many men were passed as fit for combat service, even if they were not (Imperial War Museum, London).*

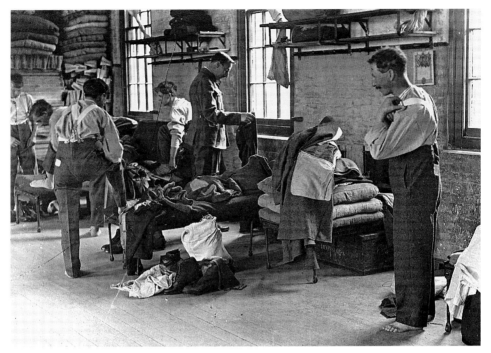

7 The initial transformation from civilians into soldiers – changing into army issue (Imperial War Museum, London).

8 Commencing 'active service' – British troops landing at Boulogne from a dazzle-painted troopship, 31 January 1918 (Imperial War Museum, London).

9 The final stages of basic training: troops at a gas training depot in France (Imperial War Museum, London).

10 The basic reality of the closed world of the trenches – mud and water. Lancashire Fusiliers in a flooded communication trench, January 1917 (Imperial War Museum, London).

11 The shock of 1918: the German Spring Offensive. It shattered the trench system and split up units. This is an outpost of the Warwicks in a ruined barn near Marquois, 13 April. Note the large amount of kit weighing down these two men, and the desecrated landscape (Imperial War Museum, London).

12 *Central kitchens in a trench near Wancourt during the Battle of Arras, 29 April 1917 (Imperial War Museum, London).*

13 *Tank Corps members at a Lewis gun post near Robecq. Cooking during a quiet spell, 17 April 1918. Men often shared resources if supplies were short or a post remote (Imperial War Museum, London).*

14 *Portioning out the bread at a roadside dump near Albert, March 1917 (Imperial War Museum, London).*

15 *Gunners sorting the mail, near Grevillers, 27 August 1918 (Imperial War Museum, London).*

THE LOUSE PROBLEM

AT THE

WESTERN FRONT,

BY

Lance-Serjeant A. D. PEACOCK, M.Sc. (Dunelm.),

ROYAL ARMY MEDICAL CORPS (TERRITORIAL FORCE),

Formerly Entomologist to the Government of Southern Nigeria;
Lecturer in Zoology, University of Durham.

LONDON :

PRINTED FOR HIS MAJESTY'S STATIONERY OFFICE,

BY HARRISON AND SONS, ST. MARTIN'S LANE, W.C.,

Printers in Ordinary to His Majesty.

—

1916.

16 *So serious were the infestations of lice among the troops that the army issued this booklet in 1916.*

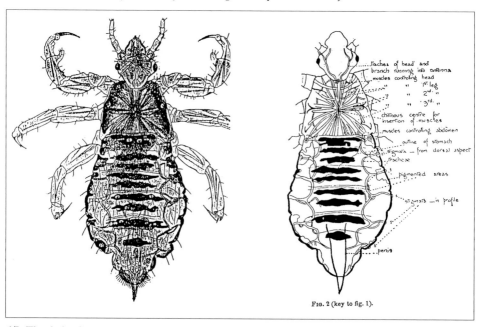

FIG. 2 (key to fig. 1).

17 *The clothes louse (*Pediculus humanus*) and (right) key to its anatomy.*

18 A classic postcard from the Western Front: infantry soldiers, September 1917. The legend 'Somewhere in France' is printed on the back.

19 Cigarettes were crucial to soldiers. This Daily Mail *card reads: Before battle, in battle, and after battle, our 'Tommies' are ready for a 'fag'. These men are lighting up after a scrap.*

WITH THE BRITISH
EXPEDITIONARY FORCE

June 24th 19

My Dear Mum & Dad,

Thank you very much indeed dear Mum for the lovely parcel you have been so kind as to send me & which has arrived quite safely, & I am sure it is more than good of you.

I must now thank you dear Dad for your nice ~~told~~ letter, which arrived along with the parcel, it is the one you wrote on the 11th & addressed to Minister & I have only just got it, it has been delayed a long time hasn't it? but still I am jolly glad I have got it.

The contents of your parcel Mum are a treat, & it is an

PTO

20 *A standard letter home from the front, written on recreation hut notepaper, in this case the YMCA. 'On Active Service' is printed above, as a caution from the censor.*

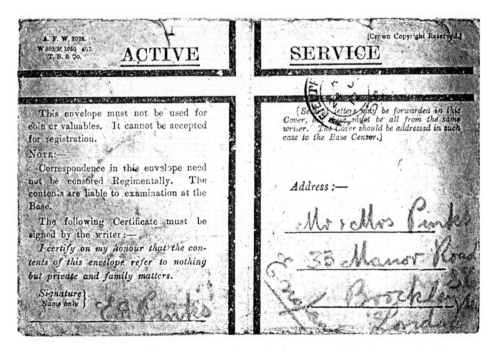

NOTHING is to be written on this side except the date and signature of the sender. Sentences not required may be erased. If anything else is added the post card will be destroyed.

[Postage must be prepaid on any letter or post card addressed to the sender of this card.]

I am quite well.

I have been admitted into hospital
{ sick } and am going on well.
{ wounded } and hope to be discharged soon.

I am being sent down to the base.

I have received your { letter dated _____
{ telegram „ _____
{ parcel „ _____

Letter follows at first opportunity.

I have received no letter from you
{ lately
{ for a long time.

Signature}
only }

Date _____

Wt W1566 R1619-18539 8000m. 6-17. G. & Co., Grange Mills, S.W.

21 A field postcard, distributed by the army to all soldiers. Regulations required these to be sent home at fixed intervals (see p. 132).

A. P. W. 3078.
W 209/M 1059 6/17.
T. B. & Co.

ACTIVE   SERVICE

[Crown Copyright Reserved.]

This envelope must not be used for coin or valuables. It cannot be accepted for registration.

NOTE:—

Correspondence in this envelope need not be censored Regimentally. The contents are liable to examination at the Base.

The following Certificate must be signed by the writer:—

I certify on my honour that the contents of this envelope refer to nothing but private and family matters.

Signature}
Name only }

[Several letters may be forwarded in this Cover; but must be all from the same writer. The Cover should be addressed in such case to the Base Censor.]

Address :—

Mr & Mrs Pinks
35 Manor Road
Brockley
London

22 A green envelope, assumed by many men to be completely uncensored. In fact one rather than two censors read these letters (see p. 132).

My Dear Mother

28ᵗʰ July 1416 Friday.

At last I have managed to get hold of some stationary, and I hope you will please forgive me for this long delay. We are encamped at a Base at present to where we came this morning, but as I am not used to this district I don't know exactly whether we came south-west or what, of our previous quarters

When we first arrived after a pleasant sea voyage, we were welcomed in a very encouraging manner, but oh, in spite of the beautiful quaintness of every street with their irregular buildings; the steep, hilly, rough & ready road-ways with white dust, inches deep, absolutely put years on us; — and the troop-trains — by Jove!, slow but not sure, rickety & decidedly not comfortable; in other words, beyond description; ~~~~ are a veritable picture or pattern of steam-snails.

My present address is as follows I think; —

No 1246 B. Company
1/5ᵗʰ East Yorks Regt.
37ᵗʰ Inf. Base Depot
A.P.O. Section 17
B.E.F.
France.

23 *Trying to outwit the censor: sample of a letter written in code in order to overcome the rule of censorship which forbade soldiers to disclose their exact location (see pp. 135–7). The first sentence spells out 'Etaples'.*

24 *Guard duty was the basis of trench routine at all times: a sentry of the 12th East Yorkshires on the firestep of a snow-covered trench near Roclincourt, 9 January 1918. He is wearing a mackintosh cape over his greatcoat (Imperial War Museum, London).*

25 *A posed photograph: the sanitised version of soldiers' lives in France. Many such were created and sent to reassure family and friends. This may be a hospital garden, as the man on the right is injured.*

*26 The real unknown soldiers of the First World War: two heavily laden conscripts trudging on,
somewhere in France – anonymous to the last (Imperial War Museum, London).*

made a stove out of an old petrol tin. He has cut a round hole in one side, and a number of small slits on top. When the flame is directed through the hole in the side the air within becomes rapidly very hot indeed, and it is easy to boil water or to cook food upon the perforated top.[16] On a daily basis stoves were 'a great benefit to us at night as we were able to cook porridge & make cocoa for our suppers. Our cook would always give us a supply of oatmeal when we asked & we used to cook this at night. He was supposed to give us oatmeal porridge for breakfast at times but preferred to dole it out to us instead & so save himself the trouble.' When supplies permitted, stoves were also used for frying potatoes, or bully beef and onions, or even Welsh rarebit, made out of bread and 'a large slab of cheese, which we have saved from our allowance at tea'.[17]

Rations were most scarce in the trenches, where men were absolutely dependent upon the supplies sent up from the reserve lines. Ration parties from each unit brought up the food every night,

> which invariably meant running the gauntlet of enemy shelling. . . . [Hot] meals cooked at the transport lines were carried on the back in metal containers with rope loops for the shoulders and reached from the neck to the hips, really quite heavy when full. Bread and jam was issued not over-generously but being based by the quarter-master on the front line strength of the previous day, as reported by each company field telephone, occasionally became a bonus from heavier casualties. These other rations [including margarine, lumps of cheese and packets of free issue cigarettes] were carried in small sacks.[18]

Yet men sometimes found themselves 'temporarily without food,' or, more often, simply hungry due to a shortage of rations: 'Thanks to our lousy Q.M.S. shortage of grub as usual – 1 loaf for 4 men for 24 hours duty!!'[19] It was in these situations that the quality and quantity of food became a relative issue, as long as it could be secured. In other words, when food was sufficient, there were complaints about taste and monotony. When it was scarce, men were interested only in getting it, whatever the quality – or even the quantity, in extreme cases. This is apparent, for example, from the diary of one conscript who kept a meticulous account of the food he was offered and consumed. The following description is typical of a scarce food situation, in which he focuses only on its actual existence: 'Rations bad:– bully for breakfast, ¼ loaf and no biscuits. Luckily Sandy had a bit of rice so made ourselves some tea. Then Asker came up from wagon line with some Quaker Oats which we had for supper.' Another solution to front line shortage was given by a conscript who claimed that 'owing to a none too plentiful supply of rations we decide to make one meal of dinner & tea, making two meals a day.'[20]

The situations of shortage were periodical, usually reflecting the location of a trench section or the state of the war, rather than any preconceived army strategy. These fluctuations were exemplified in the diary of a conscript who recorded several stints in front line trenches throughout 1917. In January he complained daily of hunger, noting that 'food awful. Breakfast ½ slice of bread (bacon or cheese). Din. 1 mug of soup. Tea 2 biscuits (jam, butter).' Early in March the 'food [is] a bit better. 1 loaf to 8 men. cheese stew and jam.' In mid-April the 'food [is] a lot better', while in his trench duty of mid-July 'food [is] pretty good.' Yet by the end of August 'food [is] not A1. Cook over tin lid with rag and candles.' In October 'conditions in trenches awful. Food not over plentiful owing to feeding of many German prisoners taken at Ypres.' His experiences in mid-November were of 'food very uncertain and scarce', a situation which deteriorated into 'suffering a wee bit from hunger. Rations have not come and have been without food all day.' His final entry on the subject, six days later, was that 'food is awfully scarce we are all weak and faint through hunger were with[out] food at all for two days'.[21]

Shortages were also apparent in reserve line trenches and camps. Frederick Voigt, who was in a labour battalion, described breakfast as 'a fragile wisp of bacon . . . [and] a piece from the previous day's bread ration'. In other camps 'the ration lorry does not come and there is no bacon for breakfast, nor bread for tea. Or an additional ten or twelve men will arrive unexpectedly and the food which was meant to serve for 48 has to be eked out to satisfy 60. Or perhaps the lorry comes but brings no fresh meat and there is only "bully beef" for dinner.' The latter comment highlights yet again the manner in which perceptions were coloured by expectations: when food was short the emphasis was laid upon the quantity distributed; when food was sufficient, the emphasis was upon quality – disappointment in the lack of fresh meat, and the reappearance of the reviled bully. This duality is apparent also in the following description of shortage: '*July 23* . . . For dinner we had boiled rabbit & we did enjoy it. We all got a decent portion & it was a welcome change to bully stew. . . . *July 25* . . . More rabbit for dinner but now we get a much smaller portion. In fact the cook called me back today & took one piece back from my dixie as he had accidently [*sic*] dropped 2 pieces in mine about 2" square.'[22] On the first day this conscript noted the quality of the food as a result of it being plentiful; on the second day his reference was merely to quantity, due to a feeling of hardship.

A common method of overcoming food shortages, especially in the rear lines where men could walk into the surrounding countryside, was scrounging. 'In other words "pinching" or picking up anything loose we might find at any neighbouring cookhouse. We visited one place where the cook very kindly gave us four tins of Pork and Beans and 4 packetfuls of biscuits.' To some men this became an instinctive measure for survival, exercised whenever the opportunity arose. And in this matter too, taste was not the most important issue: one man wrote of a train journey which had 'innumerable stops, and on one occasion somebody managed to scrounge a few bottles of champagne and tins of Nestle's Swiss milk, which made an excellent cocktail'. Another wrote that 'I have been able to confiscate 72 bars of Nestles chocolate. We don't go now for a bar or two, we want the box.' A third noted quite starkly that he 'pinched some spuds from a field on the way up last night so have a bon dinner.' Raiding potato fields was a common pursuit for many soldiers, 'to the great consternation of their owners who afterwards put in an unsuccessful claim for damages: we were therefore able to have boiled potato suppers. . . . This was a good job as our rations still consisted of biscuits and no bread.'[23]

Other men acquired the habit with greater difficulty: 'We've had a real struggle for existence lately. . . . To we novices in the art of "scrounging" it seems that the real likelihood of getting bread at a certain place is in inverse proportion to the apparent likelihood. We go to the boulangerie & are told bread is "na-poo" or "farine tout fini!" but one gets a loaf from an ironmonger's shop or perhaps a forge or a "pub" with comparative ease.' Yet hunger reduced men to behaviour they would consider unthinkable under normal circumstances. One conscript recalled marching out of the trenches. Halting 'beside a small wood . . . I saw a couple of soldiers sitting beside a fire warming a tin of food, one got up to go . . . [and] the other turned his head and in a flash I grabbed the tin and bolted between our column. . . . To what lengths hunger will drive a man.'[24]

The spring retreat of 1918, and the following summer advance, were once again the background to the greatest misery, in which hunger and scrounging appeared to have reached a peak. In the initial days of retreat any semblance of organisation collapsed, and men lived off their remaining iron rations. But within days field kitchens were set up along the road, 'at which a man was distributing soup to all who came for it, and it was good, and thick, and hot'. However, once the supply lines were restored rations were still short. 'Sometimes one loaf had to do for fifteen or twenty men for the day.'[25] Empty villages from which the civilian inhabitants had fled were a major source of scrounging at this time: 'Still retreating, we were taken to another village, where we managed to get a bit of rest (and the mail was brought up). We also had a good feed in this village, as the civilians had evacuated same & left behind them fowls, rabbits, etc. which we were soon cooking in our field kitchen.' Another man came upon a cellar full of wine and *crème de menthe*, which he consumed to the point of oblivion, sleeping soundly for the first time after a week of constant retreat.[26] The mobility of the following summer advance also made it difficult to establish permanent lines of supply. Thus in September 1918 one conscript recalled eating 'two spoonfuls of plain boiled unsweetened rice, that was the last I had for three days. . . . On the third day a three ton lorry came with boxes of rations and a little ammunition, we had hard biscuits, a tin of bully beef, jam and pork and beans.' In October another man wrote that 'no rations have turned up to-day, so we are on "iron rations".' Yet the heavy casualties suffered in this campaign also produced circumstances of abundance: 'The number of men was now so greatly reduced that . . . we had more rations than we could possibly eat – an unusual state of affairs.'[27]

Parcels from England were a 'main standby' as a supplementary source of food, representing both necessity and luxury. Besides the tangible connection with home, these parcels often contained items that assuaged pangs of hunger: 'Rations were rather short, and I can tell you I was pleased and it was nice chocolates and nice apples.' Regardless of being nice, parcels were often a major source of food: 'Bully and biscuits again, have had no bread for 5 days. Hope I have a parcel soon.' In the spring retreat of 1918 'it would have been bad for us without the contents of parcels sent from home'. In the subsequent advance one man thanked his parents for supplementing his iron rations with paste & "Tuna".'[28] Parcels were clearly created by worried families and friends aware that these men were suffering from basic shortages: 'Do not send fruit, it goes rotten. I notice you have sent a plain cake and butter, it is not so necessary now as we get bread – A.S.C. bread is not half bad.' When supplies were sufficient, parcels offered a taste of civilian life: 'This is a red letter day. My parcel came this morning with a tin of peaches, loaf and butter, fish paste, tobacco, sleeping helmet, chocolate and pair of socks and a towel. Had peaches for sweet at dinner and fish paste for tea. Grand.' One man achieved total luxury from a Christmas hamper containing roast chicken, tinned salmon, cake, crystallised figs, chocolate, raisins, nuts and fine cigars. He shared this feast with his trench-mates, who 'were just like animated chunks of mud, but still we managed to thoroughly enjoy it'.[29]

Christmas dinner was a high point of the culinary year, which the army authorities 'tried to make . . . as cheerful as possible, Officers supplying beer, oranges, and fresh meat and Christmas pudding.' Even relatively poor spreads were enhanced by a general feeling of good-will between officers and men. One conscript who was in the front line recalled his festive dinner consisting 'chiefly of stew. The Captain comes round during the meal and consoles us for the absence of Xmas puddings by telling us that owing to the activity of German submarines a large consignment of puddings have gone to the bottom of the channel. After dinner nuts and oranges and cigarettes are distributed.' This conscript found compensation two weeks later, upon receiving a plum pudding in a 'parcel of "good things"' from his mother.[30] Other men, who were located close to a YMCA canteen, combined their own resources with those of the army to make the day a memorable and satisfying one: 'Dinner of pork, potatoes, cabbage and plum pudding. Also got paid 5 francs which we all pooled to get tinned fruit etc. Tinned salmon and cake for tea, so not done so badly. . . . We had tinned pears, peaches, lobster, nuts, chocolate, biscuits etc. with beer, rum and champagne.' Yet even these achievements pale in comparison to '16 Geese, 4 Hams, plenty of vegetables & . . . Free Beer also, the men say they never had such a feed in the army before.' But reality returned together with a new year, and 'the good old Bully is getting a thrashing now'.[31]

During periods of rest behind the lines soldiers often found respite from army rations and cooking in the farms dotted around the countryside, where fresh supplies of produce and cooked meals could be secured for very reasonable prices. One conscript found himself near 'a rare country village, an "Ideal Blighty" one, we get large new laid eggs for 2*d* and milk for 3*d* a quart that's when funds permit.' Another man recalled a farmhouse from which he was 'able to obtain eggs (2½d and 3d each) and fresh milk, and took full advantage of this privilege. I also obtained some sugar and quaker oats from the village, and by lighting a fire in the brazier I picked up . . . [I] was enabled to feed very well for a fortnight.'[32]

Egg and chips was the invariable meal offered at these farmhouses. 'This was a popular feed with the "tommies" at all French estaminets. Possibly because it was reminiscent of fried fish & chips in "blighty".' Besides estaminets these men often mention going into '[an] old woman's house after tea for egg and chips'; or 'a wayside cottage where we get "Eggs, Chips & Coffee", quite a good meal for 1 franc 4 centm [sic]'.[33] Prices in estaminets and other established eateries, usually in towns rather than villages, were slightly higher. Thus one conscript described an evening in St Omer: 'Had tea at one place – awful price 2 Francs for 2 eggs pot of tea & 1 slice of bread & butter. Went to another place & had 2 eggs fried potatoes tea bread & butter galore & pastries – 2 francs 40.' A typical estaminet 'smelt of stale tobacco, burning fat and steaming clothes'. It had 'a kitchen with a smaller room opening off it. In the latter sat an old man peeling potatoes. In the larger room at the wooden table sat half a dozen soldiers enjoying the fried eggs and potatoes and coffee which the hostess made continuously upon the bright black stove. . . . At last Madame placed before me my coffee and eggs. How good they were!' In addition to the culinary satisfaction, estaminets also offered a mental respite from a military existence. One conscript had 'a fine supper in a kitchen behind a little shop – omelette, bread & butter & rum & coffee – the goods. Parlez-vousing in great style with the old girl. Made a very enjoyable evening, almost forgot about the war.'[34]

Cigarettes were another major source of comfort, sought and smoked with an ardour second only to that reserved for the pursuit of food. Each soldier received thirty cigarettes per week in their 'fag issue', but 'the ones we get are packed specifically for troops I expect & are not half so good as the ones you sent'. Smoking was a major occupation for soldiers at all times. In the front line they were a calming influence: 'After a night on the fire-step, a cigarette pulls you together wonderfully, and at other times too.' Behind the lines, in a Church Army hut 'we all sat around the fire and the chaplain provided fags. Sang a few hymns, then sat and smoked while he gave an address. Altogether a dull performance.'[35] Cigarettes were often also given as presents: 'Parade after breakfast for a distribution of cigarettes by Capt. Apted who escorted us out. . . . He is returning back today.' Another man recalled that for Christmas 1917 'some kind person, probably an officer on leave, sent us a large crate of cigarettes, we had about four hundred each'. So crucial were cigarettes, that any shortage greatly upset these men, especially when they were in the trenches: 'All the chaps dying for a smoke and sweating on "fag issue" tonight but none came up, also no mail so they are getting pretty well fed up.'[36] Cigarettes could be purchased for very reasonable prices in the mobile canteens and YMCA huts. 'You will be interested Fred to know that one of our fellows bought a tin of 50 Gold Flake cigarettes this morning in the Canteen for elevenpence, I wish I could send you some of your favourites at proportionate prices.' In comparison, an officer complained that the price was dependent on the money at hand: a larger coin bought more cigarettes than did a collection of coppers.[37]

Mobile canteens in the rear lines and rest camps were another source of food – indeed, a major one: by the end of 1918 the annual turnover of all canteen trading was £33.5 million. Long marches were punctuated by 'tea at YMCA usual tin of tea & 1*d* packet of biscuits'. Chocolate could be bought for 3½*d* a bar, and 'tin fruits, packets of biscuits, duty free cigarettes' could also be purchased.[38] At one such canteen a conscript 'saw several chaps sucking at condensed milk tins and as I craved something sweet I bought a tin, punctured a hole on each side and sucked away; it was nectar, this was my first initiation into sucking sweet condensed milk.' Scrounging was apparent here too. During the spring retreat of 1918 another man 'heard of an Expeditionary Force canteen deserted near by so went for booty. Got fags, biscuits, tins of milk and all sorts of things including umpteen bottles of whiskey. Chaps were lying about drunk all over the place.' When he got back to his unit he found 'Half the battery drunk on whiskey. Lt. Phillips opened all water bottles and emptied it out.'[39]

This was not a single or unique situation of drunkenness. Alcohol was sought by these men at every opportunity, mostly as an antidote to the nature of their existence. The basic source was the official 'rum ration', issued in the trenches by the army authorities. When first introduced in 1914, the allotment was 'one jar per 64 men and a man received a gill a day. By 1918 a division consumed 300 gallons or a third of a pint per man weekly.' As a fortifying measure in the face of nerves and the cold it was clearly effective: 'We have drawn our rum issue the last two nights for the first time. By Jove, it's strong stuff, but tres bon. We only get 3 spoonfuls but it warms you up.' Another man recalled his sergeant issued the rum, which was considered 'rough & tumble', in an empty six-cube Oxo tin, 'to steady our chattering teeth and shivering bodies. And how we loved that rum! It really is extraordinary what the human body can stand when young.'[40]

The rum issue was also instrumental in sending men into action. Writing to his parents of his first battle, one young conscript proudly noted that 'I went through it far better than I ever imagined – it must have been the rum ration I had just before we went over.' For some men, however, the prospect of battle could not be borne with the aid of 'an egg-cup full' of rum, and much more was devoured.

> Q. There's a lot of talk of the Infantrymen getting drunk when they went over the top – was that true?
>
> A. Was it true? Oh yes. I've seen them when they was drove over the top. . . . They used to count down (to zero) and then 'Over the top' and then the M[ilitary] P[olicemen] would come along and see that they had all gone over. Some was coughing, some was spewing, some was sipping, some was shouting – ah it was terrible.

Bringing in the wounded men, and rounding up the survivors of a hard battle, one man noted that 'some had so much rum they were canned. . . . by the singing and noise one would think they had been to a fair and not over the top.'[41]

Coming out of the line after action was always an occasion for the distribution of alcohol: 'We arrived in Arras about 5.30 a.m. Sunday morning, had a good tot of rum which very near knocked us all drunk, cigarettes, chocolate and cake were supplied by the Padre . . . it nearly made us wish we came out of the line every day.' Rest periods behind the lines also offered ample opportunity for drinking: 'To finish their days most of the fellows drowned themselves in cheap wines at the estaminets, and then rolled unsteadily "home," singing aloud while others more sober attempted to push them into bed.' One man frequented a farm of French peasants who gave him free beer, which was also regularly distributed at concerts: 'A good tuck-in and free booze! What more could delight a soldier's heart?'[42]

In the front line, many other things would probably have delighted a soldier's heart, such as protection or warmth. But nonetheless, the comment is very accurate: in the closed world of the army and the trenches, food and drink not only ensured survival – it also offered solace.

References to clothes and kit, and lack of them, figured quite frequently in these men's writings. As already shown, the initial issue of both was administered in several stages throughout the period of basic training in England, and supplementary battle kit was distributed in the base camps in France. Men therefore arrived at the front line as fully clothed and equipped as the state of army supplies permitted at any given time. Once there, however, distribution of fresh supplies of garments or equipment was severely limited to the annual issue of items for winter wear, and the occasional change of underclothing or shirts. A claim that 'your socks were rotted and you never had a change of anything'[43] may be extreme, but it is not necessarily implausible. In other words, within the functional institution the British Army had become in the First World War, the cleanliness, clothing and warmth of the individual soldier was basically low on the agenda, and subject to availability.

These conscripts discuss clothing and supplies as an issue reflecting upon their warmth and personal hygiene, and their various attempts to obtain both. One conscript, who arrived in France early in October 1916, kept a daily record of the minutiae of his existence as a combat soldier in France until the Armistice of November 1918. Rather than battles, this man was preoccupied with boots and baths, and his diary serves as an excellent survey both of the frequency with which these men received new issues of kit and uniform, and the sources of replacement open to them. He arrived at the front in mid-October 1916, and unexpectedly came across a large windfall of supplies in November: 'Australians all packing up. They gave me a good pair of puttees, a blanket and a clean pair of socks. Then I got a mackintosh cape, picture postcards, writing paper, books etc. which they left behind.'[44] The next day the army 'issued . . . new boots, leather jerkin and blanket', which was the standard winter kit. (These jerkins were 'lovely and warm at night – being lined with woolly material inside'. Another man claimed that instead of jerkins his unit received 'sheep skin coats, so we look like teddy bears.'[45]) Two days later he was 'marched off for a bath. Got new rigout of everything.' Yet apparently there were problems with this issue, since three days later the entire unit 'paraded before captain . . . to settle the shortage of kit. I got new trench cap and put in for a pair of spurs.' Moreover, ten days later he received an 'issue of undervest, body belt and gloves' to supplement his winter kit. All these were in his possession until the following May, when 'leather jerkins, top boots, undervest and blankets to be handed in now'. In July 1917 he received another set of new underclothes, while in September he 'got new jacket and breeches'. Apart from an issue of winter kit in November 1917, when he received another 'issue of leather jerkin and underpants' and an 'issue of top boots', this was the extent of new and clean clothing and kit received by this soldier throughout more than two years in France.[46]

Another source of clothing, and occasionally equipment, was in parcels from home, since 'we cannot get anything out in this country'.[47] The nature of these items, mostly socks, mittens, handkerchiefs, mufflers and jerseys, points to these conscripts' lack of adequate protection against the cold. In thanking his mother for a home-knitted sweater she had sent him, one man expressed his needs quite plainly: 'It will be most useful on cold nights as I can slip it on over my tunic either for sentry-go, or for sleeping in the open – it doesn't matter much what you wear out here in the trenches, I wanted some more mittens too as the one pair was quite worn out and I have lost my "issue" pair.' This comment highlights the importance these men attached to parcels of clothing, and that they often specifically requested the items, rather than awaited the undoubted thoughtfulness and foresight of their families. This letter-writer had already asked for a new pair of mittens two weeks earlier, explaining that they were 'rather worn now . . . which is not surprising – considering I have worn them on all sorts of work – day and night'.[48] His second letter was therefore a reminder. Another conscript preferred a pair of woollen gloves since 'we get some severe frosts now, [and] they would be better than mittens I think for our job dear'. One man received eight pairs of socks after hinting somewhat blatantly to his correspondent: 'If you have a pair of isle socks I can put them to extreme use here.'[49]

Once clothing or kit was secured in some way, these men were faced with the problem of its preservation and upkeep – and it was not a simple task. The dictates of warfare sometimes meant the loss of equipment. In some cases this was due to operating in official 'battle order', which meant only the clothes worn by the soldier and a groundsheet 'to keep us warm day and night'. At other times, usually of great mobility, such as the final summer advance of 1918, 'overcoats & superfluous kit were dumped & left behind'.[50] The evident shortage of kit also provoked men to take the equipment of others, either with or without intent. One conscript recalled losing both his blankets when a friend took them with him to another unit. Kit that was kept, however, was not easy to preserve in good shape. The prevalent mud of Flanders which clung to everything also ruined clothing and equipment. As already shown, one section of men resorted to removing a wide strip of material from the bottom of their overcoats, since these got coated in mud and weighed them down. Sewing was also needed for the more mundane task of darning: 'Have been trying to mend a pair of socks, but it is hopeless, you could get a brick-end through the holes, so have only now 1 pair left.'[51]

In periods of rest behind the lines men also attempted to wash their clothes: 'The usual method was to boil . . . [the clothes] (whether woollen or otherwise) in a biscuit tin that had been well scrubbed out with a body brush, saddle soap being the cleaning article and creosol the disinfectant.' This could also be done 'in a petrol can with the side cut out'. For some, who had traditionally viewed washing as 'women's work'. this chore was clearly a revelation: 'Have been washing today, its about one hour to wash a towel. I will never let a wife of mine do any washing, am using barbed wire for a cloths [*sic*] line and it seems to perforate the laundry a little.'[52] Others, who could both afford it and found themselves in a suitable location, availed themselves of the services of French women who took in washing. Thus one conscript recalled notices announcing 'Washing done', in English, in several French villages:

> It was to one of these latter that I took the bundle of dirty clothes that had been accumulating in my Kit Bag since a certain disastrous attempt of my own in which a khaki handkerchief with a bright green pattern played an important part, had decided me against washing my own clothes if it were possible to avoid doing so.
>
> The washerwoman asked for a list of the articles and when knowledge of the French word for the various pieces of under-clothing failed me she came to my help with the utmost tact.[53]

Besides the dirt of battle and life in the trenches, men's clothing became filthy simply because it was often upon their bodies for long periods: 'Have not had my shirt right off for about six weeks but you cannot help that out here.' Within the trenches themselves bathing was usually impossible, since there were no facilities, in addition to references such as 'owing to the absence of water were denied the luxury of a wash for that day'. When possible, men washed and shaved out of a biscuit tin, a 'billy can', or even 'an old "tin-hat"!'[54] One man wrote of a meeting with a friend in the trenches, in which 'we both looked very dirty and unshaven. I haven't washed or shaved since last Satdy [*sic*].' Another conscript claimed that his days in the support trench were basically preferable to those in the front-line trench because he could remove his boots and jacket for sleep, and also because there was water for washing and shaving. He also noted that in the last stages of the 1918 British advance, water for personal use other than drinking was stopped.[55]

One man suffered a severe attack of diarrhoea 'caused by the drinking of water from shell holes and I was forced to discard my braces and use a lanyard instead'. In general, bodily necessities in the trenches were catered for either by a latrine bucket or a trench toilet: 'This was a narrow trench over which a pole had been executed, being supported at each end by crossed stakes which we secured at the cross by a rope, all very primitive but there were no flush toilets on the Western Front.' A conscript recalled sitting upon such a structure when a German shell exploded 50 yards from him. 'I felt the pole shake and down into the trench I went, my back hit the rear of the trench, my feet and legs were in the filth and the seat of my breeches was wet.'[56] Unfortunately for him there were no uniform stores in his camp, and he simply had to dry out in his stained clothes.

Due to the extreme filth of their existence within the trenches, and often also behind the lines, bathing became 'one of the few luxuries a soldier gets'. Luxury is actually an understatement. The most frequent bathing record found in these writings was of a conscript who had five baths in three months.[57] One man, who enjoyed two baths in as many weeks, was moved to comment that 'we are certainly having a cushie time here'. As with their laundry, bathing was possible for these men usually only behind the lines, and it often consisted of 'very rudimentary showers'. Another man also noted that at 'the great base-camps they had steam baths, but they were not much in favour with the men, as being an unsatisfactory way of removing dirt'. The only alternative form of bathing mentioned in these writings was when three men 'lit a fire and had a good bath'.[58] Bathing, or showering, was done in the divisional baths in the vicinity of the rest camps, to which one man noted a march of 10 kilometres, and another recorded a distance of 4½ miles. Yet it was always deemed worthwhile, since bath parades were sometimes also used for the infrequent issue of fresh garments, mostly underclothes, as in the following typical description:

[Baths were] hastily constructed in say the bottom floor of a warehouse or factory. In one room we had to strip and then run from that room into another (in many cases quite a good distance away and sometimes out of the building altogether and into another). In the second room would be about half-a-dozen sprays and under each spray 2 or 3 men would stand. . . . the water . . . would be turned on coming cold at first, afterwards getting warm, and on rare occasions hot. . . . Soft soap in large buckets was provided for use. After finishing under the spray we should then line up and take our turns at receiving a clean towel and probably shirt and socks, on receipt of which we returned to the dressing room and got dried and got dressed again.[59]

The main shortcoming of these divisional baths was that 'they were always too sparing of water'; a shower could last just three minutes, and be 'a thin drip of hot water'. Another problem was that these baths afforded 'no privacy whatever'.[60] Indeed, 'during the summer, baths would sometimes be erected in a large marquee and we should undress and dress in the field adjoining irrespective of the very close proximity of houses and their inquisitive occupants'. However, the relative scarcity of bathing moved most men to ignore such problems, as in the case of a conscript who bathed in April 1917: 'I had a good bath. What a real luxury first time I had wet my body since November.' Another man remembered 'the joy of standing in a shed where piping with interspersed [jets] allowed water to refresh & clean us as if we [were] in a shower bath. Alas not often possible to indulge in.'[61]

Despite this evident pleasure in bathing, it could also be a painful experience, since 'the rough red carbolic soap stung me where the lice had bitten'. Indeed, lice were an integral part of the soldiers' experiences in France, mostly accepted by them as yet another necessary evil of their military existence. However, unlike mud, dirt, hunger and even enemy fire, all of which could be countered at least temporarily, these writings reflect a constant presence of lice, both in and out of the line: 'These pests were a continual persecution to us throughout the war, their bites causing much scratching and in some cases blood poisoning.' Many men found themselves 'lousy as coots' within a few days of their arrival in France. In the base camp at Harfleur 'ten to twelve persons in a tent did not afford much room and it was here I made the acquaintance of those little pests which are a nuisance to every soldier in France'.[62] In Etaples, another newly arrived conscript spoke to 'an "old hand" [who] made reference to lice and showed disbelief when I expressed ignorance. He suggested I should there and then inspect my underwear which I did and was astonished to find I had a family [of lice].' But it was mostly on their first journey up to the front line that men became infested: 'We slept in a ruined house on the Arras Road and here I became aware of the fact that I was lousy. I began to itch and inspection showed some promising colonies. From then until I went to the R.F.C. [as a photographer] I was never free from them.' Men also picked up these vermin in other billets such as barns or schools, where they slept upon straw which often had not been changed for many days. Even within permanent camps lice were rampant, and indeed the subject appeared to be part of soldiers' official introduction into camp life: 'I was given a warning that I would have some difficulty in keeping free from vermin as the straw in the barns was infested with lice. The blankets (grey backs we called them) could not be kept clean & I should purchase a tin of Harrison's Pomade as soon as possible & watch carefully the seams of my shirt for lice etc.'[63]

Lice also appeared to thrive within the trenches. One conscript recalled the smoke from a fire lit in a pail 'causing many lice ("chats" we called them) to fall from the roof upon us, so that they found refuge in our clothing, and within a few hours multiplied a hundredfold'. In addition, during spells in the front line men did not undress, even partially, so making it easier for lice to breed at an even greater rate. It was therefore practically impossible for a soldier to avoid infestation in the trenches, since lice were part of the environment. One man described in disgust a particularly bad trench, listing the mud, lack of rations and overcrowding as evidence of his negative experience; 'and to add to that absolutely impossible to be without lice'. Another man claimed a certain signaller 'gets on my nerves with his perpetual scratching and louse hunting and trying to be so superior to other people'.[64] In other words, lice were viewed as a negative but unavoidable characteristic of humans and trenches alike, on a par with mud, hunger and arrogance.

The breeding habits of these lice – known as 'free lice', which are hatched at a rate of five or more a day over thirty days – rendered futile anything but a thorough course of disinfection, since 'hundreds could be laid low and after an hour or so hundreds more could be unavailingly killed. After a time one took little notice of them except when they were feeding.'[65] Yet louse hunting, and killing, was a prevalent pastime for many of these soldiers when they were not in the front line, and 'it was a daily sight to see one's mates holding their shirts out and killing these tormentors'. Another conscript recalled 'burning [a] candle along the inner seams of our trousers'. But the gravest problems centred around the men's underclothes, which 'were made of loosely knit woollen material and I shall always remember seeing the gunners delousing them by candle light; a louse could be winkled out from each hole in the garment and the seams could be singed to kill the nits.' Delousing also appeared to form an accepted background to conversation and social interchange. One conscript claimed the reserve line trench latrines 'acted as a sort of social centre where we would sit relaxed, swapping gossip and delousing the accessible parts of our clothing. I remember, on one occasion, someone started to count the number of lice caught and killed and a sort of competition developed. I am not sure whether my count was 103 or 113 . . .'[66]

The army authorities recognised the severity of the louse problem, and attempted to deal with it in a number of ways. There was the warning and advice issued to men arriving in the front line. In addition the divisional baths had 'de-lousing tanks that received shirts & vests & blankets tied up in bundles of 10'. Steps were also taken against men who were particularly lousy: 'Somebody reported C battery orderly for being covered with lice, so he had to burn his clothes and take all his kit outside. Then after dinner we took all bedding etc. out to air and did the hut out with creosole [*sic*]. The chap's blankets were simply covered with lice in thousands, so the orderly officer ordered them to be burnt.'[67]

All these measures were in accordance with a 29-page pamphlet issued by the Royal Army Medical Corps. The bulk of this work was devoted to describing the louse and a series of tests designed to establish the extent of the problem, while the last chapter offered recommendations 'for a plan of campaign against the pest'. There were educational suggestions, such as the establishment of research and teaching centres in France to be attended by soldiers of all ranks – but these were apparently not implemented. However, most of the practical recommendations for the cleansing of men and uniforms were adopted, albeit often in improvised forms. These included the physical removal of both lice and eggs from clothing 'whenever possible'; and the burning of eggs either with an iron or 'a piece of hot metal or a tinder lighter.' Unfortunately the writings examined in this dissertation do not refer to the use of powders and disinfectants 'every four days' mentioned in another three recommendations. However, the focus of the delousing process suggested in this pamphlet was upon the divisional baths. A detailed diagram of the optimal bath-house depicts a structure akin to those described above, apart from the fact that instead of the sheds, huts and adapted warehouses used, baths 'should be built and not improvised . . . from permanent buildings'.[68] After bathing, most of these men did appear to receive a 'clean change of underclothing', although none of them mention having their uniform ironed. Tanks for disinfecting clothes were in use, and cresol available as a disinfectant in boiling water even for men who did their own washing.[69] Moreover, 'a keen look-out for cases acting as bad lice-carriers' was maintained, according to the above case of the lousy orderly.

It was most unfortunate that none of the recommendations regarding the cleansing of trenches and billets appears to have been implemented. No descriptions of disinfecting or scrubbing of billets exist in the writings of these conscripts, nor parades for the inspection of lousy men and trenches. And this meant that even if a soldier made the utmost effort to keep himself and his uniform clean, his attempts were doomed due to the existence of lice everywhere in his surrounding environment. One man summed up the situation by noting that 'even with the new things and a bath I still have plenty of visitors'.[70] In other words, absolute cleanliness of body and clothes became practically unattainable, especially in the trenches. A clean soldier issued with clean underclothes was still lousy; a freshly ironed uniform, or even a newly issued one, quickly became dirty during a march upon a dusty road or a stint in a muddy trench. More lice were then bred within the uniform which was not removed for some days, drawing more dirt from a body unwashed for some weeks or months. And so the sanitary experience of these men may be seen as a never-ending cycle of filth, redeemed only by occasional partial respites, such as a clean shirt or a bath, which were quickly forgotten.

Food, clothing and cleanliness: the basic facts of everyday life. To a civilian, such matters are automatic. Money, class or taste may define their availability, quantity or quality – but their existence is unquestionable. The conscripts arrived in France with these expectations relatively intact, the training camps in Britain having mostly influenced matters of taste rather than availability. But the trenches, and Flanders, radically changed everything. The very existence of these most salient facts of life became the most pressing issue confronting them. In other words, they became a question of their *own* very existence. It was, however, when circumstances were slightly less than dire that the relative perspectives of civilian and soldier came into focus. One conscript, in considering his experiences of food in the war, found himself puzzled by the grasp it – and alcohol – had over these men, and in so doing he presents an interesting appraisal of their character:

> If the other men on the section were asked whether they would rather do a twelve hours night or go without dinner for one day I do not believe that one of them would choose the latter alternative. It has been a constant source of wonder to me, the hardships and discomforts and dangers that men will put up with, if only they get their daily 'rations'. They will sleep on the ground underneath the caterpillar with the rain running in little channels below their water-proof sheets and rising gradually till it soaks their blankets and they will get up quite cheerfully in the morning ready for the day's work, but if, by any chance, there is no breakfast some day they will grumble for hours and treasure up the grievance for months. They will go up to the battery at night when the enemy is dropping shells all around and they will go about their work unconcernedly, but if they think that they are being defrauded of their 'rum ration' nothing will pacify them. They accept the fact of the war and of their part in it – one of the greatest revolutions that could take place in the life of any man, but they bitterly resent the injustice of a quarter-master-sergeant who does not give them their 'issue' of potatoes.[71]

For the conscripts, the provision of potatoes, or rum, or anything else edible was therefore a matter of dignity and continuity with their civilian background: whereas the war was something entirely beyond their control, the provision of food was their inalienable right, as civilians or soldiers. As civilians they expected to be fed, and as soldiers they expected no less. But their expectations had clearly changed. When food was to be found, it was accepted without enquiry into its merits: 'To-day we are in luck – there is a comely stew of tinned rabbit, bully & tinned "pork & beans" (e'en a goodly mix up, no doubt, but a treat to us I can tell you, Ma).' It was also devoured without ceremony: 'Bradshaw had left most of his fastidiousness on the filthy tables of the Etaples dining-huts, so drank from a stranger's mess-tin without recoiling.' Yet for all that, they never completely lost the sense of food as part of their civilian identity – as a social event, as part of a civilian life to which they still felt they belonged. Reflecting upon this issue, one conscript wrote of 'the queerest Sunday I have ever spent. 1.30 pm thinking of Sunday dinner at home. We have midday dinner as a special treat – the old bully.'[72]

Much the same is true of clothing and cleanliness: these men apparently accepted their filthy condition as a necessity for survival, and did so quite quickly. Before entering the line for the first time one young conscript observed a battalion coming out of the section: 'We were shocked to see how filthy they looked but it was not long before we were just as scruffy.' Yet at the same time they were aware of themselves as unaesthetic human beings. One conscript enjoyed his first bath after seven months, but 'still in spite of this I felt miserably dirty in my clothes and kept to myself to a great extent'.[73] In other words, his outward appearance came into conflict with his knowledge, and identity, of himself as a clean, tidy and outwardly respectable individual.

But in times of shortage, cleanliness or any civilian notion of decorum became irrelevant: these conscripts were no more than human beings striving for survival. When 'food was short . . . [men] were reaching the point of despair'. It was at these times that they would resort to behaviour which would be totally unacceptable to their civilian values – looting and scrounging. Such actions were taken instinctively in the face of hunger; however, values did become more apparent in times of relative plenty, or when observing others stooping to acts of desperation – as in a large rest camp during the summer advance of 1918: 'Went in for dinner and saw a Jerry corporal with escort, picking up all the biscuit, cheese and bully left on the floor by the first dinner sitting and putting it all in a sandbag. Then 12 prisoners came in for dinner. He dished out their tea and then divided out the contents of the sandbag. Strange to think that men should be reduced to picking up scraps off the floor.'[74]

Viewed in this light, it is understandable why the conscripts became obsessed with food, clothes and cleanliness: it had nothing to do with being soldiers or civilians, but rather with being human beings. It was a struggle for survival – not of military actions, but of circumstances.

CHAPTER 6

Contact in War

In this dismal slimy hole where I am working like a mole
See me to relieve my soul A letter
Rats and vermin bite and creep sometimes I almost weep
But what cheers me up when I can't sleep 'Your letter' . . .[1]

Being at war in the trenches was about doing battle with the enemy, with the environment, and with the circumstances. However, when a man's mind was not totally focused upon staying alive – it was totally devoted to the outside world. The one that existed in Britain, far away from the trenches: his home, family and friends; his civilian life as it was before he was conscripted. And he made every effort to keep that world, and life, alive – through dreams, letters and leave; through treats of meals and wine, when possible; through preserved images of himself as a civilian. But these conscripts were in the army, in Flanders. And keeping up such contacts was a difficult task, and one dependent upon the military framework. It was the army which had brought the conscripts to Flanders, in order to fight a war; and it was the army which also regulated many aspects of non-combat, non-military activities. Censorship, pay and home leave were chief among these. They were also the obstacles which the conscripts had to overcome in order to keep up their contact with the outside world, and civilian values. In other words, they were a major meeting point of the conscripts' military and civilian lives.

Censorship was one of the more interesting facets of the conscripts' army existence: an apparently anonymous presence, yet one that defined their experiences to the removed, civilian world. 'The Censor' loomed large in their correspondence, as a combination of an institution and an omnipotent, unknown person. Many letters contained phrases such as 'that would raise the "censor's" ire'; 'on account of the Censor'; 'it would not pass the censor.' Yet the letters were actually read by the platoon commander, an officer personally known to each of the sixty men in the unit. But curiously, even officers who actually censored letters often mentioned the issue in the same abstract and slightly awed terms, referring either to the unknown 'Censor' or to the institution: 'censorship gets stricter every day'.[2] Censorship actually worked as a paradox: on the one hand, it denied any military activity in the lives of the conscripts, since any references to battle, weapons or indeed any aspect of active army life were absolutely forbidden. On the other hand, the actual stamp of the censor permanently preserved them as 'Soldiers on Active Service' in the eyes of civilians. In other words, and at least to the outside world, censorship inhibited the conscripts from having any real military identity beyond the title of soldier.

Before reaching the point of censorship, however, it appeared there were practical restrictions upon the communication between soldier and civilian. First, there were those who could not write: 'One or two men had asked me to address their cards, and one who had trouble at home asked me to write a letter for him.' However, for those who could write, the second problem was that notepaper and envelopes were somewhat difficult to acquire in France. Many men wrote requests such as 'some note paper would be very useful when sending, we cannot get any here'. This seemed to have been a continuing problem in the area from the start of the war, as a letter of a young German soldier from October 1914 reflects: 'Also send stationery often, it's hard to find out here.'[3] Besides stationery sent from home, the notepaper provided by the YMCA huts in the larger base camps behind the lines were another major source of stationery, as were sheets torn from notebooks. But overall, stationery supplies were a recurring problem for many.

The only uncensored mail sent from overseas was a field postcard distributed by the army: 'Each week we were issued a field card which we could complete and send home, these cards were printed and just said 'I am well', they just needed signing and addressed; we could write a letter providing we had paper and envelope, but the envelopes were not sealed as the letter was strictly censured [sic]. I had sent home a card each week to my mother.'[4] In addition, each soldier received a limited issue of 'green envelopes', 'into which a letter may be sealed, unread by the regimental censor. It may be read by the base censor, though every man hopes that his one is not. On the outside is a printed declaration that the letter contains no military information. This must be signed by the sender.'[5] The declaration was: 'Correspondence in this envelope need not be censored Regimentally. The contents are liable to examination at the Base. The following certificate must be signed by the writer: I certify on my honour that the contents of this envelope refer to nothing but private and family matters.' The Green envelopes were specifically intended for 'the transmission of letters referring to *private and family matters only.* The writer will sign the certificate on the envelopes as to contents. . . . The envelope is large enough to contain several letters, the contents of all of which are covered by the certificate on the outer cover.' The letters in these envelopes were read by the base censors, who were also responsible for the monitoring of morale in the BEF.[6]

Green envelopes were comparatively scarce, and so men treasured them. One conscript recalled a kindly person sending his unit a large crate of cigarettes for Christmas 1917: 'Some of mine I exchanged for a "green envelope" in which uncensored letters could be sent home; these did not come my way very often.' Like this conscript, many men did not completely understand the green envelope system, despite the explicit explanation printed upon it and therefore lived under the misconception that these letters arrived in England completely uncensored. But others were aware of its limitations: 'I should love to tell you where I have been – and am – but suppose I mustn't, in spite of the fact that I have just been issued with my very first "green envelope".' These uncertainties were probably true to many aspects of censorship, and some conscripts seemed to have adopted a method akin to 'trial and error' in their efforts to communicate explicitly with their family: 'Will you also inform me if anything is cut out by the censor, as then I shall know what sort of matter to avoid in future – at present we are a bit hazy on the subject.'[7]

The conscripts saw censorship as a barrier between themselves and their civilian connections in a number of ways. First, there was the element of time, or the absence of it, both in the description of events and in the extended period of delivery. Men could not specify the time or schedule of their movements about the line or in action, nor could they always write at such times. 'You say it seemed ages since you last heard from me, well I always write you whenever I get the chance, of course I can't write when we are in the front lines, and then letters seem to take a long time to come and go.' In addition, the despatch of letters was delayed as a result of censorship: 'My letters take much longer to reach you than yours do to reach me, I suppose that is on account of the Censor.'[8] Indeed, mail sent from Britain usually arrived within two or three days, whereas censored letters from conscripts in France seemed to average six days in passage. Letters from Britain were sorted in London according to units, then despatched to one of three collection bases in France: Calais, Boulogne and Le Havre. There mail would be re-sorted according to current GHQ unit location lists, then sent on by train to an appropriate railhead. Mailbags would be loaded on to postal lorries attached to each supply column, and taken to the 'refilling points' at which all divisions picked up daily supplies. Each division had a field post office, which was responsible for allocating the correct bags of letters to the unit post orderly, who would then take them up the line for distribution. The mail going from the troops to England filtered through exactly the same system – with the exception of censorship in the unit and later at the base camps.[9] In other words, it seems censorship was largely responsible for the delays in despatching mail to England.

Like time, the element of place was another perceived obstacle of censorship. When the conscripts were in training, their address comprised a personal regimental number, unit details and a specific location in Britain. For example: Pte. J.R. Thompson, 26342, 'L' Coy, 45th TRB, Camp No. 2, Pertham Down. But soldiers on active service overseas were 'not allowed now to put our address, so please keep an old letter of mine dear with it in'. 'All letters to us [in France] were simply addressed to our name, number and unit, BEF, France, and on the whole the system worked well.'[10] This inhibition led to a third problem – the conscripts' desire to inform family or friends of their whereabouts as a reassurance of their safety. One man noted in his diary that they were 'not allowed to tell people at home we arrived at Le Havre'. Another wrote his wife that 'this is considered a very quiet part of the line', while a third made a joke of the entire issue: 'I'm not allowed to state that we are in the Somme area and although I'm not "writing this by the light of bursting shrapnel" still I'm about a twopenny bus ride from the trenches.'[11]

One eighteen-year-old conscript was anxious to inform his parents of his location so they should not worry that he was in Ypres. On the other hand, he wanted them to know he was not being held in reserve until he was nineteen – 'After all I was a front line soldier.' Alienation was therefore another result of the inhibition upon specifying a location. For despite the denial of action imposed by censorship, the conscripts were partaking in a war that had been raging for at least two years, and with which many civilians were familiar through the press. Phrases such as 'I believe you know where I am', which appear in most letters examined here, point to civilian cognisance of the developments of the war. The conscripts' inability to define their exact location therefore distanced them further from their civilian ties, and frustrated them: 'I am at a place

you well know but must not mention or you would not get this letter.'
The closest the men could come to openness was reference to press
reports: '. . . you would know the names of the places from the papers.
The Germans were driven out of this village in 1914.'[12]

The greatest problem presented by censorship, as a result of all these
inhibitions, was lack of narrative in the correspondence, as it is basically
dependent upon descriptions of time and place. This led to conscripts
consciously writing boring letters, since 'it's hard to know what to write about
as I can't tell you anything or this letter would be destroyed'. One man
pinpointed the trap in which the soldier found himself: 'I have no news at all
as a rule. You see we do the same things day after day and if anything out of
the common turns up we probably couldn't tell you about it on account of the
censorship.' Ultimately, these restrictions upon discussion of time, place and
events reduced the conscript experience, as it could be transmitted to a
civilian audience, to a vague existence of eating in various climatic conditions:

With the monotony of the days and the restrictions of the censor it is
indeed difficult to find material for filling a page. Anything of the
slightest interest is prohibited and one soon says all there is to say
about the weather and the food. . . . When everything else fails there
is one formula on which the men here fall back. It runs thus:

'Dear Mother,
  I'm all right
  You're all right
  That's all right.

I am not quite sure whether the last word is not spelt "write".'

The closing lines of a letter also followed a set pattern, as one conscript
remarked somewhat ironically: "Hoping this finds you in the pink as it
leaves me" (all Tommies conclude thus). Much love . . .'[13]

There were various ways in which men attempted to sidestep the
censor. One conscript placed himself by 'enclosing a cutting of a certain
advance'. Others resorted to clues: 'There is a rumour that we are for the
land where ice-creams come up in rations, shortly – compris?' One young
conscript even created an elaborate system of codes by which his parents
could identify his location: 'Don't forget the method in which I intend to
let you know my whereabouts, the letters sloping backwards thus: \ "very"
[the first three letters slope to the left (see plate no. 23)] – VER being

the first three letters of Verdun. Also whenever I move and write such a letter containing my whereabouts in detail, I shall sign myself Ted instead of Edgar, so remember.'

This letter was written in England, on the day he embarked for France. Two further letters from the front, written in his prescribed method, were decoded into Etaples, and Somme district, Maricourt and Guillemont.[14]

The censors themselves had mixed views about the soldiers' letters. The base censors, to whom all letters were genuinely anonymous, felt that in reading them, 'one is peering into vast depths where one "sees the wheels go round". . . . You see and test all the myriad cog-wheels of mentality.' But the immediate censors, the platoon commanders, did not always take such a wide view. An average quota of letters censored by such an officer was 'fifty letters daily', and they were definitely not anonymous to him: 'For weeks I used to censor the letters of a certain estimable N.C.O. who wrote a very few lines to his wife – to whom by the way he was most devoted, I know – telling her that he had only a minute or two in which to write etc. etc. and sending her his love and so on, and then proceeded to write sheet after sheet to a certain damsel in Kent, in most affectionate terms. More than once Dick and I were tempted to put the letters into the wrong envelopes – but we never did.'[15]

'Sometimes you can get some amusement from the letters you have to censor especially when a man says shells which fell quarter of a mile or even a mile away were within 100 yards of the battery. Generally they are somewhat monotonous. It is extraordinary how uninteresting other people's letters can be.' Rather than boring, one army chaplain who served as a censor divided them into imaginative and unimaginative:

One of the funniest jobs I have to do is to censor the letters occasionally. It is perfectly extraordinary how similar and how childish the majority of them are. Some tell most awful stories too. Few of these men seem possessed of any imagination but those who are – my conscience they do spread themselves out. If you believe about one half of what you hear from letters from the front you may calculate you are right as a rule. We are pretty strict here and if we catch men writing what is obviously untrue we have them up and give them a little beneficial advice. At least it seems to be beneficial for we don't find the offence repeated.[16]

This rather harsh description shows a lack of comprehension or awareness on behalf of the censor, regarding the inhibitions upon men who did not always have the option of penning creative prose unrelated to real events. In other words, this was a class problem. Censorship exposed the innermost thoughts of all troops, usually of a lower class, to the scrutiny of censoring officers, who were mostly middle or upper class. This chaplain viewed the situation with derision, but other officers realised the problem faced by the men, and in some cases even shared it. Lt Allfree, who saw action and also censored letters, noted that 'At present I believe Dolly [his wife] has the very haziest idea of what it was like, and this certainly is not her fault as I know my letters, on account of the Censor, never contained anything of the slightest interest.'[17]

Ultimately the censor was a real barrier between the conscripts' two lives, as soldiers and as civilians. As soldiers they lived through an entire spectrum of experiences which they could not transmit back to their civilian lives. In this way, and probably more than other elements within the military framework, censorship imposed another identity upon the conscripts simply because they were prohibited from sharing the immediacy of their military experiences with their civilian contacts. Yet they constantly expressed a strong desire to mix their two lives – to either create a combined identity, or else grasp on to a more comforting life. As one of them put it: 'I should love to tell you heaps more, but must trust and pray, that some day I may come home and be able to tell you myself.'[18]

Money was another issue in which civilian and military spheres overlapped, both practically and conceptually. A private soldier was entitled to one shilling per day, payable on a weekly basis. Half of this sum could be sent directly to his family as an allowance, leaving the soldier with three shillings and sixpence per week. Money sent from home, in the form of postal orders, was the only other major source of funds for most of these soldiers; and one which was not really available to most.

In theory an individual's conscription was a form of trade in which he gave himself as a soldier, and in return the state became responsible for every aspect of his existence. This meant that the purpose of money as income, equivalent to a working wage in the conscripts' civilian life, was supposedly void: they were clothed, housed and fed at the state's expense. But this reasoning proved flawed. As shown above, the army supplied three meals a day, and no more. Anyone who suffered hunger at other times had to feed himself, at his own expense. This could be done either by scrounging, or with the help of food parcels or postal orders from home, or at a local café or a YMCA canteen. Moreover, the conscript was left to his own resources when faced with the need for any item that was not strictly army issue, such as paper and envelopes, a pencil, extra socks or books. These, however, were also subject to availability, since purchasing or spending was limited to those times in which the conscripts were behind the lines, in the vicinity of base camps or French vendors.

The most basic aspect of these conscripts' perception of money was of course its purchasing power. But being in France, the currency itself also came to be a matter of fascination. Most of them had never ventured abroad before, and they had no understanding of monetary units beyond pounds, shillings and pence. Their presence in a foreign land was an introduction into the concept of exchange rates and the different purchasing power of each currency: 'It was at one of these [YMCA huts] I first had French money exchanged for English which was favourable to us our money being worth more than the French, that is to say the silver, as the copper coins passed as the same as the French. Calling for a mug of tea and a rock cake value 2s 5d & tendering a shilling to my surprise I received a silver coin similar in size to a shilling & also a penny as well. This I found was because a shilling was worth 1 franc 35 centimes.'[19]

Another conscript noted a rate which was quite similar, when he received 13.95 French francs in exchange for ten shillings. Yet adapting to the notion of two different currencies could be difficult, and often took time. One conscript wrote home after a month in France that '[I] haven't quite got into relation between French & English money.' Another man remarked upon the preference of vendors in the camps for large notes of currency that could be easily exchanged: 'For instance you can get a box of cigarettes for 11d if you give them a shilling, but if you offer a 6d and coppers it costs you 1/1.'[20]

In practical terms, these soldiers needed money for supplementary rather than basic living purposes. Supplementary, however, appears to have been a relative term. Those who had only their army pay as income existed upon military fare, with the occasional binge on wine or food on the rare occasions in which these were available: 'Once Tommy has a pay day, he usually spends it where he has the chance, as any day, any time may mean a removal.' When pay and chance collided, the former was usually quickly dispensed with: 'Paid today so went out to spend some after tea.' Those who did have recourse to private funds deemed supplementary as necessary. For example, one conscript received postal orders from his sister quite regularly, and his thank-you letters always included references to the money being used for the purchase of necessary items: 'Thanking you again for your [5 shilling] postal order which has helped to buy one or two necessities such as some food [and] a little chocolate which comes in very nice out here.'[21]

Overall, however, these conscripts were dependent upon the army, both for money and upkeep: 'We were paid this morning . . . which came very acceptable as we were all broke.' To this extent, army pay, which in France was distributed every two weeks, was really pocket money – and even as such, it was deemed inadequate by the conscripts discussed here: 'Grub is absolutely rotten here, easily the worst I have experienced. A little bit of bread dished out in the evening to last all next day. You take your chance of getting anything to go with it. To make matters worse I am running short of funds . . . & no prospect of getting more – pay comes in fits & starts out here.'[22] Lack of payment on a systematic basis was the biggest problem experienced by soldiers on active service. As already shown, while in the training camps in England the conscripts were paid once a week, in a formal parade. But the 'method of payment in the Army in France is very erratic and sometimes we were a month without pay. This goes rather hard.' Lack of money in the front line was not a practical problem since nothing could be bought. But the feeling of hardship still prevailed, since these funds were officially owed to the men. In other words, beyond the practical purchasing power of money, pay was also largely a measure of an individual's worth, which gave him a sense of independence. As one man put it, 'sometimes you had to wait a month for it [pay] – you'd never got no money. There was nowhere to spend it but we used to gamble it.'[23]

Army pay therefore created a duality of consciousness in the conscripts. On the one hand, these soldiers were aware that their upkeep and existence in the front line was totally dependent upon their external identity as soldiers in the British Army. On the other hand, they still possessed their civilian concept of a work ethic rewarded by monetary payment in the civilian world, regardless of the circumstances. And it was this concept that instilled within them a feeling of rights denied. Rights, however, belonged to those who worked for a living, and not to those who received pocket-money. And so, despite the small sum involved, it seems that these conscripts still viewed their pay as wages given in exchange for a job of work, and not pocket money. In other words, it gave these conscripts an identity of workers in uniform, whose job description was that of fighting. This is emphasised by the following diary entry: 'Major says we get no pay till he finds out who made a hole in a water trough the officers pinched from the men, so there is a general opinion of "no pay, no work".' Deduction of pay in the army was a known disciplinary measure, but it is interesting to note that here it is interpreted by the men within the context of a civilian workplace. The major, by denying the men pay as a form of sanction, clearly assumed the mantle of employer in their eyes – and they responded as employees in an industrial dispute. For at heart, the conscripts still saw themselves as working men, in the civilian sense of the word, employed by the army for a specific job – at an unsatisfactory rate of pay: 'We got no bonus, boot money, danger money, dirty money or any other sops now expected by the average working man.'[24]

Home leave was a major focal point for these conscripts. The possibility of somehow going home was the highest aim; a sustaining desire; an exceedingly rare treat. They lived from rumour to hope that it would happen, rebuilding hope from each new disappointment. In this way, after continuously promising his wife he would arrive home shortly, one man wrote: 'Am afraid I shall not get leave this year, but hope to get some before we again get up to the front.' Conscripts knew that in theory army regulation entitled them to seven days leave every six months, much as they knew that their chances of actually receiving it were slim: 'I hope I shall get my leave before we go [up the line again]. I expect it will be knocked on the head altogether, if I don't. I wish the days would pass a little more quickly for that leave seems a long time coming doesn't it?'[25]

Denis Winter claimed that in the early part of the war leave from France was seldom granted, but that after 1916 'leave became as well administered as most of the other admin. matters in our war. Lists were kept and a strict rota followed.' As an example he noted that in the first two years of fighting in France 'Ellison had a typical ration of three leaves in two years, one of four days, another two of ten days each.' This quota far exceeded anything enjoyed by the conscripts discussed here, since most of them either went on one home leave from the front or not at all: 'From Christmas, 1917, I never had a single days leave until I was demobilised in 1919.'[26] Leave, like every other organisational aspect of the army, was a function of the developments of war. This did not contradict the establishment of lists and a rota system, but rather diminished their steady enactment. Winter also wrote that compassion 'certainly had no part in the process. Fairness and the rota were the only criteria.' Yet in this study several references are made to men going on special leave due to illness in the family or other circumstances. But above all, as one conscript explained, luck was as important as organisation when it came to leave: 'The "leaves" have commenced & Jimmy Rourke is the first to go. Of course us newcomers are at the bottom of the list but it seems our turn will come in about 9 months time if we are lucky.'[27] Leave was so important to these men that they would do much to gain it. One conscript recalled spending an 'exciting evening looking for two German prisoners as capture means a months leave.' Another man, who did not usually care too much about army regulations, claimed he returned two Prussian bayonets he had kept as souvenirs: 'We had orders that we were not to bring anything at all in the way of souvenirs – we were going to have ten days leave and I thought "Well, I don't want to lose my leave," so I puts them down and the chap behind me picks them up and he gets through – and he went through with them. That was just the luck – and I should like to have kept them but, you see, ten days leave was worth more than that – (after all that time, we had no leave in 13 months).'[28]

On the whole, these conscripts never relinquished their desire for leave. As one of them put it, the soldier always 'lays claim with unfailing persistence . . . [to] his rations, his pay, and his "leave"'.[29] Yet at the same time they identified the established hierarchical system of the army working against them: 'Major fired a lot of rounds today. He has got a month's leave and we can't get a day.' This insight is borne out by the observation of a conscripted junior officer, who found himself similarly confronted with the system: 'Bob is home on leave. How he worked it I don't know. I am digging myself well in with my C.O. by dint mainly of being a good listener to his stories of Simla in the year one; but even then I don't see much prospect of leave before December – and before then we might be in some push or other one never knows.[30]

As with every other aspect of the conscripts' future movements, leave was also shrouded in mystery, and therefore germinated many stories:

'Rumours of the Division going home on leave and then going to India.'
In the same way, notice of leave was usually given unexpectedly, and
implemented immediately: 'We had been waiting for seventeen months
when, without warning, a leave allotment was assigned to our unit. About
half a dozen men were going every day and no one knew whose turn
would come next. We were full of intense excitement and glad
expectation, but also of anxiety in case something should happen to stop
our leave altogether.'[31] Another man recalled that 'one evening there was
brought to me the very pleasant information that I should pack up and
be ready to go back to [the] depot with the ration limbers . . . [once
there] I spent some hours removing all traces of mud, had a shower-bath,
and polished my buttons and waited.' Indeed, when possible the men
made every effort to make themselves physically presentable for civilian
eyes. One conscript recalled a pal going on leave borrowing one man's
tunic, and 'Bob's leggings and Harry's British warmer and Tom's puttees.
This guy's going to make a splash in London, I can tell you.'[32]

The journey across France to England usually involved all forms of
transportation, and since these were invariably slow a certain part of a
soldier's leave was wasted. One conscript recalled that starting 'from La-
Gorie station I travelled to Bethune by a light railway and from there
proceeded via cattle trucks to Boulogne, this distance being covered in
2 days. On the following day we set sail for Folkestone at 9 A.M. arriving
at 11 A.M. from whence we entrained for Victoria reaching this
destination at 3 P.M.' Another man travelled for a day and a half by train
to Le Havre, where he embarked upon a waiting vessel at 4 p.m. 'We went
downstairs and finding a nice spot very soon fell asleep on the floor of a
passage where we remained oblivious of everything until awakened about
five o'clock next morning. Our first enquiry naturally was 'Where are we'
but much to our disappointment we received the reply that we were still
in the Harbour at HAVRE.'[33] After a further delay of twelve hours, during
which the troops disembarked and had 'a sing-song', the ship finally
sailed to England.

The conscripts' experiences on leave were rarely documented in these
writings, probably because they quickly reverted to their civilian lives and
identities and so felt this period to be removed from their military
experience. Typically, leave is summarised in a few sentences, if at all: 'I
need not enter here into the happiness of the days I spent on leave. Every
moment was one of joy and each of the 15 days was like a day in heaven.'
One conscript, who kept a very detailed diary in France, went on leave

after two years at the front. His entries for the period of leave are minimal, often skipping two or three days at a time.[34] For many men the initial contact with British civilians was shocking, in that it starkly contrasted the existence both populations had become accustomed to in the conscripts' period of absence. One man recalled arriving in Victoria station during a German bombing raid in January 1918. He entered the underground and boarded a train which was 'full of scared women and children who did not realise how safe they were in such deep tunnels. As we passed by some exclaimed "Poor boys!" Little did they know our true feelings.' However, since their experiences while on leave are not discussed, it is difficult to establish from these writings to what extent, if any, these conscripts did actually voice their true feelings. The only explicit reference made to this issue was by a young conscript who arrived home on his first leave just after the Armistice of 1918. When questioned by his father he found himself unable to discuss his army experiences in full, since 'I was young and confused about man's inhumanity to man. I did say it was bloody horrible and I told him I had seen a trench full of parts of American soldiers which had been blown to pieces.'[35]

The return to France and to their military existence appears to have been traumatic for many conscripts: 'The scene at the station was indescribable; thousands of people were there to see their husbands, sons, sweethearts, and friends off . . . it was indeed an effort . . . to keep from breaking down.' The trains were 'full of soldiers returning from leave and apparently all were feeling like myself, fed up as not a word was spoken on the journey each being engrossed with his own thoughts'. It is difficult to gauge these thoughts precisely, but they probably summarised the short civilian interlude of leave: 'These delightful experiences which seemed like an oasis in the desert and to which I had been looking forward to so eagerly, came to an end all too quickly and . . . I had to return to France with a heavy heart.' And upon reaching their camps, most men simply embarked upon another flight of fantasy about 'the next leave – it might come in eight or nine months – it was something to look forward to and I began to think of all the things I would do then. Nothing seemed to matter save my next leave.'[36]

Life in the trenches was clearly dominated by the struggle for subsistence and survival: it was the overwhelming reality of existence. But within this total world, it was the notion and memory of the outside civilian world which sustained these conscripts. Whether through letters, attitude to money or home leave, it was their image of themselves as civilians which carried them from day to day. Moreover, they persisted with this image despite the huge obstacles imposed by the army: censorship delayed their letters and allowed them little substance in correspondence; pay was minimal and often late in coming; and leave was exceptionally rare. Yet perhaps they persisted in their image *because* of these barriers: unable to write about their military activities, the conscripts could only communicate on civilian matters, and those which occurred in their life before conscription. Being denied regular pay, or having too little of it, simply threw them back to similar situations in their previous civilian lives. And living in such dire circumstances, and being unable to escape, ultimately recreated home as a haven – a refuge. But in either case, whether the army framework was an obstacle or a catalyst, it is clear that in their attitude to the outside world, the conscripts clung on to their civilian lives and identities.

PART THREE

Soldiers of War

He knew that the essence of war is violence,
and that moderation in war is imbecility.

Lord Nugent's *Memorials of Hampden*

CHAPTER 7

The Backbone – Discipline

To drop your rifle on foot of Second Lt
is bad luck – for him.
To drop ditto on foot of Sergeant Major
is bad luck – for you.[1]

An army is basically an extremely hierarchical institution engaged in the deployment of organised violence. As such, discipline is central to it. The character of each army is often determined by the emphases laid upon different aspects of discipline, since officer–man relations, *esprit de corps* and morale are directly affected by it. As already shown in the chapter on training, discipline instils the acceptance of a hierarchy and unquestioning obedience within the military unit, and at the same time the use of violence outside it. In other words, it is the underlying force behind extremes of repressive and expressive behaviour. Michel Foucault explains this paradoxical duality in noting that the 'chief function of the disciplinary power is to "train", rather than to select and to levy; or, no doubt, to train in order to levy and select all the more. It does not link forces together in order to reduce them; it seeks to bind them together in such a way as to multiply and use them.'[2] Taking this principle to extremes, one could say that the ultimate role of military discipline is the creation of a robot who obeys all orders docilely behind the lines, yet roars into tremendous displays of aggression when sent into action.

The conscripts were not robots. They were men who had been put into uniform; civilians whose values had supposedly been made invalid by the discipline of the military framework. That was the theory; but the reality was slightly different. Many aspects of their army experiences – such as food, mud or cleanliness – were basically human, rather than military or civilian. They were about survival. At most, they could therefore involve expectations rather than values. But there is no human level to discipline, which is designed to eliminate any semblance of individuality or character. Or as one conscript put it: 'What is a "crime" in a soldier is usually a pardonable eccentricity in a civilian – and what is regarded as a good military quality is usually one which would stamp a civilian as being socially impossible. The army therefore being based on an immoral hypothesis – viz war – is simply an inversion of moral codes.'[3]

In other words, discipline was the sphere in which civilian and military values came into conflict. Understanding this conflict is therefore a way of understanding how the conscripts saw their two lives, or two identities, as civilians and soldiers.

The most informative insight into the these men's perceptions of military discipline was written by a conscripted schoolteacher, who devoted an entire chapter of his lengthy account to the issue: 'The discipline in the army is maintained by threats. On this fact I make no criticism: I merely state it. 'You refuse to obey my order. Very well. Fall in two men and march him off to the guard room.' 'Do this at once or I'll bring you up before the officer tomorrow.' Yes, that expresses the attitude better than anything else. "Do this or —".'[4] In other words, discipline was seen in the strictest sense of obedience and disobedience, isolated from other considerations such as comprehension, compassion or even morale. An order given by a person of a higher rank, thus better placed than a conscripted private within the hierarchy, was to be obeyed – regardless of the circumstances. This perception was borne out in the writings of these men in several ways. One conscript, who was interviewed in an oral history project, recalled that 'we was never allowed . . . to take a photograph. If they caught you with a camera, they'd damn well shoot you. That's what they used to threaten us, anyway.'[5] Most commonly conscripts were threatened with various punishments due to sloppy appearance, such as hair of an unmilitary length or unpolished boots: 'Every man must shave once in twenty four hours. Buttons . . . cap badges and numerals must be cleaned thoroughly once a day. Box-respirators and steel helmets will always be carried. Except when it is raining, great-coats or waterproofs will not be worn when men are working. . . . Unless there is an improvement in future the coompany [*sic*] will parade each evening at 5.30 and on Sunday afternoon for extra drill.'[6]

Threats were also carried out, especially if superiors felt their authority was not absolute. In other words, bullying through threats and punishments was the method used, mostly by NCOs, to keep an awareness of the hierarchy within the army, and the conscripts' lowly place within it: '[The NCO] was bullied by his superiors just as we were bullied by ours. He was bullied into being a bully. And his superiors were bullied by their superiors. The army is ruled by fear – and it is this constant fear that brutalizes men not naturally brutal.' Bullying could be done in a number of ways, as in the issue of pointless orders which, if unfulfilled, left the soldier open to punishment: 'I remember . . . one corporal in particular, who seemed almost to take a delight in issuing useless orders. That man is the only man in the army for whom I have felt anything like hate.'[7] The following sequence of diary entries highlighted another method of bullying, whence disciplinary measures, which ultimately affected the private soldier most, were used as a tool within a power struggle between officer and NCO:

18 February 1917	Carter, Lock and Bdr. Anchers were late for O.P. this a.m. and are under arrest.
19 February 1917	Carter and party up before major who reprimanded them.
20 February 1917	Sgt. Petty got up in a bad temper and put Carter under arrest because he was not washed and ready for duty by 8 a.m. prompt. He was remanded for colonel.
21 February 1917	Carter got five days No. 2 [punishment] and sent down to Wagon Line.

Field punishment number two 'meant a note in the pay book, pay forfeit, sleeping under guard and the performance of such fatigues and pack drills as could be crammed into the day. All the while the offender would be on a diet of water and biscuit. Worse, he would not be allowed to smoke.'[8]

The most common cause of resentment and feeling of hardship aroused within these men was the absence of explanation and reasoning.

There is, in the army, a feeling that an order for which the reason is explained tends to slacken discipline. Men must learn to do things because they are told to do them not because there is a good reason for doing them.

'Do it because I tell you to do it.'
'Never you mind why: remember you're speaking to an N.C.O. and get on with the job.'

'It doesn't matter whether there is a better way of doing it. I'm orderly sergeant and I've given you an order.'

These are typical of much that goes by the name of discipline.

One conscript wrote of a solo balloon ascent he attempted while on training, in which he nearly crashed due to circumstances beyond his control: 'The crowning insult was hurled at me the following day by the C.O. who designated me "an insolent young puppy" for expressing my opinion of the ascent in my balloon report, as "extremely unwise" – that is one of the reasons I dislike the army. Of course I wasn't allowed the luxury of a protest and had perforce to "turn about" from the presence of the "all highest".' Another conscript, who was in the line, noted that 'two men were nearly arrested for answering back.'[9] And a gunner recalled an inspection held by a new Regimental Sergeant Major, who discovered that all the men in his unit had removed the heavy ammunition from their bandoliers, and then padded them out with paper:

> Consequently he reported us all to the Colonel as the most slovenly and ill equipped squad he had ever inspected. The old Colonel was awfully decent about it and lectured us in a kindly way reminding us . . . what a terrible predicament we should be in should trouble arise & we find ourselves without ammunition. As however we were not carrying rifles I am afraid we failed to appreciate carrying a bandolier . . . [with] 28 lbs of 'ammo' while we had nothing to fire it with. Still it was not our place to argue the point.[10]

Conscripts, like any other British soldier, rarely argued with their superiors. But it seems these men abstained out of considerations which were of a civilian rather than a military nature. Moreover, it was this attitude which ultimately shaped their identity in the eyes of others in the army – who persisted in a view that the conscripts were an alien, and dangerous, civilian element.

> . . . both junior officers and the [regular and voluntary] rank and file seemingly unite in their suspicions of the conscripts, [and] it is hardly surprising that such fears were also prevalent at higher levels. . . . Major-General Sir Wyndham Childs, who as Deputy Adjutant-

General and then Director of Personal Services in the War Office from 1916 to 1919 had dealt with disciplinary matters, was in no doubt that after the war crime in the army and especially desertion was more prevalent after the introduction of conscription.[11]

In fact, only one case of desertion was mentioned in these writings, and it occurred in England. On the train to Southampton Alfred Hale recalled 'the voice of the Sergeant-Major calling out that no one was to leave the train under threat of dire penalties. But this did not prevent Ist A-M Matthews, who all along had said that he would not proceed overseas whether ordered to or not, from leaving the train and the squadron altogether; deserting in fact.' Warnings issued by the army authorities in the face of possible desertions, and the expected punishment, are noted twice. The first occurrence was also in England, when troops were stationed in Woolwich for two days prior to embarkation to France: 'Am now warned not to leave barracks as absence from roll call means liable to be tried by District Court Martial.' The second was in France, when a conscript who had fought in the infamous Polygon Wood, where much blood had been shed by both sides, recalled that on the night before his departure from this site 'an officer had read us a warning concerning the penalties of deserting. This was the only time we ever heard this warning.'[12]

Within the spectrum of military disciplinary devices, death was the ultimate penalty hovering over the men. The offences punishable by death included 'mutiny, cowardice before the enemy, disobedience of a lawful order, desertion or attempted desertion, sleeping or being drunk on post, striking a superior officer, casting away arms or ammunition in the presence of the enemy, leaving a post without orders, abandoning a position, and treacherously communicating with or in any way assisting the enemy'.[13] Out of this list, the most questionable issue was actually 'cowardice before the enemy', since it turned death into a permanent fixture in the men's lives. The basic purpose of an individual's conscription into the army was to fight; but this clause meant that a refusal to do so was cause for his death. In this sense, a combat soldier was caught within a paradox, since both fighting or an abstention from it, for whatever reason, could lead to his death:

I've seen them when they was drove over the top. If they didn't go they was shot. They used to count down (to zero) and then 'Over the top' and then the Military Police would come along and see that they had all gone over.

Q.   And what happened if anybody decided they weren't going to get out of the trenches?

A.   Oh well, they shot 'em.

Once a soldier went over the top the death threat was not eliminated, since he could refuse to proceed and fight. One conscript who was promoted to the status of NCO recalled his personal dilemma during an attack in which 'there was sufficient light from bursting shells to enable me to see one of our men running back . . . I believe we NCO's were supposed to shoot any man we saw running away from action but in the vast confusion of battle, even in daylight, how could one be sure?'[14]

A refusal to fight was the most frightening crime punishable by death, simply because it did not necessitate a court martial. There is no data on the number of men, conscripts or others, who were shot in this manner. However, from the outbreak of the war to the end of March 1920 '3,080 men had been condemned to death [by court martial] and 346 of them, 11.23 per cent, had been executed'. Of these, only nine appear to be conscripts, though the data is not sufficient to make a clear or absolute calculation. For all men, the sentences were carried out 'in a secluded place with men of their own unit as witness. Twelve men chosen at random would be issued with a mixed live and dummy dozen of bullets to ease their consciences. Each death was reported simply as a casualty on active service.' In general, there was a huge increase in the number of courts martial held throughout the war. In 1913 3,690 cases were heard, whereas between 1914 and 1918 252,773 cases were tried – an average of 160 per day.[15]

Two courts martial are mentioned in the writings examined here. In the first, which took place in a training camp on Salisbury Plain, a conscript was put on trial for striking a NCO who had cheated in a card game. After being held for several days in the guard room he was marched to a tribunal – a forum composed of a major, captain and lieutenant. The prisoner was prosecuted by his own adjutant, and defended by a company officer. When he entered, the conscript was asked if he had hit the NCO: 'I could only answer yes. I did have one officer defending me and I remember him saying something about extenuating circumstances. The sergeant in charge of my escort was told to take me outside and wait; but it was not long before I was back inside to hear the president of the court say "you have committed a serious offence, the court finds you guilty, your punishment is sixty days in H.M. military prison".'[16]

In the second instance a soldier was found asleep while on guard duty in the front line. This offence was punishable by death under any circumstances. His NCO, however, pleaded on his behalf, claiming that because of a bout of influenza the company was short of men, which meant the fit ones were on duty all night in addition to a rotation of two hours on and off during the day. In more regular circumstances, men on guard duty were usually given several hours of rest the next day. The sentence passed on the guard was one of death commuted, and was served by him during the periods in which the company was out of the front line – as a result of the Army Suspension of Sentences Act (1915). This Act 'fulfilled the basic tenet of military law in that the penalty did nothing to precipitate a man-power shortage. In consequence, an offender might remain on active service despite conviction, the army reserving the right to acquit or impose sentence at will.'[17]

A soldier was legally army property; any attempt to 'damage' him was therefore also punishable by court martial. Throughout the war, with a marked increase after the Somme campaign of August 1916, four thousand men were charged with causing a self-inflicted wound. A chaplain attached to a front-line unit wrote of a case in which a man was put 'under arrest for having tried to injure himself and will probably get two years for it'. The conscripts were aware of their status as property, which was another cause for resentment. One young conscript, noted above, was thankful for having missed a rat poised on the tip of his boot which he attempted to stab, since he could have been court martialled for 'self inflicted wound.' To this extent, army discipline had instilled in this man a sense that as an individual his life was worth less than that of a rat – in addition to a thorough understanding of the negative implications of a court martial.[18]

One conscript recalled an amusing incident in which a court martial was narrowly averted. In his account, he also reveals the latent attitude of these conscripts to the disciplinary framework in which they found themselves. A somewhat pompous young officer arrived in the front line directly after his training in England. Appalled by what he deemed as lack of discipline among the troops, he attempted to enforce the 'King's regulations'. These were all very well in a training camp but some were out of place in the front line. Having got drunk one night he decided to make the men more alert to the possibilities of spies, by lining them up and then disarming them. Standing in front of a well-built Irishman, who was a building labourer in civilian life, the officer addressed him:

'Now, I'm a German spy and you are all quite defenceless.' Mike said 'Am I, begorrah!' and laid him out flat in the mud of the trench with a straight right. The corporal, after helping him to his feet, had to explain that if he tried to court martial Mike for hitting an officer he would lay himself open to the charge of disarming his men in face of the enemy. After this incident Mike was heard to remark that 'I've been wanting to do that for weeks but I never thought that he would give me such a wonderful excuse for doing it.'[19]

Several men mention guard duty as a focal point of discipline, basically because it was a regular feature of their lives, in addition to their other duties. However, it was here that a human need for sleep often came into conflict with the military need to mount a guard – but military discipline took consideration only of the latter. One man, who was struck by the Spanish influenza epidemic that ravaged Europe in the summer of 1918, remained the sole survivor of a signal section which was sent up the line. Arriving at his post, 'I lay down on a mattress in the cellar of a ruined farmhouse, checked that all my telephone connections were in order and knew nothing more until I was rudely shaken by the company commander who asked me if I knew that, for a soldier on duty sleeping at his post, the sentence was death. I explained my condition which he apparently understood and that was the end of it and my Spanish 'flu.' Another conscript recorded a more common occurrence of sleeping on duty:

While I was on [night] duty about 11 o/c I saw someone standing not far away whom I took to be one of the wheelwrights as their bivvy was close by so did not challenge him. All of a sudden it dawned on me it was an officer so I at once challenged him & found to my dismay it was the Captain. 'So this is how you keep guard is it,' he said . . . 'Call out the guard' said he. This was a fine predicament as I knew they were all fast asleep in their bivvies. . . . I told him I thought that as it was a wet night & we had no guard tents that the NCO had let them go to their bivvies . . . The next morning the NCO got a lecture from the Captain but nothing worse.[20]

There were usually six soldiers on each night guard duty rota, thus two men for each watch. One conscript recalled a lightening German raid in which one sentry was stunned by a blow over his head, while his partner was seized from their post in the middle of the night. 'Next day all remaining five men were sent out for court-martial, and eventually discharged; the captain and colonel were suspended for some time after this affair.' Following this incident the company went out for a week's rest behind the lines; however 'we had no rest whatever . . . for the authorities seemed to be bent upon punishing us all for losing that man. Our company had to work all day doing odd jobs . . . we were glad to push off again to the [front] line.'[21]

This case highlights four aspects of military discipline which were important to the conscripts discussed here. First, their perception of 'the authorities' as a vague and threatening power, above themselves as private soldiers. In other words, discipline was really understood as the underlying force of the hierarchy, in which their own place was exceedingly low. Second, that in rest periods discipline was not relaxed – in fact, the contrary was true. In this case the company was obviously being punished with extra duties, but units often resumed a regime of drill and parades while out on rest.[22] This means that discipline was seen as the tool used by 'the authorities' in any attempt to return the army to its more rigid pre-war structure, since discipline in the front line was influenced more by the dictates of war than of principle. The commuted death sentence noted above was another example of this situation: while in the line a soldier was expected to fight and to keep alive, but behind the lines he could be subject to disciplinary dictates.

The third aspect of discipline apparent here was the concept of collective punishment, for offences committed both by superiors and by the men within their own ranks. In the incident described above the entire company was punished for the loss of one man; this in addition to the individual punishments meted out to those who were directly involved and responsible. It was a double principle of responsibility, in which each man was responsible for the perceived offences of himself – and of his fellow soldiers and his superiors. In this way one conscript noted in his diary that the 'Skipper [was] disgusted with battery staff yesterday, so gave us a cross-country run as punishment. . . . When we got back he sent us over the jumps. I had a job getting mine [horse] over but eventually did.'[23] The fourth tenet of discipline was that, with no exception, there *always* had to be someone responsible for a perceived offence. For example, in the following occurrence: 'I saw a grenade accident where the sergeant technically responsible was court martialled and demoted. While the responsibility was his in theory, supervision under battle field conditions was almost impossible and the undiscriminating response of the army did not give us a good opinion of staff sense since he was a good man & we did not like to see him broken in this way.'[24]

This description also reflects upon the other side of collectivity, in which the men felt themselves as one in opposition to their superiors. The group spirit appeared to instil a measure of strength within the individuals, alongside a sense of justice – punishment for an offence committed by everyone was more acceptable than punishment suffered by all for the offence of one. This contrast between the weakness of the individual and the strength of the group was highlighted in the account of one young conscript. At one point, he described a French peasant child attempting to steal some chocolate from the pack of a marching soldier. 'She must have known that no British soldier would leave the ranks to chase her.' This may be seen as a typical example of an individual soldier's perception of discipline, against which he was helpless. Yet as part of a group his perception is different. In the base camp at Etaples his unit was drilled by an unpleasant NCO who was nicknamed the 'Black Bastard'. This led to the entire draft refusing to budge at one time, and 'blowing raspberries' at the hated superior, who was ultimately replaced.[25] In other words, when individuals combined, the elements of strength and justice allowed for the resurgence of civilian values and sensibilities within the group, which were expressed as a united front against the military values: 'During one of the frequent marches, one day we were plodding along when to everyone's dismay, we saw a man crucified to the wheel of a gun in the middle of a field. Everyone immediately stopped, and the whole regiment refused to go any further until they had taken the man down. Within the next half hour we saw the man taken down when we then continued marching.'[26]

The man in question was undergoing 'No.1 Field Punishment': 'The police fastened the soldier to a fixed object, usually a wheel, in full view of his comrades for two hours on three of four consecutive days. This notorious part of the punishment was known as "crucifixion" because of the stance adopted. It could be a brutal practice, especially when inflicted by an old-fashioned disciplinarian.' In some cases, pay was also deducted from the offending soldier's army wages, and his family informed of the matter on an official form designed for the purpose. At base, the sight of the bound man offended the sensibilities of these conscripts, probably for two reasons. First, regarding the punishment itself, the group spirit instilled a sense of shared experience. The tied man was an individual who was equal to each and every one of the passing soldiers, and as such the outrage felt was personal: this was an act of empathy as well as sympathy. Second, the visibility of the punishment was offensive. 'In a survey of Warrant Officers and NCO's public exposure was one of the commonest complaints about punishments.' For this sight was not only shaming in absolute terms – it was also an element of discipline from which civilian offenders were spared. Since the beginning of the nineteenth century 'the great spectacle of physical punishment disappeared; the tortured body was avoided; the theatrical representation of pain was excluded from punishment.'[27] This reversion to antiquated, and somewhat primitive concepts of punishment by the army therefore offended the conscripts both as individuals accustomed to a measure of military discipline, and also as civilians. For it seems that these men did not entirely differentiate between a military or a civilian ethos of justice and discipline. As individuals, their civilian perspective existed only latently, since they felt themselves in a relatively weak position within the hierarchy. But as a group, their acceptance of military discipline was strictly within the context of military necessities – as perceived from an essentially civilian point of view.

A classic example of this trend was given by one conscript who noted 'two turn-outs (air raid practice) tonight and almost a row, shouting at officers and stone throwing etc.' In other words, turn-outs were not deemed a military necessity by these men, and they therefore refused to accept them as part of their duty, or within their definition of collective discipline. It is also interesting to note that even in cases in which the group tactic failed, the context was still within a civilian evaluation of the situation. For example, when a concert was arranged in a neighbouring camp to which no soldier ventured due to bad weather, 'we were paraded and marched down to it, a good one for "John Bull".'[28]

Discipline in the British army was notoriously harsh, to an extent that caused a German officer to comment upon it in his diary in December 1917: 'The administration of discipline by the English is very rigid. Whilst on our side there is known to me only a single case in which a soldier on account of aggravated refusal of duty in the face of the enemy was shot, I gather from a compilation of the British orders which have been found, that at least 67 English soldiers have been shot under martial law in the period between 27 October 1916 and 30 August 1917.'[29] Although the use of the death penalty may not be an adequate measure of the daily practices of discipline, it was clear that in an environment of probable death, such as a battlefield, any use of it appeared brutal and extreme. The Allied troops, who were also acquainted with discipline in the British Army, often found it unacceptable, and there were a number of references to these men protesting against it. One conscript noted a row that erupted over a British soldier tied to a wheel in 'No. 1 Field Punishment'. A group of New Zealand troops 'in a camp nearby cut him loose and threatened to tie anybody up who interfered. Major Bray ordered a machine gun to be put near the wagon and turned on anybody who came near. Then they tied the chap up again. A parley between officers resulted in N.Z.'s [sic] being confined to camp.'

On a comparative basis the conscripts were also aware of their extreme disciplinary conditions. In a base camp 'some Colonial troops came in conflict with the military police. The Colonials did not believe in being "penned up" like cattle, nor were they accustomed to that exasperating discipline to which we Tommies generally assented.'[30] Another conscript, whose unit was loaned to an Australian tunnelling company, was amazed by the relaxed but effective discipline in which these Allied soldiers existed. His description highlighted the discipline to which he was accustomed in the British Army, and its resulting low morale: 'We were charmed by the camaraderie we found among the Australians – and also their casual ways. There was none of that fall-in, right turn, quick march on the way to the job. We were simply told what to do & expected to go away and do it. We had a break of 5 minutes every hour & were expected to use common sense as to the best moment to take it. There was no scrounging – everyone worked with a will, the way one should. The officers trusted the men and the men did not let the officers down.'[31] Lack of trust within an authoritarian framework may also be seen in the following diary entry: 'Friday evening – Rum arrived but ordered to be drunk in front of Captain – therefore refused.'[32] In this case, the conscript saw himself as an adult, and refused to be treated as a child by an officer, who did not trust him.

By emphasising the lack of common sense and trust in their perception of the discipline in the British Army, these conscripts offered an insight into the issue as an extension of British education. Frederick Voigt was apparently put on a charge after writing the following description in a letter: 'Being in the army is just like being back at school; the only difference is that whereas at school your superiors generally know a little bit more about things than you do, in the army that is not the case.' The conscripted teacher mentioned earlier expounded upon this parallel: 'The most startling thing that I have learned about teaching is the similarity between many of our methods in School and the methods of officers and N.C.O.'s in the army. How often have I resented the bullying manner and truculent tone of sergeants and corporals and then suddenly remembered that I have, on occasion, used the same words and adopted the same tone to my boys in School.'[33] This description of the contemporary British school system was well substantiated in a collection of memoirs about the experiences of childhood in Edwardian England. Most of the interviewees, apart from those who went away to boarding school, described their education as a minor event, centring mostly around discipline. For example, Clifford Hills, who was raised in a village, recalled: 'No, I can't say that I did enjoy school. We were glad to get away from school. We got the cane and played truant.' Annie Wilson, who grew up in Nottingham, claimed that 'we were all terrified of teachers you know. "You wait till you get to school. The teacher'll soon straighten you out", if you'd been naughty at home you see. And you went to school in fear.' In his autobiography, the author V.S. Pritchett offered a succinct summary of the issue: 'In most schools such a crowd was kept in order by the cane. . . . To talk in class was a crime, to leave one's desk inconceivable. Discipline was meant to encourage subservience, and to squash rebellion – very undesirable in children who would grow up to obey orders from their betters.'[34]

In this light, discipline in the British Army, especially as perceived by these conscripts, may be seen as a one-way system of orders to be obeyed, unquestioningly. 'Early in my army life I discovered that thinking for oneself was one of the most useless things that any soldier could attempt to do. Over and over again I have tried to use my intelligence, to seize the idea of some movement and to act accordingly, and when I have been asked what I meant by thus acting and have replied that I *thought* that was what was wanted I have been told "Don't think. In the army just do as you're told. It doesn't pay to think." How I have resented that scornful retort: how unjust I have felt it!' Another conscript recalled being very surprised by a new commanding officer who expected him to take the initiative. 'This was something quite new to me, up to now initiative had been frowned upon.'[35]

A further parallel to military discipline perceived by these men was with the civilian workplace. There too initiative was expected only from those situated higher up in the hierarchy, while a group spirit often existed on the shopfloor, giving the workers a degree of strength and control over their conditions. However, whereas management in the workplace imposed discipline, the ethos of this civilian structure also offered protective measures – and this ethos was transferred by the conscripts into their army life. This may be seen, for example, in the case noted above in the discussion of money, when an unpaid section adopted the approach of 'no pay, no work', which was, and is, an attitude taken usually in an industrial dispute. In other words, beyond the group effort, the principle behind this incident was taken directly from the civilian world of trade relations, which was conceptually alien to the military establishment. However, many of these men had come from a background in which it was prevalent, and their attitude was clearly determined by it. As already noted, one conscript framed his entire approach to his military experience in the comparative terms of a job of work, when he noted that as a soldier he got no bonuses or 'any other sops'. Another man, following a similar line of reasoning, claimed that during the war, 'Engineers, Miners, Railwaymen etc. threat[ened] to strike for increases in their wages, whilst we in the Army had not even the option of lodging a complaint and in addition to existing on very meagre rations and experiencing the hardships of a bitter campaign, were daily risking our lives for a mere pittance.'[36]

One hierarchical institution, the army, therefore seemed to emulate another, industry. The conscripts were the workers; the NCOs were the supervisors; and the officers, coupled with the ambiguous 'authorities' such as GHQ, were the management. Most of the literature dealing with the subject of labour history appears to agree that the concept, if not the implementation, of labour organisation and negotiations existed in the British labour force by 1914. Indeed, as the labour historian Jonathan Zeitlin notes, 'few nations have the unbroken record of trade union organisation and collective bargaining which distinguishes the history of industrial relations in Britain'. In the period 1880–1914 membership in trade unions rose from 4 per cent to 25 per cent, and even traditional craft unions were invaded by unskilled workers, thereby expanding the concept of collectivity beyond the 'preserve of a privileged minority'. Within this emerging structure of industrial relations, 'it is clear that the foreman formed the vital link in the chain of command (and still does),

[but] the collective discipline of the work group or squad was often more important than formal directives from management. Many firms were pressing for efficient subordination of workmen to managerial authority . . . but others recognized the value of a "responsible autonomy" in the execution of certain tasks.'[37] Based upon this paradigm, it is possible to assert that the conscripts often saw themselves as workers detailed to do a job of work – fighting a war – and as such expected a degree of 'responsible autonomy'. As will be shown in the following chapter, they were often granted this autonomy due to the circumstances of war and the imposed functional character of the BEF. It was not an army decision; it was a reality. But the sphere in which this autonomy was still elusive was that of military discipline.

The army authorities, who had a prevailing concept of discipline from pre-war days, had accepted civilians as volunteers. The conscripts, having failed to volunteer, were categorised as unwilling. Unwillingness was a trait identified in schoolchildren – and it was in this way that the army treated the conscripts. The latter, on the other hand, saw themselves as responsible adults used to doing a job of work. As such, they responded only to those elements within the military disciplinary framework which were relevant to what they considered their job description – fighting a war. The other elements, those related to the professional ethos of soldiering, were of no interest to them, and as such were either reviled, avoided or disregarded.

CHAPTER 8

The Framework – Daily Schedule

What did they expect of our toil and extreme
Hunger – the perfect drawing of a heart's dream?
Did they look for a book of wrought art's perfection,
Who promised no reading, nor praise, nor publication?

Ivor Gurney, *War Books*

On 30 October 1915, just five weeks before his resignation, Sir John French, Commander-in-Chief of the British Expeditionary Force in France, sent King George V a telegram: 'There is no sacrifice the troops are not prepared to make to uphold the honour and traditions of Your Majesty's Army and to secure final and complete victory.'[1]

French was responding to the king's congratulations on the ostensibly successful Loos offensive which was launched on 25 September 1915. As such, he was speaking for an army made up of the remnants of the pre-war regular army and the Territorials, and a large number of the volunteers of Kitchener's New Armies. This is the army which has since become immortalised in the public mind as the force that fought and won the First World War. Yet barely two months later conscription was introduced, and by the end of the war it was the conscripts who were dominant in the BEF. And while their commitment to final and complete victory was undoubted, their attitude to the honour and traditions of the British Army cannot be taken for granted in the same way. They may have had respect for the army as a national institution, but they took a much dimmer view of its wartime organisation – especially as they experienced it on a daily basis in Flanders. For the army was in fact a paradox in their lives: it was responsible for bringing them out to the trenches, putting them into combat, and possibly getting them killed. Yet it was also responsible for their most basic human survival, at least in theory. It was from within this paradox that the conscripts viewed the army and its organisation, and not necessarily favourably. As one of them put it, in explaining why he wrote a memoir of his service, he wanted people to know 'how the soldiers were treated whilst fighting for their King and

162

Country and of the lack of proper arrangements which marked every movement undertaken by the Army in France'.[2] It is a statement, and a perception, worth exploring.

The conscription of an individual into the army was basically a bureaucratic process, enacted by the civilian branches of government for the benefit of the military. Once in the army, the army became the absolute authority in the conscripts' lives, which both set the schedule of their existence, and provided their needs. These were the two aspects of its organisation that were most apparent to the conscripts throughout their service. That said, there is no doubt that their experiences of this organisation during their training, in England and in France, were very distinct from those in the combat zone. First, training camps were placed within civilian populations largely unaffected by the battles and devastation of the war. As such, they offered the conscripts an accessible non-military option to their army existence – from company and society to food and drink. This situation was almost the reverse of that found in the combat zone: 'The British army was complete in itself and contact with French people was not very necessary, nor were there so many French as English in the war-zone.'[3] In addition, the civilians were not only few, but they too suffered from the war. The conscripts could therefore find wine, food and even good cheer in these villages or towns, but not a normal and detached civilian existence.

Second, the regime within the camps adhered, as much as possible, to the rigid and intentionalist structure of the pre-war British Army. And while this may have been an hierarchic and disciplinary life, it was also a reliable and strictly regulated existence in which all the conscripts' needs were provided for. In the combat zone a conscript was subject to discipline, rotas of duties and parades, yet these were relatively relaxed. In addition, and much more significantly, the essence of his existence was far more self-reliant, incorporating at most the other men of his section. It was each man, rather than the army as an organisation, who effectively offered his close comrades a support system. 'With a few exceptions as in any circumstance in life the one "in action" required that all should support one another and so as regards the individual war brought out the best in each.'[4] Moreover, men had to be resourceful and self-reliant at all times, not only in action. This fact has been amply reflected throughout earlier chapters above, from their scrounging for food, through the independent construction of dug-outs in the line, or even the search for billets behind the lines. For example, a conscript who arrived in Ypres after being relieved in the front line, had to 'search for a place to sleep in. Found one at last.'[5] Another recalled that 'We marched (or shall I say straggled) back to FLESQUIERS where we sat on the pavement for over an hour whilst the Officers in charge endeavoured to find us billets for the night, but getting properly fed up, impatient, and being dead tired, we entered the cellar of a big ruined house and after a bit of patching up succeeded in making it comfortable; someone gathered together some fuel and a fire was made then one by one we fell asleep on the floor and remained so until the morning.'[6] In other words, the army organisation could be relied upon to decide where these men would go and what their duties should be, yet its role as provider was much diminished. The removal of the conscript to the front line was therefore his removal from a situation of near-total reliance upon the army as a protector and provider, to one of greatly increased self-sufficiency and reliance upon a small group of comrades.

The schedule in the combat zone was based upon the principle of rotation, both within the line itself and between different sections of it. This was clearly an attempt to spread the onus of duties and exposure to the enemy as evenly as possible among all the available manpower. As a result, one conscript could write that 'some time ago I had to do three night sentries in a small shell hole, at the end of a sap called Lunatic Sap – only about 15 yards from the Hun lines! that was very rotten!' In contrast, another man could recall a tour of duty in a sector of the front line which was relatively quiet: 'For the first two weeks at 'Ypres' nothing occurred of very great importance.'[7] Two duty rotas were permanent fixtures not only in the front and rest lines, but also throughout every corps and unit in the combat zone: gas guard and sentry duty.[8] Parallel to these were the schedules of military and combat duties, working parties, and finally rest periods.

Once in the line, the rotation of trench duties followed a set pattern: 'The usual routine for infantrymen in France was as follows: three weeks or a month moving between the front, support, and reserve lines, passing five or six days in each, though variations occurred in more strenuous or quieter times; then followed perhaps ten days at a rest camp eight or ten miles back, or occasionally a still longer period twenty or thirty miles to the rear.'[9] The foremost line was also known as the 'advanced' post, and the rest line was sometimes the 'reserve'. The distance between the first two lines was approximately 100 yards, while the reserve, or third line, was one or two miles back. Six days in each line was the maximum period referred to in these writings, though men also note three- and four-day rotations. Three general and somewhat flexible rules appear to have determined these routines. First, that the length of time spent at the front was dependent upon the activity in a given area, the shortest time being spent in a quiet sector. Second, that a unit would spend equal amounts of time in each line of the sector, though the period in the rest line could be longer. And third, that the principle of rotation meant that a unit would always occupy all three lines within a given sector, not just the front or the reserve line, for example. However, the sequence of rotation would not always commence with the front line.[10]

The basic problem with the front-line schedule was that men were usually on duty rotas divided into hours rather than days: 'When we were in an advanced post we were all on duty throughout the night, and during the day we did two hour spells on and two, perhaps four, hours off, according to the number of points we had to man and the number of men available for duty.'[11] Another common routine was 24- or even 48-hour duty, in which men were constantly rotating each other in blocks of two hours on and off. These two-hourly formations secured constant attention to the enemy, but they also meant that even in a quiet sector the men got little respite or rest. 'Two hours in a dug-out where thirteen men filled a space barely large enough for eight was not conducive to sleep.' In comparison, life in the support line was usually divided between night and day. During the day men were often cramped together in a bivouac or a dug-out, or performed duties under cover, since they were not allowed to be seen.[12] Sleep was therefore difficult in this case too – though very necessary, since the night hours were devoted to work parties up the line. These comprised activities such as trench digging or carrying ammunition, which in quiet periods was often beneficial to the men themselves: 'Working parties . . . [were] organised from the different Companies who were in the "line", by which means the trenches were made habitable, new "dug-outs" were built, the direct front of the line and all "craters" were well wired, the trenches were deepened, and I think in every sense the whole position was made much more secure, and although "Tommy" often complained of "overwork" and very little sleep, yet when all was done, we all felt that those who had instigated the work were fully justified.'

Men who were on working parties during bouts of shelling did not usually echo the latter sentiment: 'The strain of these nights upon us was very great, so that it was not unusual to see a man burst into tears on the return journey, or to give himself up to cursing everything and everybody, after falling heavily in the darkness.'[13] The tension, lack of rest and hard work which characterised the conscripts' existence in the two forward lines led them to prefer life in the third, or reserve, line. This was considered overall to be the best location in the combat zone, since it was 'far enough back to be out of range of minnies, good deep trenches, well maintained, off duty spells even at night and . . . no working parties even at night'.[14] These conditions, coupled with the fatigue accumulated during the days in the front lines, meant that the conscripts spent as much of their time as possible in the third line resting or sleeping.[15]

It was the infantrymen who mostly experienced this schedule of existence, since they manned the trenches and ultimately suffered the heaviest losses. As a result, the image of the soldiers' experience in the First World War is also largely limited to this form of front-line duty; yet gunners and artillerymen were also at the front. The guns were usually fixed in one line, which was set slightly back from the front line, and so the rotation in these positions was usually between two rather than three lines: 'We had 24 hours off and 24 hours on [the gun]. When it came your turn to do 24 hours off, you went back perhaps a mile to a camp of some sort for 24 hours rest.' Yet in some positions this schedule, or any other form of short period rotation, was impossible. In the case of the infantry it was the men who relocated, and despite cumbersome battle order and heavy overcoats this could be achieved with relative ease. Gunners were dependent upon the guns, and once these were in position they had to be constantly manned. Sometimes gun lines were set far from a rest line, due to topographic and strategic reasons, in which case gunners found themselves in the line for much longer periods than 24 hours. One conscript recalled spending two weeks in such a situation, when posted to a gun line that 'was very important as it kept a lot of the enemy artillery engaged'. Alongside descriptions of filth and misery, he makes it clear that rest or sleep evaded him and his fellow gunners throughout much of the time they spent there: 'First of all it was foolhardy to wander about the site during the day as it was under enemy observation, secondly the guns could not be fired at night as the flashes would expose the exact position and invite a hail of shells, so it meant that on order from our observation officer we had to dash from cover fire a salvo of shots on fixed targets and then dash for cover again. . . . [as a result] we were on the quiver [sic] all day long waiting for the command "Action".'[16]

The fourth line occupied by soldiers within the schedule of rotation in the combat zone was the rest line, usually located a few miles behind the reserve line. The routines of extended physical exertion coupled with fear, tension and fatigue which these conscripts experienced in the front lines could lead to the logical assumption that they eagerly awaited their days in the rest line. Their preferences, however, appear to have been in direct contradiction to this line of reasoning. As one conscript, a signaller in the RFA, wrote in his diary: '12.30 PM. Am now all ready to leave and rejoin section [behind the lines] . . . I am rather sorry for I should like to have kept in action as a telephonist as a rest really means hard work in the horse lines just behind the firing line.' This sentiment is expressed in many of these writings, by soldiers of every unit. An infantryman noted that 'they were called rest days but in these 4 days we did carrying parties, taking food and ammunition to the men in the front every night after dark and sometimes it was morning before we got back'. Another man noted in his diary: 'Some rest! Up to the trenches again for fatigue at night.'[17] A gunner claimed that 'instead of having a rest, you were carrying ammunition up . . . to the guns. You were better off on the guns than you were having time off. If you had nothing to do on the guns, you could get a bit of sleep in the dugouts.' The issue is best summarised by the conscript who recalled that 'since life was more difficult when we were only a little way back, we felt relieved to be making our way towards the front line on Christmas Eve'.[18]

Periods of rest in camps located even further back were also considered unwelcome to some conscripts: 'Went in Brigade rest at Bouchier. Working parties during the day and guard at night. Hardest time of my life. About 2 hours rest out of 24 every day.' Even a week of rest in a town, which potentially offered the option of better food and evenings in an estaminet, was sometimes deemed worse than a tour of trench duty: 'Truly we had no rest whatever. . . . Our company had to work all day doing odd jobs for the Town Major . . . we were glad to push off again to the line a week later.'[19] The major referred to was the liaison officer appointed by the British Army to work in conjunction with the local mayor or dignitary; there was one appointed in each town occupied by British troops.

Training and practice camps far from the front were another form of respite, if not rest from the front-line routine. One conscript spent two weeks at a Trench Mortar School in Beauval: 'Here we were billeted in a barn, along with 500 others, up a flight of stairs. Our hours of instruction were 9 am to 10.30, 11.0 to 12.0 and 2.0 to 4.0. This was a very easy time for us, our only grievance being that we were insufficiently fed.'[20] But another conscript, who was sent on a signalling course at Henesourt complained: 'it was a miserable place, no money, no fags, no nothing, and it lasted for 3 weeks, I was glad to get away.' Others also found these periods of relative relaxation 'not very congenial in a time of war as there is too much time at one's disposal for thinking of possibilities which might easily become realities'. Uncongenial thoughts were sometimes an abstraction of a further aspect of routine: boredom. Even if a schedule incorporated much hard work and fear, the fact that it was set within fixed divisions of time and labour reduced it to routine. Many of these conscripts complained of being bored, even when exhausted. While in the line one man claimed that 'the four day routine was rather boring'. A gunner and driver in the RFA who spent two months in a training camp located near a village far behind the line uttered a similar opinion, despite his days being completely filled with practice and horse-care. As a result he was quite happy to go on a two week signalling course, even though it meant a three mile walk each way, 'and be relieved of the boring fatigue duties with our wagon line.'[21]

This apparent dislike of rest periods stemmed not only from the extra work allotted to the men, or even the possibility of boredom, but also, and perhaps largely, from another facet of days spent away from the front lines: '. . . a special rest [was] granted to the division for its good work, but after all there's not much rest, it is all parade, parade every day, and plenty of field days'.[22] In other words, within these conscripts' understanding of army organisation, 'rest' merely implied the removal of combat duties, and therefore also the explicit onus of fear and tension. All of these, however, were replaced by extra fatigues, alongside drills and parades – both the latter having been diminished to the point of extinction in the front line. Indeed, life in the combat zone was practically devoid of the routines and outer trappings of the British Army as a professional institution, such as emphasis on dress and appearance, or even regular inspection parades. But outside this area and its exclusive focus upon battle and survival, all such elements became apparent. And the further a camp was removed from the front line, the stricter and more formal the regime within it. Life in a retreat sap, according to one conscript, incorporated daily rifle drills, saluting and equipment parade. The schedule of a week's 'rest' slightly further back, in a wagon line, comprised labour fatigues, drills, exercises and 'dress [parade] this morning then harness cleaning'. Still further back, at a Divisional Headquarters to which a conscript was sent on guard duty for a week, a brigadier held several inspection parades since he was dissatisfied with the shine upon the men's buttons and straps.[23] Even marching between camps and sectors behind the lines, entailed, at each point, 'the full marching order inspection prior to moving. They were a constant nuisance.' The ultimate reversion to a strict army regime was found in the large base camps on the coast, which strongly resembled those in England. As one conscript wrote of Etaples: 'It's dreadful to be in a place so full of rules and regulations.'[24] And conscripts clearly had little interest in the rules and regulations of the British Expeditionary Force.

Four main conclusions may be drawn from these conscripts' perceptions of their schedule, both in and out of the line. First, that it was predictable: a stint in the front line would lead to one in the support line and then the reserve, after which a few days would be spent out at rest. The cycle would then inevitably repeat itself, or be delayed by a train journey on cattle trucks and a march to another sector. As a result of this routine, the second conclusion is that location as a point of identification was irrelevant. A sector was deemed to be 'quiet' or 'windy' rather than in Arras or Verdun, and it was always divided into three lines. The mud and general desolation of the war zone also wrought a uniform landscape throughout much of the front line, which meant there was little singularity in any given geographical location. For example, one conscript was part of a working party sent to build a dug-out at the front. 'At about 5.0 P.M. . . . we got lost and kept getting in the road of the shells. It became dark and still we were stumbling and slipping about along the muddy tracks with a guide to help us. . . . all this district is the picture of the most dreary ruination and desolation that has ever been.' In addition, men often had no idea of their exact situation, since they were not told, nor did they usually have any maps. As a result, foreign names in an unknown area meant little. This explains the many references such as '[going] somewhere up the line for the 13th Batt'.[25] However, this situation made any form of army organisation absolutely crucial, since men mainly identified themselves as part of a unit which was in or out of the line. This was well illustrated in a diary entry written by a driver who went down the line with his unit:

Coming back, my horses got behind and finally stopped and I had to lead them and got lost. Nobody seemed to know where our lines were and I wandered through theirs. Finally got near a red cross station near our lines but it was getting dark. I landed at 187 Bde where they told me to stay, fed the horses, gave me some supper and I slept in a forage tent. [Next day] Fed horses again then set off without any directions, as even the major of 187 Bde didn't know where we were, but I got a note to say I had reported there.[26]

The third conclusion is that time and its normative divisions became a somewhat abstract notion in the front line. As one conscript put it: 'One loses all count of time during war.' Civilian measures of time in years, months and days were replaced at the front by a continuous existence of hours; which battle could then further distort into 'little stirring minutes, that seemed hours'.[27] Two or four or 24 hours on or off duty marked progress through daylight, in which men had to keep under cover, and night in which most of the routine combat duty occurred. This existence also greatly diminished the possibilities of rest and sleep – a situation compounded by the fear and tension which were integral features of the combat zone. The mental strain of this schedule therefore distorted these men's perceptions of time still further. Diarists, or men with access to a diary, could keep a formal track of time by referring to a calendar. But in effect this was meaningless, since the implication of time passing as represented by a date was unsubstantiated. They had not lived through a day's work and a night's rest, but rather through so many hours on and off duty. The point at which 23:59 became 00:00 as a mark of a time-cycle completed was irrelevant to a man who had already completed several cycles of two-hour duties, and was in the midst of another. In other words, these men existed not only in a desolate combat zone, but also in a detached time zone.

This mental and physical isolation, however, appears to have been acceptable to the conscripts within the context of their front-line existence, since it was an integral part of combat. And to them, combat – and ultimately victory – was the purpose of their placement in the trenches, away from their civilian lives. Anything else, however, was unacceptable. The fourth conclusion is therefore that they resented any element within the schedule that was not strictly concerned with combat or survival – as is apparent in their dislike of rest periods which were filled with drills and parades. And as with their attitude to discipline, this conclusion reflects that their perception remained intrinsically that of civilians. In other words, though clearly combat soldiers, these conscripts saw themselves as men hired to do a job of work, which was fighting a war on behalf of their country. That they were commissioned to do so within the confines of a professional organisation, which also had other aims and ethos, interested them little. The issue was best illustrated in the account of a conscript who was 'warned by Orderly Sergt . . . to report with Wilkie and O'Burne as officers' servants. Did not like the idea at all, so we and Eades went to see C.S.M. and told him we joined the army to fight so he asked us whether we wanted to be put on draft. We said we did and so we were told we would be for a draft on Saturday.'[28]

And so, returning to Sir John French's telegram, it is clear these conscripts were definitely willing to 'secure final and complete victory', but not necessarily to uphold the traditions of the British Army. Victory was the sole purpose and justification of their conscription – but the army was nothing but a constant bane.

CHAPTER 9

The Identity of Conscripts

There's something amazingly commonplace in
the whole huge drama; and something amazingly
dramatic in the commonplaceness of it all.
Anyway it's *all* very silly.[1]

The preceding chapters present everyday life in the trenches, from the
conscripts' perspective, and in their own words. It was an appalling life,
of that there can be no doubt. But as their world unfolded, it was also
possible to glean their own insights into it. To understand how they saw
themselves within each facet of their lives, whether it was the filth of their
own flesh or their views on the organisation of the army in which they
found themselves. It now remains to bring all these strands together, in
order to reflect how they defined themselves: undoubtedly British men
and British conscripts – but had they become British soldiers, like the
volunteers before them, or did they remain civilians in uniform?

The army is the most apt point of departure in search for an answer to
such a question. It has already been shown to be the organisation that
regulated every aspect of the conscripts' existence. But in more abstract
terms, it was also what the sociologist Erving Goffman defined as a 'total
institution', one in which the three major spheres of life – sleep, work
and play – are no longer separated, for a number of reasons:

First, all aspects of life are conducted in the same place and under
the same single authority. Second, each phase of the member's daily
activity is carried on in the immediate company of a large batch of
others, all of whom are treated alike and required to do the same
thing together. Third, all phases of the day's activities are tightly
scheduled, with one activity leading at a prearranged time into the
next, the whole sequence of activities being imposed from above by a
system of explicit rulings and a body of officials. Finally, the various
enforced activities are brought together into a single rational plan
purportedly designed to fulfil the official aims of the institution.

It is also important to note Goffman's depiction of individuals initiated into the world of total institutions: 'The recruit comes into the establishment with a conception of himself made possible by certain stable social arrangements in his home world. Upon entrance, he is immediately stripped of the support provided by these arrangements.' By alienating the inmate from his previous concept of existence, from the outer elements of singular clothing to daily schedules of collective work and rest, as opposed to the personal and private ones of civilian life, a totally new identity is imposed upon him.[2]

Both elements of the definition, the institution and the inmates, clearly correspond to the life and framework reflected throughout this book. The conscripts were the inmates, and the British Expeditionary Force was the total institution – at least in theory. Each of Goffman's attributes may be applied, to a certain extent, to the way in which it operated, especially as depicted by these conscripts. They were brought together under a single authority – the army. Henceforth they ate, drank, smoked, slept, fought, bathed, hunted lice, marched through mud, and shared parcels and fear together. None of these men, unless he became lost or detached from his unit, ever experienced any aspect of life, in or out of the line, as an individual. Their existence was conceptually, and practically, collective. Moreover, despite the sudden developments of war, this was done within a tight, imposed and predictable schedule over which they had no control. To this extent, it was a paradigmatic life. However, the ultimate paradox of their existence was that within the confines of this total institution they often had to fend for themselves.

The validity of the first three elements of Goffman's definition, unity of place, company and schedule, led inevitably to the fourth: the official aims of the institution. But it was the very rationality of the army's plan, to fight and win the war, which reduced the conscripts' existence to irrationality. The circumstances of an extended and stagnant war drained every reserve within the BEF, yet imposed increasing responsibilities upon it. Conscription meant a massive influx of men who were totally dependent upon it – and they arrived after the previous wave of outsiders, the volunteers, had already put the system under severe strain. The organisation reflected in their writings was stretched to its absolute limits, often defaulting on the two issues which were most crucial to their survival outside battle: food and shelter. In other words, the reality of the conscripts' front-line existence reflected upon the devolvement of the BEF into a functionalist organisation which provided its men with a framework for survival, rather than a structured and reliable existence. As such, its ability to be a total institution should have been much reduced, and in practical terms, it was. However, this army continued to operate as a total institution, and this was largely due to the implicit and explicit acceptance of it as one by the inmates – in this case the conscripts.

The conscripts persisted in seeing the army as a total institution. It was a seemingly irrational perspective for them to hold, matched only by the irrationality of the army as they had come to experience it. But it was a necessity to them, and an inbred trait, despite their complaints and their basic lack of interest in military formalities. Their training in England, where the army as an institution could indeed meet its definition, led them to view it initially in this light. But their subsequent placement overseas, in alien and often hostile territory, left them with little option other than to perpetuate this perception. For beyond rebellion, which not one of them mentions even in passing, no other formation or organisation appeared to them as a possible replacement. And they obviously felt a need to see themselves as part of an organisation which bestowed upon them a framework, even if it could never be more than an abstraction. For as John Keegan has pointed out, modern warfare is intensely impersonal, which means that 'the soldier is coerced, certainly at times by people whom he can identify, but more frequently, more continuously and harshly by vast, unlocalized forces against which he may rail, but at which he cannot strike back and to which he must ultimately submit'.[3] The conscripts may have not liked the BEF, but at least it was a known and familiar entity to which they could belong.

An acceptance of the army as an impersonal but total institution was therefore a tenet of the conscripts' perception of it – and themselves within it. The fact that its totality was apparent mainly in the schedule it set rather than its reliability as a provider resulted in the second tenet of their perception: human survival. Hence the sustained emphasis upon rest and sleep as a focus of their attitude to the schedule, both in and out of the line; their obsessive interest in food; their reliance upon cigarettes and drink; and their fear and intense dislike of the mud and the rain. Any aspect of their existence which did not reflect upon any of these or combat was totally rejected by them:

We were regrouped [in Etaples] and parted with our insignia identifying us with the 19th City of London Regiment. Our cap badges, shoulder names, fancy buttons we all discarded to be replaced by insignia linking us now to the 2nd Battalion Worcestershire Regiment. As I had never developed any particular loyalty for the London Regiment, into which I had been unceremoniously thrust a few months previously, and no one had taken time or trouble to tell us anything about the traditions or battle honours of the regiment it was not difficult to transfer to a new regiment equally unknown.[4]

Another conscript put the issue in even more stark and severe terms: '[A general] told us that we were leaving the Third Army and joining the Fifth, or vice versa, as though a great honour was being bestowed upon us. As we thought it was most unlikely that this would make any improvement in our rations or living conditions the news left us cold.'[5] In these two sentences lie the essence of the conscripts' attitude to the army: rejection of the military establishment, and a focus upon means of survival. And within these two was embedded their identity, as apparent in the following account:

> It was always a joy to us to get away from the 'line' for a little recuperation, and I may say that as a rule Tommies' rest consisted of numerous drills, inspections and working parties, polishing our buttons and brasses which to my mind is a farce, and was a thing with which we had to occupy our time when out on rest, and I can fully understand now why so many of the photographs of the British Tommy in the Press were headed with the words – 'The bright and cheerful Tommy' and 'He is happy, are you?' and I have often thought that the true 'heading' should have been:– 'Underneath a bright uniform lies a heavy heart'.[6]

The retrospectively positive words with which this conscript started the passage deteriorate in the face of his description of the drills and parades of the military establishment; then disappear entirely with the word 'farce', which is particularly striking. Yet he was not alone in using it when describing his existence. Another man wrote of 'a medical exam which as usual is a formal farce'; while a third reflected upon the 'colossal farce of one charming Englishman crawling on his state-fed tummy across a state-battered strip of "every-man's-land",'[7] in order to shoot a state-fed German of similar intent. A farce, according to the *Oxford English Dictionary* is a 'hollow pretence, a mockery', and it was in this manner that these conscripts viewed themselves and their existence: they were civilian soldiers whose identity was neither.

The BEF gave these men a schedule of existence, and also offered them a framework for identification. But they deemed the military establishment to be farcical, and as such inappropriate for identification; yet the basic implication of conscription was enforced attachment to it, and so being presented as soldiers to civilian eyes. But they were 'amateurs'[8] who felt no desire to become professionals, beyond the qualifications required for doing the job of fighting a war. They had also lost their physical contact with daily civilian life: 'We existed in a little world of our own, when we were in the line we had little time for social calls on neighbours and when we were out we did not normally wander far from our billet or canteen.'[9] Their previous, known, civilian life was even further removed. Leave was an 'oasis in the desert' which was often dreamed of, but rarely attained. Their letters were filtered through the barriers of censorship and experiences which could not be translated into civilian terms. Communications from home perpetuated their past, while diaries marked the time spent away from both. One gunner, who was married with two children, commenced his entries every Monday with the sentence 'In the army x [e.g. 22] weeks', followed by 'Away from home x weeks' every Thursday, and 'On Active Service x weeks' every Saturday.[10] The present, the military existence, filled with routine and sheer horror, was constantly measured in the face of the past, and basically refuted. This meant that beyond their knowledge of themselves as human beings who had to function and survive, there was no viable or tangible element in their daily lives in France with which they could identify. Ultimately, therefore, these conscripts were neither soldiers nor civilians; at best, they could be defined as alienated civilians. It was a non-identity – a 'No Man's Land':

I'm asleep at present – I've signed on to be & I'm not allowed to be anything else. I sit in clubs & estaminets with my own poor uniformed self in hundreds. We say & do the same silly things. We've *got* to.[11]

EPILOGUE

It is more arduous to honour the memory of the nameless than that of the renowned. Historical construction is devoted to the memory of the nameless.

Walter Benjamin

The Forgotten Memory

'There is one aspect of the war which I do not as yet
hear that you have treated . . . and that is its effect on civilians.'

Gordon Bottomley to Paul Nash, 22 August 1918

Richard Lovat Somers was conscripted in 1916 and rejected as unfit due
to ill-health. In 1917 he was resummoned, with the passing of the second
Military Service Act, and put into category C3: unfit for military service,
but fit for light non-military duties. But he was not called up to serve. In
September 1918, during the desperate battles of the last Allied offensive,
he was summoned for a third time and recategorised as C2: fit for non-
military service. But the Armistice of November 1918 arrived before he
was called up. Since Somers had no interest in serving he was essentially
saved by his ill-health, yet he felt deeply wounded: by the summons, by
the medical examinations and by the rejections.

Richard Lovat Somers was really an alter ego: the hero of D.H.
Lawrence's autobiographical novel *Kangaroo* (1923). Like many of his
writings, it dwells endlessly upon the predicament of men, the
impossible power of women, and the deep failings of society. In this
book these themes are densely interwoven to produce a story of
bitterness verging on despair, which finds its pinnacle in 'The
Nightmare', a chapter in which Lawrence depicts his ordeal of
conscription and rejection in the First World War. As such, it is one of
the few literary, or non-literary, allusions to the experience of
conscription; and for all its self-obsession, it is therefore one that may
offer an insight into the alienation and negative imagery of the
conscripts during the war, and their subsequent disappearance from the
imagery after it ended, and the British collective memory of the event
throughout the century. For the conscripts discussed in the previous
chapters were those who actually served in the trenches: men who
sought to preserve their past civilian lives within the reality of the front,
but without any substantive contact with civilian life.`And as a result,

their writings reflected their identity as alienated civilians. Lawrence presents the opposite experience – life within Britain during the period of conscription, as a man known to have been conscripted, even if he was rejected. And curiously, this too is ultimately a narrative of alienation: from his fellow conscripted men, from the system that summoned them, and from wartime British society. It is a narrative of difference and otherness. In truth, Lawrence was so removed from the mainstream that he was probably an alienated citizen, not just a civilian. Nonetheless, he depicts the common conscript situation as much as his personal one: he writes of being publicly singled out, examined, and in his case cast aside as unfit. But above all it is the public element, the full glare, about which he is most biting – and for good reason, for it was the real issue at the root of the conscripts' predicament. To the wartime British public they were neither fit men, nor fit citizens. More significantly, they did not fit the public image of the soldier.

The correlation between manliness and war is an axiom of humanity: in the name of a sanctioned cause men take up arms, exert physical power and kill other men. It is both an essence of masculinity and a route to achieving it. This cultural configuration lies at the heart of the imagery of the soldier of the First World War, often portrayed as a patriotic rush to the colours, yet essentially acknowledged as such by both contemporaries and subsequent generations. C.E. Carrington, better known as Charles Edmonds, reflected seventy years after the war that his rush to volunteer may be summed up as an attempt 'to demonstrate my manhood, and to be allowed to indulge a taste for anti-social violence'. George Coppard volunteered in August 1914, when he was sixteen and enchanted by marching soldiers and military bands: 'This was too much for me to resist, and as if drawn by a magnet I knew I had to enlist straight away.' After the war George Orwell simply claimed that 'You felt yourself a little less than a man, because you had missed it.' Elaborating upon this theme, writer C.H. Rolph recalled that as a young policeman in the 1920s 'I was always miserably ashamed of my ribbonless uniform jacket: it was like the odd nakedness of a Freudian nightmare in which the fact that no one notices your nudity seems only to make it worse.'[1]

Being a soldier was therefore one of the most defining male experiences of the period. But during the war, *becoming* a soldier, being transformed from a civilian into a soldier, was equally crucial, not only as an act of patriotism, but as a social statement. For it was this transformation which was seen by the British public, not acts of bravery, or survival, in the battlefield. And it was the British public that decided the imagery of the First World War soldiers, as an act of judgement upon the men of the nation. The focus of this process was the recruiting office, as the meeting point between the civilian and military campaigns of the war. It was the location to which an individual man arrived as a subject of the former in order to become a participant in the latter: 'Go to the nearest Post Office or Labour Exchange. There you will get the address of the nearest Recruiting Office, where you can enlist.'[2] This was one of the earliest posters issued by the Parliamentary Recruiting Committee, but its language of urging each man to take himself – as a self-motivated act – to the recruiting office was echoed in over one hundred subsequent posters. In addition, newspapers reported daily on recruiting statistics throughout the land, and carried pictures of the crowds in and around recruiting offices. Within a community each man was seen, and often known, as he approached the local office. In other words, it was the public platform of judgement upon men as members of society; an openly viewed location to which a man came in order to be transformed from a civilian into a soldier – but within the established social, not military, definitions of the term. And to contemporary civilians, a soldier was basically a model of duty, self-sacrifice and masculinity. A real man sacrificed himself in order to aid others, while a real citizen put the nation above his own personal needs. In these terms, a real man and citizen was a volunteer. However, this definition implied that one who did not sacrifice himself, who did not exhibit his sense of duty, was half a man and no patriot. He was one who had to be brought to the recruiting office, one who had the duty of citizenship imposed upon him. He was a conscript.

This may seem a harsh construction, but nonetheless one that appears to have emerged in wartime Britain as an immense social force. It is the one behind the woman who told her husband in 1915 that he was 'nothing but a coward and . . . if he were half a man he would be away in France, where the bravest were, defending his country'. It is also the one which compelled a conscript to see himself, and be seen by others, as 'a number in uniform'.[3] Moreover, it was a force that was assisted by the legislation of the war: men who arrived in the recruiting office before 1916 could only have been volunteers, whereas those who appeared after this date were conscripts. And the chronology of appearance was crucial to the wartime British civilians, far removed from the front line, and to whom combat criteria were irrelevant. It was the external appearance of a civilian in uniform which defined him as a soldier, and the method by which he achieved this transformation that defined him as either hero or failed man. In other words, in his single act of self-motivation, committed in the public eye, the volunteer became equated with an ideal of masculine warrior, and elevated to the status of hero – regardless of any subsequent performance in the army. Within such a construction, achievement in battle was of no importance, since it was not seen. However, taken in reverse it meant that an individual who did not undertake the act of volunteering, with all its surrounding connotations, would be denied the public definitions of masculinity and heroism. A conscript was such an individual. And while these may seem both extreme and abstract notions, they were precisely the parameters within which the British public defined the image of the First World War soldier. And it was this image which stretched on into this century after the war, enshrining the volunteers and deleting the conscripts. However, in order to fully understand this process, it is important to first reach back into the complex web of nineteenth-century conceptions regarding soldiering, citizenship and masculinity, and to then see how these were imposed upon the wartime population. From there it may be possible to proceed first into the immediate postwar era, when wartime images were reshaped into memory, and then into the second half of the twentieth century, when memory became myth.

The British public image of the soldier in August 1914 was based on ignorance: 'The ordinary English man and woman knew nothing about war. That it would all be over soon was the first reaction. It was not in any case expected to affect the lives of the ordinary citizen. Wars were fought by soldiers and sailors, who came on leave and were made a fuss of.' Children's author Noel Streatfeild, born in 1898, was reflecting upon the First World War as the event in which she 'grew up all in one minute',[4] leaving behind her Victorian and Edwardian childhood world. It was a world of Empire that celebrated wars and soldiers, and enshrined the army – yet one in which combat soldiers and battles were merely ideas and images, devoid of any meaning to civilians. Such innocence was hardly surprising, given that the standing regular army numbered under 300,000, and there was no conscription or any form of national service.

In other words, there was no system which could have taken the civilian populace beyond the external image of the army.

The only event of mass interaction between army and society in the nineteenth century occurred long before 1914, during the Napoleonic wars, when the threat of invasion led to an immense enlistment of volunteers. But with the cessation of hostilities they all returned to civilian life, and the army reverted to its previous identity as a relatively small professional organisation. And yet, as Linda Colley has shown in her examination of the British nation in the early nineteenth century, this period of wars was highly influential in establishing a centrally controlled widespread patriotism, within which the army assumed an important role. And so, while the reality of military life receded and was gradually forgotten, a sanitised and carefully staged image of the army came into being, through state-sponsored glamorous parades and military spectacles. These were watched and eagerly consumed by the British public, which by the end of the century expressed its disapproval if military splendour was absent from any official occasion. Indeed, Queen Victoria's Golden Jubilee in 1897 has been described as a 'Roman triumph', with a march-past of British and native troops from all over the Dominions and colonies. And a triumph it was, since through its ceremonial façade the army ultimately became a major cultural institution, with a permanent presence and influence upon various aspects of life – from evolving modes of dress to the emergence of war games and toys, such as tin and paper soldiers. More significantly, elements of army organisation, such as discipline and singular dress, made a deep impact upon the industrial workplace, whilst the spirit of militarism pervaded civilian spheres such as church organisations, the Volunteer Force and the Boys' Brigade, which were part-time and quasi-military organisations.[5]

Alongside the army as an institution, the image of the soldier within it also acquired a certain glamour, infused with civilian notions that were equally detached from the reality of warfare. In fact, it was the image of the upper-class officer that was promoted, since the actual profession of soldiering was much despised among the lower classes throughout much of the nineteenth century, because of the low rate of pay, extended period of service and bad living conditions. As a result it mostly lured only those men who could find no other source of employment, such as Irish immigrants escaping from famine, or untrained, unemployed labourers. Such men – often in company with their officers – frequently indulged in scenes of drunkenness and rowdiness, a situation which led the respectability-driven middle classes also to hold the profession in disdain. In an attempt to combat these wide social perceptions a series of reforms in pay and terms of service were initiated in the late nineteenth and early twentieth centuries, while the 1885 manual of army regulations specifically stated that soldiers in the ranks must be disciplined as to 'the propriety of civility and courtesy in their intercourse with all ranks and classes of society.' But such measures did little to improve the standing of the profession, and recruits were still drawn mainly from the lowest elements of society, as is apparent in a report issued by a public commission in 1903: 'If the terms offered are attractive only to men whose intelligence is underdeveloped, it is impossible to make them soldiers of the class required in modern warfare.'[6]

Soldiering therefore reflected a paradox of imagery, composed of a disliked profession and an increasingly admired external image. However, the admiration went deeper than the virile splendour of uniform and insignia, to the role of the soldier in war, about which British society knew even less than the reality of army life. For wars were events enacted by British soldiers far from civilian eyes, or as John Galsworthy put it, the 'Boer wars, and all those other little wars, Ashanti, Afghan, Soudan, expeditionary adventures, professional affairs far away'.[7] However, with the emergence of Empire and the spirit of imperialism in the nineteenth century, the battles fought by the army in far-off lands assumed growing importance as national focal points. Images of these battles were re-created for popular consumption upon the stage, postcards, paintings and the pages of newspapers, magazines and books, in prose, poetry and verse. And much as a glittering exterior image of the army was created, war became a glorious event in which a fantastic image of the soldier in action was established, infused with concepts such as adventure, bravery, sacrifice and heroism. George Bernard Shaw reflected the wide currency of this imagery in his satirical play *Arms and the Man* (1894), in which the cavalry charge of the Bulgarians against the Serbs, led by Sergius who is betrothed to Raina, is described in glowing terms by her mother: 'You can't guess how splendid it is. A cavalry charge! think of that! He defied our Russian commanders – acted without orders – led a charge on his own responsibility – headed it himself – was the first man to sweep through their guns. Can't you see it, Raina: our gallant splendid Bulgarians with their swords and eyes flashing, thundering down like an avalanche and scattering the wretched Serbs and their dandified Austrian officers like chaff.' But then Petkoff, a seasoned soldier who fought with the defeated Serb forces, hides in Raina's bedroom and explains to her that the leader of a cavalry charge is usually pulling at his horse, which is running away with him:

Petkoff: . . . do you suppose the fellow wants to get there before the others and be killed?

Raina: Ugh! But I dont believe the first man is a coward. I know he's a hero!

Petkoff: Thats what youd have said if youd seen the first man in the charge today [Sergius]. . . . He did it like an operatic tenor. A regular handsome fellow, with flashing eyes and lovely moustache, shouting his war-cry and charging like Don Quixote at the windmills. We did laugh.

More telling still was Shaw's 1898 preface to the play, in which he settled scores with the critics who had found his depiction of the old soldier and his view of war as 'fantastically improbable and cynically unnatural'. He claimed their rejection was due to the image being 'unromantic . . . [since] it implied to them a denial of the existence of courage, patriotism, faith, hope, and charity'.[8]

Shaw's play and criticism highlight the two most important aspects of the imagery of soldiers in the decades before the war: individualism and romanticism. Heroism was promoted as an individual achievement, committed in daring moments of adventure and superhuman ability, leading to great feats of patriotism and bravery. And within this, emphasis was laid upon the self-motivation – and self-sacrifice – of the individual, as one who came forth willingly for the greater good: the volunteer. He was the leader of the charge, the man who faced the enemy single-handedly. Such notions were in fact part of the medieval code of chivalry, which was renewed within the nineteenth century spirit of Romanticism. And as in older times, the neo-chivalry laid great emphasis upon honour, justice, duty, personal commitment and fighting. A knight fought a duel or went into battle in the name of a sacred, just cause, and in so doing exhibited his nobility of spirit, regardless of the outcome of his endeavour. The act itself became hallowed, often in isolation from the context in which it was performed. As Mark Girouard noted, 'Victorian and Edwardian chivalry produced its own world of myth and legend, just as much as Medieval chivalry. And, as in the case of medieval chivalry, the inspiring images are sometimes out of touch with the reality.'[9]

The knightly ethos was removed from context not merely for the creation of national military legend, but also for the promotion of ideals of masculinity within all ranks of society, as a correlate of patriotism. The most popular manifestation of this trend was in children's adventure stories published in magazines such as the *Boys' Own Paper*, and also in books – the eighty works penned by George Alfred Henty being by far the most renowned, with titles such as *The Boy Knight* (1880) and *When London Burned* (1894). The tales usually involved a hero of high breeding who single-handedly faced and fought danger, often in far-flung corners of the Empire, and in so doing saved the nation. The exemplary physical and moral traits of the hero were emphasised throughout the stories, and the large audience of boys who read them were constantly made aware of his manliness, and urged to emulate it. Adult adventure stories, such as those by John Buchan, were also available to an expanding readership, especially in the decades before the war. A classic example was Baroness Orczy's immensely popular *The Scarlet Pimpernel* (1905), which transformed a handsome British aristocrat into the ultimate knight through his daring endeavours in saving French aristocrats during the Revolution.

Non-fiction books on knightly masculinity also reached a wide audience. In Samuel Smiles's *Self Help* (1859), which had sold 250,000 copies by the turn of the century, 'the glory of manly character' was dependent upon the 'honest and upright performance of individual duty'. Defining the highest patriotism as the exhibition of such activity, the author fused together notions of national strength, personal endeavour, and man as knightly soldier, regardless of class: 'Though only the generals' names may be remembered in the history of any great campaign, it has been mainly through the individual valour and heroism of the privates that victories have been won. And life, too, is "a soldier's battle".' Smiles repeatedly emphasised the unity of personal and national strength; but above all he stressed that self-help was possible only with the existence of self-will, as 'the very central power of character in a man – in a word, it is the Man itself', whereas national decay resulted from 'individual idleness, selfishness and vice'.[10]

Man, knight and nation were also fused together in *Scouting for Boys* (1908) by Lord Baden-Powell, founder of the Boy Scout Movement, and one who became a national legend in his own lifetime as defender of Mafeking during the Boer War. Originally published in six fortnightly parts, the book set out to inculcate boys with the ethos of patriotism as individual endeavour. In the opening chapter scouts were defined as 'strong and plucky, ready to face danger . . . accustomed to take their lives in their hands, and to risk them without hesitation if they can help their country by so doing'. An entire section of three chapters was devoted to chivalry, the first, 'Chivalry to Others', relating the code of medieval knights; 'Self Discipline', focusing upon duty, loyalty and courage; and 'Self Improvement', emphasising religion and individual commitment. The book was an immediate success, inspiring boys to form Scout Troops, and Baden-Powell to resign from the army and found the movement in 1910, with its telling motto: Be Prepared! To Baden-Powell preparation meant physical endurance and health, as traits not only crucial to the scout but also dependent upon an upright character. Defining smoking and drinking as unsuitable for boys and enabling masculinity for adults only when taken in moderation, he deemed masturbation the most ruinous vice, which 'tends to lower both health and spirits. . . . if you have any manliness in you, you will throw off such temptation at once.'[11]

The linking of duty, voluntary service, masculinity and nation, as also the emphasis upon vice and especially masturbation, were not unique to the works of Smiles and Baden-Powell. These were the tenets of the emerging middle-class morality, which became the overriding social force. Much effort was invested throughout the nineteenth century in educating boys and young men to such traits, whether through religious instruction, stirring speeches or manly literature. Above all, games were considered an activity which enabled both mental endurance and physical health – and one that channelled the energies of boys away from immoral practices such as masturbation. The compulsory Education Act of 1870 undoubtedly expanded the role of schools in diffusing these ideals in all classes of society, but it was in the grammar and public schools that it was mostly promoted. Writer V.S. Pritchett, who attended Alleyn Grammar School from 1912, recalled he was not considered 'a "healthy-minded boy". I liked games but only in an undisciplined way – unable to keep my place in the field. I hated the popular adventure books . . . [but] I was told not to be a prig and to read John Buchan. I found his thrillers unreadable. The characters were not like human beings.' Just for good measure, Pritchett completed his image of priggishness by refusing to join 'the masturbation gang who met in the lavatories', which says much about the air of active sexuality which pervaded the school despite, or possibly because of, the rigorous physical regime it imposed upon the boys. Robert Graves, who attended the more prestigious public school Charterhouse during the same period, was initially horrified by 'the many refinements of sex constantly referred to in school conversation'. Activity replaced conversation at night in the dormitories, and overall 'the atmosphere was always heavy with romance of a conventional early-Victorian type, complicated by cynicism and foulness'.[12]

Boys and men of the lower classes were also targeted for inculcation with the ethos of nation and duty translated into voluntary action. This was done through a vast network of middle-class social workers, reform projects and philanthropic agencies, which by the end of the nineteenth century handled more money than that distributed by the state Poor Law. Within these were many frameworks created for males, such as clubs for working boys, working men's co-operatives, religious associations, cricket and rowing societies, and improving projects such as social and literary clubs and university extension classes. The YMCA, for example, was instigated largely to cater for young men of lower classes emigrating to big cities in search of work. In 1856 it was defined by the Earl of Shaftesbury, a fervent reformer on purely religious grounds who was involved with over two hundred voluntary associations throughout his life, as an organisation 'to bring within the pale of morality and Christian knowledge, the thousands of the young men of the British Empire, young men who are to . . . do much to determine the character and condition of the country'. And among the advantages of workers' co-operative associations, as specified in 1884, were the 'encouragement of sympathy with public aims, and a desire for the well-being of the community generally. . . . The development of intelligence, self-reliance and business knowledge in a manner that has had a real educational and political value.' But national well-being was not merely an abstract notion of morality or spiritual strength: it had a very tangible connection with soldiers and defence. For example, largely lamenting the failure of the Repton Club founded for boys in a university settlement in East London, its head Hugh Legge wrote in 1901: 'in view of possible military requirement, we have to remember that children bred in over-crowded cities tend to become a degenerate race; and, in spite of patriotic dreams, it is idle to suppose that men of . . . [urban slums] could lend much effective aid in repelling foreign invasion – they have neither the physique nor the morale for such a purpose.'[13]

Long before the war, therefore, there were clear and strongly established images of men, and soldiers. But these were actually one and the same, since the vast majority of the civilian population had no notion of any military reality, whether in the army or at war. As a result, this image of the ideal male/soldier was actually a fusion of romantic ideas of heroism and self-sacrifice with the middle-class ethos of duty and voluntary service – and shrouded with a thick layer of morality. It had taken a century to create this image, but it took the First World War not only to expose it, but to put it to the service of the state. For the outbreak of hostilities was promoted as a long-awaited opportunity to make real all the concepts imposed upon the glittering façades of the army and the soldier, as the embodiment of national strength and manhood. It was now up to the men of the nation to seize the opportunity, and prove themselves equal to it: to volunteer. And even if men may have volunteered out of a variety of reasons – from patriotism to unemployment – the overriding imagery of fulfilled masculinity and citizenship encompassed them from the moment they appeared at a recruiting station. For their personal endeavour was daily defined as such by the recruiting propaganda, upon stage and screen, at recruiting rallies, and above all upon millions of posters, newspapers, magazines, pamphlets and postcards.[14]

The posters probably made the greatest impact of the campaign, with slogans such as 'Your Country Needs You!' and 'Daddy, What Did You Do in the War?' plastered over every conceivable surface in the land. However, while such messages obviously inspired guilt and a sense of duty, a close examination of the one hundred and sixty posters issued by the Parliamentary Recruiting Committee (PRC) reveals that they were the outcome of a structured campaign, that promoted volunteering as a cause in itself, no less than recruiting.[15] And the parameters within which both issues were defined corresponded almost exactly to those of the ideal male/soldier image created in the nineteenth century. For the two common denominators of all the PRC posters were a focus upon the individual as a moral subject, and masculinity – or rather the romantic civilian conception of the masculine spirit, since hardly any of the posters dwelt upon the battlefield, or even the army, but upon the male and the image of the soldier. The subtlety of the recruiting campaign was in the immutable combination of these two factors into a single imperative which differentiated between a male and a man, with only one route of transformation from the former into the latter: if one was born a male, one became a soldier, and one became a soldier only by volunteering.

On a pictorial level, this was achieved in a number of ways. First, all the posters were extremely personalised, targeting the individual, often in huge block capitals – as was the case with this poster: 'Thousands Have Answered the Nation's Call, But **YOU** May be the ONE to Turn the Scale at a Critical Moment. Do You Realize This?' Second, the war was presented as a moral event – with messages such as 'Can Britons Stand by while Germany Crushes an Innocent People?', 'Take Up the Sword of Justice' and 'Avenge This Devil's Work' – and also one collectively sanctioned by state and society: 'Thousands Have Answered the Nation's Call', 'Make Us as Proud of You as We Are of Him!'[16] The third method was the construction of femininity, since women were reflected as the embodiment of patriotism, whose role was to send men out to war: 'Women of Britain Say – "Go"!' and 'Go! It's Your Duty Lad.'[17] But at the same time, and within the same construction, women were also portrayed as the obstacle to men in their search for true masculine fulfilment: 'Some of your men folk are holding back on your account. Won't you prove your love for your country by persuading them to go?'; 'When the war is over and someone asks your husband or your son what he did in the Great War, is he to hang his head because you would not let him go? Won't you help and send a man to join the army today?' The underlying assumption in these messages is that men are volunteers in their own conception of masculinity, inhibited only by their sense of moral responsibility to their dependants. In other words, these posters placed the moral commitment to nation above the moral commitment to family, by making the latter dependent on the former: 'Do you realise that the safety of your home and children depends on our getting more men NOW?'[18]

On a more notional level, women and children as defenceless targets were also used within the context of chivalry, which was constantly evoked by references to duty, honour and nobility: 'Your rights of citizenship give you the privilege of joining your fellows in the defence of your Honour and your Homes'; 'Show Your Appreciation by Following Their [the volunteers] Noble Example'.[19] However, given the moral framework of the war, such messages also assumed moral significance. Therefore, by consistently placing the individual male in potential opposition to them – through the use of questions or iconography, for example – the posters essentially brought into question the moral character of each man: 'There Are Three Types of Men: Those who hear the call and Obey, Those who Delay, And – The Others. To which do you belong?'; 'Be honest with yourself. Be certain that your so-called reason is not a selfish excuse.'[20] As a logical conclusion to this situation, the appeal to enlist – as a volunteer – also assumed a moral significance: a man who volunteered had morals, whereas a man who did not, lacked them. As one poster blatantly put it within the context of women: 'If your young man neglects his duty to his King and Country, the time may come when he will NEGLECT YOU.' Within all these parameters, the recruiting posters shifted the emphasis of the campaign from the soldier needed for war, to the act of enlistment – from the end result to the point of transformation from civilian into soldier. As a result, the traditional role of the soldier came to be redefined, from a warrior to a volunteer. But this also meant that the PRC posters evolved into a campaign against those men who did not voluntarily enlist, thus establishing them in the public eye as lacking in morality, and unmasculine: 'Every Fit Briton Should Join Our Brave Men at the Front'; 'Does the call of Duty find no response in you until reinforced – let us say superseded – by the call of compulsion?'[21]

It was the repetition of these messages over fifteen months and millions of posters which left the conscripts who enlisted after the campaign bereft of public support in their transformation into soldiers. The corresponding equations of man as soldier and soldier as volunteer became fixed within the public eye and consciousness, based upon every aspect of the pre-war construction of the male/soldier. And if any doubt still existed as to the moral and masculine superiority of the volunteer over the conscript, the last months of the campaign were used to systematically quash them: 'Do not force your country to force you to fight, but come of your own free will.'[22] This poster was issued during the Derby Scheme, which started in October 1915, in which men were canvassed in their homes as to their willingness to attest – a system which basically revoked the premise of volunteering as a self-motivated act. However, the scheme was promoted as a last chance for voluntarism as the sole honourable option: 'Will You March too or Wait till March 2', the date on which the January 1916 conscription bill came into force; 'The new Military Service Bill need not apply to you if you ENLIST NOW under the Group System' promoted by the Derby Scheme; 'Your duty is to fight the COMMON FOE and to get your comrades to join you'.[23]

Such a pointed reference makes clear the perceived existence of another foe, within British society, that did not do its duty: the non-volunteer, who very shortly became the conscript. This image was apparent in a number of posters, such as 'Forward!' and 'An Appeal To You!', which placed the civilian onlooker as the focus of military onslaughts. 'Are You In This?' reflected a young civilian, hands in pockets, on the side of the enemy, and in opposition to symbolic figures representing the national effort. The poster was conceived and drawn by Baden-Powell, and reflected almost exactly his definition of immoral and unmasculine young men, in a speech he made before the war, as 'loafing about with your hands in your pockets, doing nothing to keep it [the Empire] up.'[24] The non-volunteer was therefore an enemy: lazy, unpatriotic and, above all, immoral. This premise was once again most apparent during the Derby Scheme, which Lord Derby presented as resting entirely upon it: 'I believe the moral effect of showing to our enemies that England is perfectly determined by the voluntary method to put into the field all that could be got by the compulsory method will be such that it will bring the war to a far quicker conclusion.'[25]

Voluntarism was thus firmly enshrined as an exponent of morality, with compulsion damned on a negative basis. However, such a sweeping condemnation threatened to bring shame upon many men – those who would possibly be conscripted. As a result, the married non-volunteers were set apart from those single, within the premise of family responsibility – a separation reflected by the scheme, which promised to take the single men before the married. It was also apparent in the public discourse of the period. In *The Times*, for example, many letters appeared concerning the plight of the 'young professional married man who is entirely dependent for the support of himself and his family upon what he can earn by his own personal exertions'. Pointing out that the separation allowances would be totally insufficient for such men, the letter asked: 'Are they unpatriotic if they say "No"? Have they no right to expect that the unmarried men with no responsibilities should be taken first?' The populist *Daily Mail* was exceedingly forceful in highlighting this issue, with screaming headlines such as: 'Meanwhile the single slackers wait to be fetched', and articles stating that 'there are still in the London area alone 750,000 young unmarried men'.[26]

The married men were therefore brought within the ideal image of the male/soldier, but portrayed as trapped within a moral dilemma. And if in the earlier days of the war women were called upon to release them from their internal conflict, the state, through the Derby Scheme, now officially stepped in to resolve the issue, as long as the married men expressed the minimal measure of self-motivation by attesting their willingness to enlist. In this way a moral stratification was put in place, headed by the married volunteers, as men who resolved the conflict of morality entirely due to their own self-will. Coupled to them were the single volunteers, as the idealised image of masculinity within the conception of youth. Beneath these two came the married non-volunteers, as men deemed to have self-motivation, yet lacking the salient tenet of commitment to nation. And finally, there were the young, single non-volunteers: those who were depicted and despised as neither moral nor masculine. Or, as the *Cornish Post* and *Mining News* from 11 November 1915 put it, the men that 'remained impervious and cold' to the recruiter, who had appealed 'to your cupidity, your patriotism, your manhood and your selfishness, all with small success'. As such, society set these men apart, as unfit men and citizens, and ultimately, unfit soldiers. And these non-volunteers were the men who became conscripts.

The conscripts clearly had a negative image right from the start, and it remained with them throughout their military careers, regardless of their subsequent achievements in holding the line and ultimately bringing a victory. But they were also afflicted by exceedingly bad timing, for they were fielded as of 1916. The war, which everyone had foreseen as being short and victorious, had by this time been dragging on for sixteen months. Rather than being over by Christmas 1914, as had been popularly predicted, it now seemed to be in danger of lasting for many more months and even years, with no victory of any kind in sight. In this early, voluntary period great battles such as the First and Second Ypres and Loos had already been fought, with immense losses. But the strong public sentiment which had encouraged the volunteers was still intact at that stage, upholding its vision of war as an heroic, knightly endeavour – and it was within this context that the escalating death toll was viewed: as undoubtedly awful, yet also magnificent and patriotic. Death gave the final seal to the notion of supreme, self-sacrificing heroism exhibited by young, single, upper-class knights, best embodied in one such as Rupert Brooke, but reflected also in many memorial tributes to soldiers throughout the land. A pamphlet in memoriam of a Lt Warneford, aged twenty-three, for example, published by a little-known organisation called The Patriots' League, chronicled his life and bravery, followed by a specially composed poem:

> WHAT DID HE DO? Why, the whole world knows
> The foeman he fought alone,
> And to save the lives of children and wives
> He gallantly risked his own.
>
> Since Cressy the blood has been just the same
> And that is the reason why
> THIS NATION LIVES ON – for her gallant sons
> *In a cause that is JUST* WILL DIE![27]

Unfortunately, it was not merely public opinion which viewed battle, and death, as heroic and magnificent, but also the military command: 'The officer corps still looked for battlefields where there was a place for individual acts of heroism. The advent of industrialised society had in fact meant the end of the type of war such men dreamed of. Battle was now simply a matter of numbers, and the heroism of the individual, or even the unit, was now an irrelevancy.'[28] This irrelevancy was becoming apparent to the British public by late 1916, when the battles of Verdun and the Somme had also been fought, the latter accounting for 60,000 men killed and wounded on the first day alone. The awfulness of war had thus come to overshadow its magnificence, especially since the increasing toll of death and destruction was coupled to a steady deterioration in the economy, with many women leaving the home to work, and rationing being introduced. Throughout the last two years of the war the spirit of the home front therefore deteriorated into one of grim determination in the face of protracted hardship, and it was in this mood that the civilians viewed the huge battles of Arras and Passchendaele – the Third Ypres – in 1917, and the German offensive in the spring of 1918. Only in the midst of the Allied advance of that summer did public sentiment become more uplifted. And so, rather than a spirit of romantic acceptance and grief, the conscripts' major military efforts, both successful and disastrous, were greeted with mounting disinterest and fear – of death and of loss. For by the end of the war, much of the population was inconsolable. Never before had the modern western world known such mass annihilation: over ten million men in all were killed, of which 702,410 were British.[29] Civilians had no real cognisance of battle, nor even of the realities of life within or without the front line. But death, though unseen in its enactment, was felt in every corner; those who did not suffer the personal loss of a family member, a friend or a lover, knew of many that did. It quickly became the most overwhelming reality of the First World War, and one which rendered everyone, civilians and soldiers, helpless. The confrontation with death therefore became the underlying purpose of any attempt to make the war more comprehensible, and ultimately acceptable. For this purpose myth, far more than fact, and the image of the volunteers rather than the conscripts, could provide suitable frameworks.

The public association of myth, mythology and the First World War began but a few years after the guns were silenced, and has continued to this day. It involved the fusion of personal memoirs, war poetry and historiography, alongside concerted efforts on behalf of the state. As George Mosse has shown, the creation of myths in all the former warring nations was a national endeavour, perpetrated as a means of preserving the nation while also offering consolation to the bereaved: 'Those concerned with the image and the continuing appeal of the nation worked at constructing a myth which would draw the sting from death in war and emphasize the meaningfulness of the fighting and sacrifice. . . . The aim was to make an inherently unpalatable past acceptable, important not just for the purpose of consolation but above all for the justification of the nation in whose name the war had been fought.' The outcome of this process was, according to Mosse, the transformation of reality in all the warring nations into the 'Myth of the War Experience'.[30] But in the case of Britain, it seems a prior myth was forged: the 'Myth of Participation in the War'. It evolved because it was the only nation which consciously differentiated between volunteers and conscripts. In comparison, France and Germany, for example, upheld traditions of compulsion which confirmed, rather than questioned, the concept of citizenship, since it had been a tenet of forging their modern nation states. So from the outbreak of war in 1914 many volunteered for the army in both states, alongside the conscripts who were called up. In this way ideals such as voluntarism and patriotism could exist alongside conscription, and be applicable to the entire populace of civilian-soldiers.

In Britain, however, conscription and voluntarism were clearly and firmly opposed. And if, as reflected above, this was initially due to a propaganda campaign that ruthlessly equated the male/soldier with the volunteer, the years of slaughter which followed only served to embellish this image, which had become hollow, as a form of ideological compensation for the immense human toll. For if the image of the soldier remained that of a committed individual who chose to fight, his death could be accepted as a just sacrifice to an ideal which he himself believed in. The collective responsibility of state, society and the individual remained intact. But since the ideological commitment of a conscript was not sought, and actually emphasised in its absence in comparison to a volunteer, his death had to be borne by those who sent him out: society and state. Moreover, if the conscripts were equated with the volunteers, the purpose of the latter could be nullified. For as a conceptual movement they volunteered out of a belief in the war as a justified action, and thus they died. They had singled themselves out of society as unique men, capable of fulfilling an ideal. However, a basic implication of conscription was that any and every man, regardless of his commitment, was adequate for the job of soldiering and dying. But for society, which had endorsed the volunteers, and especially for those within it who suffered loss and mutilation, this was untenable. And so, for the sake of national unity and justification it was in the interests of the state and society to uphold a monolithic image of the volunteer throughout the war, and after. To create war memorials such as the one to the men of the Metropolitan Railway Company, in Baker Street station, who 'left all that was dear to them, endured hardness, faced danger and finally passed out of sight of men by the path of duty and self sacrifice, giving up their own lives that others might live in freedom.' To create the 'Myth of Participation'.

In the decades that immediately followed the war, the two myths, of the War Experience and Participation, became imperceptibly but completely intertwined in Britain. Moreover, this happened not necessarily as an intentional measure, but rather as a way of transforming the painful reality of the war into an abstraction.

For its part, the state set about this through a variety of ceremonial and symbolic means. For example, an annual Remembrance Day ceremony was introduced, focused upon the Tomb of the Unknown Soldier in Westminster Abbey, created specifically for this purpose, and containing a body exhumed from a Flanders battlefield. However, since the official tomb in the Abbey was inappropriate for mass ceremonies, being confined to a small enclosure within, an accompanying Cenotaph was erected in Whitehall, around which the yearly ceremony could be enacted. In this way the pain and sacrifice inflicted by the war were taken out of the personal realm of the bereaved and placed within the public, collective and state-sanctioned domain: the fallen became the glorious dead of the entire nation. This effort was further enhanced by the red paper poppy, which was introduced as a symbol of the blood of the fallen. By selling poppies for some days prior to the ceremony, during which time they were worn by the purchasing public, the period of open grief was extended beyond a single day, yet limited to a clearly defined period. In other words, by sublimating the implications of the war into permanent symbols, and allotting a fixed period of annual public grief, the state created a framework in which daily collective life could resume on a strictly civilian basis. The war was acknowledged as a pivotal and crucial event in the life of the nation – yet removed as an overwhelming daily reality.[31]

Within a remarkably short span of time the war went through another transformation, from a receding reality into an imaginary event. In 1929, in a short introductory note to the second edition of his war memoir *Combed Out*, Frederick Voigt wrote that '[The book] is not a piece of imaginative writing. It is a record of the Great War as seen by a private soldier in the British Army.' In 1931, Edmund Blunden further underlined the impression that the First World War had already become an imaginary event in his introduction to W.V. Tilsley's *Other Ranks*, written in 1931: 'Were I of the new generation, should I have the imaginative sympathy to turn away from present delights and perplexities and to bind my thoughts to the monotonous emplacement of an obviously absurd and long finished war?'[32] Such words point to a transformation of the war within public consciousness: from a sequence of real events enacted over an extended period of time within living memory, to a singular, imaginative event – relegated to the archives of collective memory.

These two literary examples were not isolated in their perception of the First World War as an imaginary event; but they were distinct, in that they were written by private soldiers who were not volunteers. Tilsley enlisted under the Derby Scheme, whereas Voigt was conscripted; and, as already noted in the introduction, their books number among the five known memoirs published by men who were not volunteers. Tilsley's book follows the hero, Bradshaw, through his mental and physical journey in the war zone, as a Derbyite who quickly became assimilated into trench life. Voigt's book, however, offers an interesting insight into the public image of conscripts, both during the war and after. It was first published in 1920, a remarkably early date considering that the mass of memoirs came out nearly a decade later. In this first edition no autobiographical data was given, beyond that which may be gleaned from the narrative itself. In the second edition, published in 1929 – when the image of war had begun to recede – the author added a note, dating his conscription to 1916. In addition, he claimed that the second edition was identical to the first, 'and save for some rearrangement and some excisions nothing has been changed'. Yet, it is curious that the author chose to excise the following passage, in which a soldier cursed his situation as a conscript: 'The man could find no other way of expressing himself with adequate force and crudity. At times he became incoherent. He was not grumbling at the little hardships and discomforts of this particular morning. He was grumbling at an entire life of discomfort. He was rebelling against his degrading slavery and enforced misery, and it was the harrowing consciousness of his own impotence that added such bitterness to his anger.'[33]

It is possible that Voigt chose to delete this passage in 1929, and to admit to his conscription, because his anger against the war and his placement within it had dimmed somewhat. It is also possible, however, that by this date the public image of the war was accepted as that of an horrific yet heroic sacrifice; and as such he could not express such strong feelings against it. And given the overall anti-war stance exhibited throughout the book even without this passage, he felt the need to explain his participation in it by his conscription.

One passage, written and excised by one man, in one book, cannot be accepted as typical. And yet, because so few conscripts had identified themselves as such by this time, or published their experiences, Voigt's case may be used as a form of explanation for this trend. Since being a conscript was established during the war as socially unacceptable, an individual could rail against his emplacement as such, but without admitting to it. This is applicable to the 1920 edition of *Combed Out* in which Voigt omitted the autobiographical note, and so could possibly be identified as a disillusioned volunteer. If, however, an individual identified himself as a conscript he refrained from condemning his 'degrading slavery and enforced misery', since this could completely ostracise him from society and state – hence the 1929 edition of the book. For by this date Voigt, as a conscript, was battling not only with the imagery of volunteer soldiers as established in the war, but also with the mythical imagery which had been created by the flood of war memoirs.

Between 1926 and 1933 a large number of war memoirs were published, at an amazing rate. For example, six such books appeared in 1926, fifteen in 1927, twenty-one in 1928, and twenty-nine in 1929. The public impact of these war books was immense: in the first eleven months of 1929, for example, R.C. Sherriff's play *Journey's End* was reprinted thirteen times, and sold 45,000 copies; while in 1930 *Her Privates We* by Frederic Manning was issued four times in the space of a month.[34] Robert Graves's *Goodbye to All That*, originally published in 1929, 'sold well enough in England and the United States, despite the Depression which had just set in, to pay my debts and leave me free to live and write in Majorca without immediate anxiety for the future. The title became a catch-word, and my sole contribution to Bartlett's *Dictionary of Familiar Quotations.*'[35] Overall, the interwar publishing history of Edmund Blunden's *Undertones of War* offers a most illuminating, and typical example of the appeal of the war books: in 1928 it was reprinted three times in one month, and three times throughout 1929. In June 1930 a 'second and cheap edition (revised)' was reprinted twice, and once in 1935; in March 1937 it became a Penguin book which went into its fourth impression in November 1938.

The issue at stake is not only the clear and vast popularity of these volumes, but also their pivotal role in establishing the war as a mythical event. This was achieved by the threefold manner in which most of the authors set about their task. First, many of them related the experiences of one person; however, since that individual was a soldier, who despite often being an officer was externally similar to many millions, he could be accepted as typical: an everyman. Second, by adopting a literary rather than a documentary approach to their subject – the experiences of war – they removed it from reality. The third point is that by placing these experiences within the context of an event which had really occurred, they created an image of it which could be accepted as fact. And the image itself was basically that of an officer who had volunteered for service out of a belief in the war as justified. This individual then found himself exposed to the horrors of trench warfare, which were often described in detail, and as a result he experienced a process of disillusionment. And yet out of a sense of duty and patriotism the individual officer remained in the trenches and participated heroically in battle.

This assessment is not intended as a criticism of these authors, who had suffered harrowing experiences in war, and probably set about writing of them in order to preserve their own personal history of the event.

However, the cumulative effect of many such volumes written in the same manner and vein, and eagerly read, was to establish the literary version of the war as the prevailing one. In other words, the memoirs created a myth. And ultimately, it was this myth which established the public image of the First World War to later generations – and even affected the historiographical depiction of it. Basil Liddell Hart wrote a history of the war, which was widely upheld as definitive alongside the government publication of the official history. In the preface to the first edition of the book, in 1930, which was then titled *The Real War*, he already acknowledged the impact of the literary memoirs: 'Because the war affected individual lives so greatly, because these individuals were numbered by millions, because the roots of their fate lay so deep in the past, it is all the more necessary to see the war in perspective, and to disentangle its main threads from the accidents of human misery. Perhaps this attempt is all the more desirable by reason of the trend of recent war literature, which is not merely individualistic but focuses light in the past four years.'[36]

Other critics were less understanding. Two other books were also published in 1930, strongly attacking the memoirs. Douglas Jerrold, an ex-officer of the regular army who had served in Gallipoli and France, and an author of two histories of the war, wrote *The Lie about the War: A Note on Some Contemporary War Books*: 'The object, conscious or unconscious, of all these books is to simplify and sentimentalise the problem of war and peace until the problem disappears in a silly gesture of complacent moral superiority, and the four years of war shown idiotically as four years of disastrous, sanguinary and futile battles in which everything was lost and nothing gained, a struggle begun for no purpose and continued for no reason.' The second book was *War Books* by Cyril Falls, a former staff officer who had already written two military histories, and was then working in the History Section of the Committee of Imperial Defence. It was a critical bibliography of 728 books – a number indicative in itself of the immense flow of words the war induced – written both in Britain and in other belligerent countries, and covering both documentary and literary titles. The purpose of the memoirs, he maintained in his introduction, was 'to prove that the First World War was engineered by knaves or fools on both sides, that the men who died in it were driven like beasts to the slaughter, and died like beasts'. Joining with Jerrold's claim of a lie, he went on to note that 'the falsest of false evidence is produced in another way: by closing up scenes which in themselves may be true. Every sector becomes a bad one, every working-party is shot to pieces; . . . The soldier is represented as a depressed and mournful spectre helplessly wandering about until death brought his miseries to an end.'[37]

By 1934, when he published the second edition of his history, Liddell Hart was also remonstrating against the image created by the war literature, claiming that 'decisive impressions were received and made in the cabinets and in the military headquarters, not in the ranks of the infantry or in the solitude of stricken homes'. And yet he follows this assessment with another that not only publicly linked the historiography of the war with mythology, but also explained how it evolved: 'The more that any writer of history has himself been at hand when history is being made, or in contact with the makers, the more does he come to see that a history based solely on formal documents is essentially superficial. Too often, also, it is the unwitting handmaiden of "mythology".'

Both literary and formal official sources were therefore seen as unreliable by the historian, who clearly feared the power of myth. And yet, by 1938, with the publication of the third edition of the book, under the telling title *Through the Fog of War*, Liddell Hart deemed the official sources the less worthy of the two: 'Nothing can deceive like a document. . . . After twenty years of such work pure documentary history seems to me akin to mythology.'[38]

And so, just twenty years after the end of the First World War, its image was openly associated with myth. The official documents available up to that point appeared to reflect a mythical image to an historian who had observed the events in their enactment; while the image offered by the amassed war memoirs could not be anything but mythical, since it was based upon literary works of an intensely personal nature. Yet it was this latter image, created mostly by people of the middle- and upper-class officer caste, which prevailed. For these writings presented a delicate duality – of a real war experienced by a fictitious yet typical hero – with which a wide audience could identify. Moreover, these books also offered an acceptable image of the war, in which heroism and futility existed side by side: the young man who volunteered to fight for his country persevered in his task despite the disillusionment and sense of futility which his prolonged exposure to warfare afforded him. And in accepting this image of the war, and the soldiers' nobility within it, the First World War as a catastrophic event could be publicly acknowledged, while the role of the soldier within it could be glorified.

Ultimately, therefore, the Unknown Soldier of the war memorials took on the image of a young volunteer officer, who fought patriotically and heroically on the Western Front, in the face of horror and disillusionment. It was a mythical image, the postwar version of the wartime male/soldier one. And the conscripts were, of course, excluded from it. For more than any other element, this image of a soldier rested upon the ideal of personal commitment: both to his country and to the cause for which he had volunteered, despite its emerging futility. In other words, as in the war, so in the subsequent interwar years, public imagery was decided by the ideological stance taken by the soldiers, and not by their actual endeavours. The conscripts were therefore excluded from the image of First World War soldiers because they were not volunteers, and not because they did not fight determinedly and heroically – for this was never an issue under debate, as a crucial element of imagery. As a result, the Myth of Participation which had been created during the event itself prevailed, and became an integral part of the Myth of the War Experience in Britain.

The Second World War brought the process of imagery-making, as also the dispute between the memorialists and the historians, to an abrupt halt. Indeed, it was only in 1964 that mass interest was rekindled, when another generation set about commemorating the fiftieth anniversary of the First World War – and embellishing its myths. But by this time the Great War had become the First World War, another one having superseded it in living memory, and it could therefore be relegated to distant history. And in order to recreate it, the modern commemorators used a new and exceedingly powerful tool: the electronic media, and especially television. And through this medium the image of the war created for the anniversary would become absolute to an entire generation that had no immediate knowledge of it. As a result, the Myth of Participation in the war would also be confirmed as absolute.

A flood of books, albums, films and ceremonies marked the anniversary, yet the most forceful and enduring product was the 'Great War' series produced by the BBC. It was this series, more than any other commemorative effort, which established an image of the war within public consciousness, which has persevered to this day, for two reasons. First, because since the fiftieth anniversary it has been screened three more times, thereby delivering its image and message to subsequent generations of viewers. Second, because the Imperial War Museum was a partner to the production of the series, and therefore holds a copy of it, which allows for independent screenings of the programmes to additional groups of viewers – especially schoolchildren. In addition, the original material collected during the production of the series, and most especially the letters of response to it by veterans, were all lodged in the Department of Documents in the museum. They still form a substantial part of it, and are also used extensively in the exhibition halls of the museum.

The 'Great War' was the first serious documentary history series, which in many ways is still upheld as a model of its kind. Two years of research and one year of production resulted in twenty-six programmes, each thirty minutes in length, which attempted to reflect the war both chronologically, and from the perspective of all the combatant nations. Moreover, the intent of the producers, Tony Essex and Gordon Watkins of the BBC, was clearly to broach the subject with objectivity, and in this way to create a document of historical integrity, since both the script-writers and the sources used were of the highest standing. Sir Basil Liddell Hart was the official adviser to the series, and the scripts of each programme were sent to him. These, in turn, were written by military historians such as John Terraine, Alistair Horne and Correlli Barnett. Source material was drawn from both official and private archives in all the countries in which they were attainable. Yet a focal point of all the programmes, which also shaped the concept of the series, was the personal testimony and memorabilia given by veterans of the war, and other surviving contemporaries. It was these narratives, however, which greatly enhanced the Myth of Participation in the War.

The creators of the series obviously gave great credence to the testimonies of the veterans, allotting them a prominent place from the start. Appeals were put out in search of veterans and photographs, through all manner of media – newspapers, radio and television – with a specific emphasis on memory. As the producers noted in a press conference on 3 July 1963, we 'want to know what you [veterans] can remember most vividly. . . . We want to draw on the memories of those who went through the war.' And such was the response that a pool of 'twenty girls to handle correspondence and file information' was established to handle the incoming flow, which ultimately reached 20,000 letters.[39] Yet, the veterans they sought were those 'who served on any front up to the end of 1915'. This specification was further emphasised in the prominent advertisement which appeared the following day, 4 July in the *Radio Times*: 'The BBC invites anyone who served on any front during the First World War, UP TO THE END OF 1915, to write briefly. . . .' The block capitals appeared as such in the original text, and the notice attracted a massive response from veterans. Indeed, the overwhelming majority of letters to the BBC were written in July and August 1963, as a result of a publicity campaign which combined these advertisements with news items, mostly seeking surviving volunteers.

There were subsequent public appeals, in which the producers specified other groups they sought, such as women who participated in the White Feather Movement, yet at no time did they put out an explicit appeal for men who enlisted after 1916. In fact, the only appeal relevant to conscripts appeared in the *Daily Mirror* of 9 September 1963; and rather than an advertisement, it was part of a small news item which called 'for personal experiences from readers who served in the First World War from 1916–1918'. Apart from the fact that no other paper, most significantly the *Radio Times*, carried this appeal, its wording clearly had a very strong impact. For while it may appear that it was relevant to those who enlisted after 1916, the relatively few letters of response to this paragraph clearly show that it was understood as a search for those who had experiences of the years specified, rather than those who had enlisted at this time. As a result, it was mainly volunteers who survived the latter two years of the war who gave testimony about them, rather than conscripts. The result of these efforts was that the episode dealing with British military enlistment during the war was limited to the recruiting efforts of the first sixteen months, and defined by the producers as a question of 'what sort of men made up Kitchener's Army of 1916?'[40]

Nearly fifty years after the First World War had ended, the major commemorative creation of the state-owned television ignored over half of the British soldiers who fought in it. They were not sought after or publicly acknowledged as conscripts, and the image of the volunteers not only survived intact but became further embellished by personal testimony. The question is – why?

The two producers of the 'Great War' series are no longer alive, though Gordon Watkins had been interviewed for this study, with other members of the production team. A salient feature of conversation with them all was the total conviction that the story of the conscripts had not been omitted by decision, since the issue had never arisen. In other words, a question about the conscripts brought into focus an entire aspect of the war which had never occurred to them – since the story of the war in their eyes was that of the volunteers. As John Terraine explained: 'The volunteering story was a very fantastic one', while conscription was 'always regarded as very un-English'. Correlli Barnett concurred with this latter statement, comparing the English tendency to enshrine the image of the volunteers in the First World War with that of Queen Victoria enshrining the memory of Albert, as a perpetuation of a once glorious past. Both historians agreed that the story of the conscripts had been neglected, and that an 'element of self justification [was] running throughout' the English attitude to the First World War. With regard to the television series, this attitude translated itself into 'the traditional image of the war', in other words that of the volunteers, which the two producers upheld as a conceptual framework for its creation.[41]

In a sense, the image of the soldiers as volunteers portrayed throughout the series may actually be seen as a tribute to the Myth of Participation in the War, since it stemmed from an image already established in the minds of the series producers and writers. None of these men had experienced the war, and most of them were actually born many years after the Armistice of 1918. As such, their approach really was informed by imagery, as much as any fact gleaned from a document or a book. Yet it is clear that even for well-informed historians this image did not include the conscripts in any way. In other words, in their sincere attempts to re-evaluate the events of 1914–18, both producers and writers did so within the confines of the imagery which had been shaped by the war and the following decades, which focused upon the plight of the volunteers. And so, for the generation that set about commemorating the fiftieth anniversary of the war, myth had become fact: the soldiers of the First World War had been volunteers, recruited mainly in the first two years of the war. The conscripts who came after them did not have to be excluded from this image, because they had never had any place in it. Moreover, it appears that the conscripts accepted this image. As soldiers, they had felt themselves to be alienated civilians, and after the war, in an attempt to shed their alienation, they had apparently discarded the blemish of conscription: they never contributed significantly to the flood of memoirs, nor did they put themselves forward in the commemorative attempts. But in so doing, they had also negated their own participation in the war. For in allowing the volunteers to speak for them, the conscripts by default accepted the public image of the war, from which they were excluded. In other words, the image of the war, as resulting from the Myth of Participation in it, influenced both the public at large and the conscripts themselves.

The fiftieth anniversary, and the genre of personal testimony established by the television series, ultimately unleashed a new round of interest in the First World War, which has not significantly abated to this day. On the one hand, the dispute between the memorialists and the historians re-emerged, and strengthened, but this time conducted between academics. Strict military history of the war slowly expanded to social studies of the event and the army, based upon official documents; but these were countered by works of cultural historians and literary critics, who developed an intense interest in the literary output of the war, alongside other cultural artefacts such as songs and films. On the other hand, popular histories of the war emerged as a major new trend in publishing. Based upon the written and oral testimonies of veterans, these volumes brought into focus the common soldier, honing in on the tragedy and hardship of the experience of war. Needless to say, none of these categories included any reference to the conscripts, and all discussion of soldiers was firmly entrenched within the image of the volunteers.[42]

In other spheres, the war slowly gained immense popularity. Starting with the biting stage and film hit, *Oh! What A Lovely War!* in the 1960s, the war came to be depicted in a variety of artistic media. On television, for example, several episodes of the popular series *Upstairs Downstairs* were devoted to the period – with both master and footman volunteering with the outbreak of hostilities. More recently, the satiric series *Blackadder Goes Forth* was set in the war, with all the characters reflecting caricatures of the accepted stock images of volunteers – from the benighted Tommy to the disillusioned officer. In latter years the event has also become the subject of serious literary works, such as Sebastian Faulks' *Birdsong* and Pat Barker's Regeneration trilogy – all works of great integrity that offer a serious re-evaluation of the war, but not of its soldiers.

Perhaps the most compelling and pervasive reflection of the Myth of Participation is in the First World War exhibition in the Imperial Museum. This institution has assumed a central role in informing and educating the public about the wars in which Britain has participated in this century, with an annual intake of visitors numbering over half a million. A large proportion of these are schoolchildren, who make their way through the exhibits with the aid of questionnaires and 'information packs'. Like the 'Great War' series before it, the exhibition clearly attempts to display the war objectively, with an emphasis upon the British contribution offset by items from all the participating countries. Following the chronological development of the war, the visitor is led through displays documenting the political background to the war; its outbreak; the recruiting efforts; the method of warfare and existence on the Western Front; summaries of the main battles; the home front in Britain; and the Armistice. And yet despite this comprehensive approach, the image of the British soldier is firmly reflected as that of the volunteer, due to both the form and the content of the exhibition. The form is established through the emboldened signs heading the various stages of the exhibition. The first is 'Origins and Outbreak of the War', followed by 'Recruiting in Britain 1914–15', 'The Western Front' and then 'Home Front' and 'End of the War'. In vain will the onlooker search for a sign introducing 'Recruiting in Britain 1916–18', for none such exists. In other words, if a visitor were simply to drift through the exhibition quickly, following the main signs rather than the content of the display cases, his impression would be that Britain recruited its First World War army between the years 1914 and 1915.

The content of the cases is of greater importance. The section devoted to the period of voluntary recruitment opens with the information that 'nearly two and a half million men joined the British Army before the end of 1915'. However, the overall size of the wartime army, as eventually numbering over five million men, is then explained in light of voluntarism: 'The 'New Armies' created by Field Marshal Lord Kitchener in 1914–1915 included thirty infantry divisions. Although their training was hampered initially by shortages of instructors, weapons and equipment, all these divisions had gone overseas by June 1916. Together with new units of the Territorial Force they formed a large part of the biggest army in British history. In all, 5,704,000 men served in the British Army during the First World War.' From this passage, which is prominently displayed, one may conclude that the five million men in the wartime army were either volunteers, Territorial soldiers or regulars. It is only in another passage, located further on in the exhibition, which explains the roles of Lord Kitchener and the Parliamentary Recruiting Committee, that the option of conscription is mentioned – but not the conscripts: 'By the end of the year [1915] Britain was ready to break with its long tradition of voluntary enlistment and to introduce conscription.' This, in effect, is both the summary and an assessment of the British recruiting efforts in the First World War, as shown by the Imperial War Museum. Having established the image of the soldiers as that of volunteers, the displays relating to the Western Front and the other battles are seen in this light. Conscription is eventually mentioned again as part of the exhibits relating to the home front in Britain, and explained as part of the massive reorganisation of the wartime economy: 'In May 1915 the Munitions of War Act empowered the government to exercise much greater control over factories engaged in war production. Following the sharp decline in voluntary recruiting for the Army, conscription was introduced for single men in January 1916 and extended in May to include all males between 18 and 41.' This passage then goes on to explain Asquith's resignation, rationing, and the establishment of ministries for shipping, national service and food. In the accompanying display case conscription is effectively shown through items relating mostly to the Conscientious Objectors, and those who appeared before military tribunals in an attempt to escape conscription. Once again, therefore, it is the efforts of approximately 16,500 men which are enshrined, rather than the efforts of 2.5 million men.

The explanation of the form and content of the exhibition, as given to me in conversation with members of the Imperial War Museum staff, was simple: all the displays are created as a reflection of the material lodged in the archives of the museum. And since the mass of the material relating to the First World War concerns the volunteers, the display merely reflects this trend. In addition, the importance of the letters from the 'Great War' series within this material was especially emphasised. In other words, it is still the image of the series which is being promoted by the museum, nearly thirty years after its creation. Moreover, in its emphasis upon the role of the letters within the archive, it is apparent that the museum still views them as totally representative of the soldiers of the First World War. For the museum, like all other elements of contemporary Britain, the Myth of Participation is a fact.

The First World War wrought untold destruction upon Britain, and not only through the death of over 700,000 men. The implication of the war, which lasted for many years more than originally predicted, was that the British no longer had sole control over their destiny. The length of the war, the mutual financial and military dependency upon the other Allies, most especially the United States, and also the immense loss of life – all these signified a loss of power. Moreover, as the century proceeded this trend was both accelerated and accentuated, culminating in the dual loss of Empire and financial prominence after the Second World War. The myth of the volunteer soldier in the First World War offered great solace throughout this extended period, not only because it supplied a form of justification for the deaths of that war, but also because it contributed greatly to an ideal of British identity. The volunteer was a hero in his commitment to an ideological cause, in his patriotism, and mostly in his perseverance in the face of loss, destruction and futility – salient factors in modern British history. Moreover, by eliminating any element of dissent from this image of the soldiers of the First World War, such as the conscripts, it became possible to portray the war, despite its losses, as a collective endeavour of the state, society and the individual. The projection of this image made it possible to place the war in a favourable light within the collective memory of the nation, and in this way to create an identity which dwelt upon ideals rather than events. And for the sake of national unity, and historical coherence, such an identity was an imperative. For the fact is that even eighty years later, and even to an aged veteran who was a conscript, the events themselves remain incomprehensible:

Looking back and after twice visiting old battlefields with the countless cemeteries, and memorials to those who have no known grave, one is stunned by the horrific loss of young lives from all nations engaged in a war which as time went on the reasons for it faded. In my time I can't think of any special hatred of an enemy who in the early days was known as 'The Hun' or 'The Boche' but to me was the almost friendly 'Gerry'. Then one must think of the unrelieved anxiety of relatives at home in whose mind was the fear of that fateful War Office telegram 'Killed in Action'. Did the years that followed really disclose any victory measured against the world's suffering?[43]

Notes

INTRODUCTION

1. Sigmund Freud, 'Thoughts for the Time on War and Death (1915)'. in *Civilization, Society and Religion* (The Pelican Freud Library, Vol. 12, Penguin, 1985), p. 65.
2. *Statistics of the Military Effort of the British Empire during the Great War* (HMSO, 1922), p. 364.
3. The only known scholarly work written about the conscripts is Ian F.W. Beckett's 'The Real Unknown Army: British Conscripts 1916–1919', *The Great War*, Vol. 2, No.1 (November 1989), pp. 4–13. On the Conscientious Objectors, throughout the century a wealth of biographies and autobiographies have appeared, alongside two major monographs: John Rae, *Conscience and Politics* (OUP, 1970); and Thomas C. Kennedy, *The Hound of Conscience: A History of the No-Conscription Fellowship 1914–1919* (University of Arkansas Press, 1981). For a comprehensive list of publications and sources on the subject, see Kennedy, 'An Essay on Sources', pp. 303–16.
4. Lloyd George, *War Memoirs* (Odhams Press, 1938), Vol. I, p. 428.
5. James Arthur Salter, *Memoirs of a Public Servant* (Faber & Faber, 1961), pp. 73–4. On military and economic planning, see for example David French, *British Economic and Strategic Planning, 1905–1915* (Allen & Unwin, 1982); idem, *British Strategy and War Aims, 1914–1916* (Allen & Unwin, 1986); Keith Grieves, *The Politics of Manpower, 1914–18* (MUP, 1988); Avner Offer, *The First World War: An Agrarian Interpretation* (OUP, 1989).
6. Theodore Ropp, 'Conscription in Great Britain, 1900–1914: A Failure in Civil-Military Communications?' *Military Affairs*, 20 (1956), p. 75.
7. On Haldane's reforms, and the overall changes and evolution of the army 1901–14, see for example Correlli Barnett, *Britain and Her Army, 1509–1970* (Penguin, 1974), chs 12–15; Ian F. Beckett and Keith Simpson (eds), *A Nation in Arms: A Social Study of the British Army in the First World War* (MUP, 1985); Brian Bond, *The Victorian Army and the Staff College* (London, 1972); Tim Travers, *The Killing Ground: The British Army, the Western Front and the Emergence of Modern Warfare 1900–1918* (Allen & Unwin, 1987). On pre-war forms of militarism, see for example Hugh Cunningham, *The Volunteer Force* (Croom Helm, 1975); Scott Hughes Myerly, '"The Eye Must Entrap the Mind": Army Spectacle and Paradigm in Nineteenth-century Britain', *Journal of Social History*, Vol. 26, No. 1 (1992); Anne Summers, 'Militarism in Britain before the Great War', *History Workshop Journal*, No. 2 (1976), pp. 104–23.
8. R.J.Q. Adams and P.P. Poirier, *The Conscription Controversy in Great Britain, 1900–18* (Macmillan, 1987), p. 11, *passim*. See also Dennis Hayes, *Conscription Conflict: The Conflict of Ideas in the Struggle For and Against Military Conscription in Britain between 1901–1939* (Sheppard Press, 1949).

9. On the tabloids' spread of menace, see Avner Offer, 'The Working Classes, British Naval Plans and the Coming of the First World War', *Past and Present*, No. 107 (May 1985). On the press propaganda on conscription, see for example Michael Sanders and Phillip M. Taylor, *British Propaganda during the First World War* (London, 1982); Cate Haste, *Keep the Home Fires Burning: Propaganda in the First World War* (Allen Lane, 1977).

10. Peter Simkins, *Kitchener's Army: The Raising of the New Armies* (MUP, 1988), p. 104.

11. 'National Registration Act, 1915', *1914–16 Public General Acts* (Eyre & Spottiswoode, 1917), Ch. 60.

12. Ibid.

13. S.P. Vivien, *Confidential Memorandum on the National Registration Scheme*, PRO RG 28/1, p. 1.

14. Ibid., pp. 3–4. The emphasis appears in the original.

15. *Memorandum of Registrar-General*, 20.7.1915, PRO RG 28/1.

16. *Memorandum on the National Register*, 1915-1919, p. 38.

17. Adams and Poirier, p. 98.

18. *Mr Vivien's Second Memorandum*, PRO RG 28/1, pp. 2, 6.

19. *Memorandum on the National Register, 1915–1919*, 31.5.1919, PRO RG 28/1, pp. 18, 25.

20. Letter of Mrs Violet Carruthers to S.P. Vivien, 14.3.1916, PRO RG 28/1.

21. Quoted in Adams and Poirier, p. 96; see also Michael Fry, 'Political Change in Britain, August 1914 to December 1916: Lloyd George Replaces Asquith: The Issues Underlying the Drama', *The Historical Journal*, 31, 3 (1988).

22. Figures from Lord Derby's report to the Cabinet, reproduced in Adams and Poirier, p. 135.

23. Quoted in Hayes, p. 201.

24. Quoted in French, *British Strategy and War Aims, 1914–1916*, p. 187; Memo to the Cabinet by Sir William Robertson, Chief of the Imperial General Staff, 21 March 1916, in Lloyd George, Vol. I, p. 438.

25. Wilson, p. 400.

26. E.J. Leed, *No Man's Land: Combat and Identity in World War I* (CUP, 1979), p. x.

27. Tony Ashworth, *Trench Warfare 1914–1918: The Live and Let Live System* (Macmillan, 1980), p. 56. See also idem, 'The Sociology of Trench Warfare 1914–18', *British Journal of Sociology*, XIX, 4 (December 1968), pp. 407–20; Leed, p. 15.

28. Northrop Frye, *Anatomy of Criticism* (Princeton University Press, 1957), p. 41.

29. Leon Wolff, *In Flanders Fields* (Readers Union: Longmans, Green & Co., 1960), p. xxi; Denis Winter, *Death's Men: Soldiers of the Great War* (Penguin, 1987), p. 16.

30. Haig to Lord Derby, 3 October 1917, quoted in Beckett, 'The Real Unknown Army', p. 5. On the attitude of the high command, see for example Adams and Poirier; French, *British Economic and Strategic Planning*, chs. 2, 8, *passim*; Grieves, chs 1–2.

31. Martin Stone, 'Shell Shock and the Psychologists', in W.F. Bynum, R. Porter and M. Shepherd (eds), *The Anatomy of Madness* (Tavistock, London, 1985), pp. 242–71. For the prominence of shell shock as a crucial issue within the British medical establishment both throughout the war and subsequently, see for example G. Elliot-Smith and T.H. Pear, *Shell Shock and Its Lessons* (Longman, Green, London, 1917); E. Jones, 'War Shock and Freud's Theory of the Neuroses' (1918), *Papers on Psychoanalysis*

(3rd edn, William Wood, New York, 1923); A. Leri, *Shell Shock, Commotional and Emotional Aspects* (University of London Press, London, 1919); F.W. Mott, *War Neuroses and Shell Shock* (Hodder & Stoughton, London, 1919); L.R. Yealland, *Hysterical Disorders and Warfare* (Macmillan, London, 1918).

32. Elliot-Smith and Pear, p. 22.

33. Jose Brunner, 'Psychiatry, Psychoanalysis and Politics During the First World War', paper presented at the Israeli Political Science Association, Tel Aviv University, May 1988, pp. 2–3. On similar British treatment, see for example Stone, pp. 253–4, *passim*; Elaine Showalter, *The Female Malady: Women, Madness, and English Culture* (1985; Virago, London, 1987), ch. 7: 'Male Hysteria: W.H.R. Rivers and the Lessons of Shell Shock', pp. 167–94.

34. Meyer S. Gunther and Harry Trosman, 'Freud as Expert Witness: Wagner-Jauregg and the Problem of War Neuroses', *Annual of Psychoanalysis*, Vol. 2 (1974), pp. 5, 6, 9, 12; pp. 4–9 are a full transcript of the discussion held before the commission.

35. *Report of the War Office Committee of Inquiry into Shellshock* (HMSO, London, 1922), p. 165.

36. P.E. Dewey, 'Military Recruiting and the British Labour Force during the First World War', *The Historical Journal*, 27, I (1984), pp. 210-11; *passim.*

37. Kenneth Boulding, *The Image* (University of Michigan Press, 1959), p. 69.

38. The known books are: F. Gray, *Confessions of a Private* (Blackwell, 1929); F.A. Voigt, *Combed Out* (Cape, 1929); Paul Fussell (ed.), *The Ordeal of Alfred M. Hale* (Leo Cooper, 1975); F.A.J. Taylor, *The Bottom of the Barrel* (Regency Press, 1978); W.V. Tilsley, Other Ranks (Cobden-Sanderson, 1931).

39. Voigt, p. 7; p. 22.

40. E.D. Bishop, IWM 77/111/1; W.R. Acklam, IWM 83/23/1.

41. Erving Goffman, *The Presentation of Self in Everyday Life* (Allen Lane, 1971), pp. 38–9.

42. Michel Foucault, *The History of Sexuality: An Introduction* (Penguin, 1984), pp. 61–2.

43. Sigmund Freud, 'Thoughts for the Times on War and Death (1915)', p. 67.

44. A.J. Abraham, IWM P.191; p. 44.

CHAPTER ONE

1. Richard Holmes, *Firing Line* (Penguin, 1987), p. 32.

2. E.J.O. Bird, undated letter, IWM BBC/'Great War' series.

3. Military Service Act (No. 2), 1916, in Public General Acts, 5 & 6 George V, Chapter 104. The first section of the Act, regarding attestation, was identical in all the Military Service Acts in the war.

4. W. Cobb, unpublished account, IWM 73/188/1, p. 1.

5. Army Form B. 2513, *Record of Service Paper*, PRO WO 32Y/ 76545.

6. *Memorandum on the National Register, 1915–1919*, p. 19; pp. 19–20; p. 22.

7. W.D. Tonkyn, *Diary*, IWM Con Shelf.

8. E.C. Barraclough, unpublished account, IWM 86/86/1, p. 1.

9. John William Binns, undated letter, IWM/BBC, 'Great War' series.

10. R.L. Angel, unpublished account, IWM; p. 1.

11. Taylor, *The Bottom of the Barrel*, p. 16.

12. *Punch*, October 1915.
13. S. Bradbury, unpublished account, IWM 81/35/1; preface.
14. Lt E.C. Allfree, unpublished account, IWM 77/14/1, p. 10.
15. Ibid, p. 11.
16. Simkins, *Kitchener's Army*, p. 176.
17. Leonard Preuss, letter, 22.7.1963, IWM/BBC, 'Great War' series.
18. B. Rudge, Oral History Project interview, IWM 85/39/1, p. 3.
19. Barraclough, p. 1.
20. Paul Fussell (ed.), *The Ordeal of Alfred M. Hale*, pp. 36–40.
21. Tonkyn, op.cit.
22. Doron Lamm, 'British Soldiers of the First World War', *Historical Social Research*, Vol. 14, No. 4, 1988, p. 63.
23. W.L. Fisher, diary entry, 20.2.1917, IWM 85/32/1; Cobb, p. 1.
24. *Lancet*, 26.2.1916, p. 490. The British Medical Association did not appear to intervene in this use of the medical profession. Neither the *British Medical Journal* nor the *Lancet* commented on the doctors' role in these medical examinations. Their concern appears to have centred far more on the enlistment and/or conscription of medical students, and the feared subsequent loss of potential doctors.
25. Humphrey Gleave to Edward Gleave, letter of 21.2.1916, IWM 78/31/1 T.
26. D.H. Lawrence, *Kangaroo* (Penguin, 1950), pp. 237–8.
27. J.M. Winter, 'Military Fitness and Civilian Health in Britain in the First World War', *Journal of Contemporary History*, Vol. 15, 1980, pp. 215–16.
28. F.P. Crozier, *Brasshat in No Man's Land* (Cape, 1930), p. 216; quoted in J.C. Dunn, *The War the Infantry Knew 1914–1919* (Cardinal Sphere, 1989), p. 246.
29. Military Service Act, 1916 (Session 2), May 1916, *Public General Acts*, 6 & 7, George V, Chapter 15.
30. Abraham, p. 8a; *The Bottom of the Barrel*, p. 43.
31. Dunn, p. 245.
32. Humphrey Gleave to Edward Gleave, letter of 12.2.1916.
33. W.B. Henderson, unpublished novel, IWM 81/19/1, pp. 6–7.
34. J.M. Winter, *The Great War and the British People* (Macmillan, 1986), p. 52.
35. K. Grieves, *The Politics*, pp. 131–2. This was the Shortt Committee, chaired by Edward Shortt, which convened initially in July 1917 to discuss the methods of examination and the rates of exemption apparent in the year's recruiting statistics. For a full discussion of the committee, see ibid, pp. 130–3; for its decisions on medical classification see J.M. Winter, *The Great War*, pp. 50–55.
36. J.F. Thompson, undated letter, IWM 72/119/1.
37. Holmes, p. 32.
38. Lord Derby's speech at the Mansion House, 19.10.1915, in which he presented his scheme. *The Times*, 20.10.1915, p. 10.
39. Cobb, p. 1.
40. Tonkyn, diary entry for 15.2.1917.
41. Lt P. Creek, unpublished account, IWM 87/31/1, p. 20.
42. W.L. Fisher, op. cit.
43. Norman F. Dixon, *On the Psychology of Military Incompetence* (Futura, 1988), p. 81.

CHAPTER TWO

1. A ditty sung by the room orderly in Bulford Camp, quoted in Creek, p. 22. A 'rumen' is the 'first stomach of a ruminant animal', *The Shorter Oxford English Dictionary.*
2. H.L. Adams, unpublished account, IWM 83/50/1; B.W. Hughes, diary, IWM 85/43/1.
3. Barraclough, p. 1.
4. Creek, p. 21.
5. W.L. Fisher, diary entry for 2.3.1917; A.J. Jamieson, IWM 88/52/1, p. 3.
6. J.F. Thompson, letters of 6.10.1917, 12.10.1917; Hale, p. 58; Adams, p. 1.
7. Creek, p. 23.
8. P.G. Copson, unpublished account, IWM 86/30/1, p. 1; Allfree, p. 20.
9. Allfree, p. 15; Thompson, letter of 18.10.1917.
10. Creek, pp. 22–3.
11. Taylor, p. 21; Allfree, pp. 15–16.
12. Creek, pp. 23–4.
13. Copson, p. 1.
14. E.A. Pinks, IWM 85/43/1, letter of 4.1.1917.
15. Tonkyn, letter of 16.3.1917.
16. Creek, p. 24; Thompson, letter of 6.10.1917.
17. Creek, pp. 24, 22; Hale, pp. 44, 47.
18. Thompson, postcard of 8.10.1917.
19. Allfree, p. 30.
20. Thompson, letters of 18.10.1917, 25.10.1917.
21. Adams, p. 1; Bradbury, p. 2; Allfree, p. 22.
22. Jamieson, p. 3; Allfree, p. 24. On the organisation of training in Kitchener's Armies, see Simkins, *Kitchener's Army*, pp. 185–95, *passim.*
23. *Statistics of the Military Effort*, p. 834.
24. P.R. Hall, unpublished account, IWM 87/55/1, p. 3; Allfree, p. 29; Cobb, p. 3.
25. *Statistics of the Military Effort*, p. 833.
26. W.L. Fisher, diary entry for 3.5.1917; Thompson, letter of 6.10.1917; Creek, p. 22.
27. Allfree, p. 32. His major comment on the main meal of the day was its lack of accompanying bread or salt.
28. Thompson, letter of 13.10.1917.
29. E.A. Pinks, letter of 7.1.1917. It must be noted that within the context of this correspondence the comment was written as an objective assessment, and not in a vein of irony or as an attempt to pacify his worried mother.
30. W.L. Fisher, diary entry for 4.5.1917.
31. Taylor, pp. 26–33.
32. S. Pinks, IWM 85/43/1, letter of 18.5.1917.
33. Trevor Wilson, *The Myriad Faces of War*, p. 51;. P.E. Dewey, 'Military Recruiting and the British labour force during the First World War', p. 204; 'Military Tribunal Papers: The Case of Leek Local Tribunal in the First World War', in *Archives*, Vol. xvi, No. 70 (October 1983), p. 150.
34. Bradbury, p. 1; Thompson, letter of 16.10.1917; Jamieson, p. 5.
35. Hale, p. 51; A. Hynd, IWM WWI 78/4; letter of 20.10.1917.

36. Hynd, letter of 25.11.1917; Allfree, pp. 20, 21; S. Pinks, letter of 15.5.1917.

37. S. Pinks, letters of 7.6.1917, 28.8.1917; Hale, p. 56.

38. Thompson, letters of 9.10.1917, 21.11.1917.

39. Tonkyn, letter of 24.3.1917.

40. Creek, p. 23; Jamieson, p. 4.

41. J. Bennet; Tonkyn, letters of 9.3.1917, 16.3.1917; Thompson, letters of 12.10.1917, 29.11.1917; P.G. Preston, IWM M6/160-167/1, diary entry for 6.6.1917.

42. Taylor, p. 21; Adams, p. 1.

43. For a discussion of public health in Britain during the First World War see: J.M. Winter, *The Great War and the British People*, Part II; Bradbury, p. 2; Taylor, pp. 25–6.

44. Statistics in the *Lancet*, 22.8.1914, p. 522; parliamentary debate of 25.1.1916, quoted in the *Lancet*, 29.1.1916, p. 275.

45. Tonkyn, letter of 14.3.1917; W.L. Fisher, diary entry for 19.3.1917; Copson, p. 1.

46. Hale, p. 107; Jamieson, p. 5; Barraclough, p. 1; Taylor, p. 41.

47. C.H. Cox, unpublished account, IWM 88/11/1, p. 1.

48. Thompson, letters of 6.10.1917, 12.10.1917, 20.12.1917.

49. Tonkyn, letter of 14.3.1917.

50. Thompson, letter of 9.10.1917; Hale, p. 70.

51. E.A. Pinks, letter of 24.1.1917; Thompson, letter of 21.10.1917; Hale, p. 92.

52. On training during voluntarism, see for example Simkins, ch. 12; Denis Winter, *Death's Men*, ch. 2; Wilson, ch. 22. Nearly all of the many published memoirs of volunteer soldiers and officers, and novels based upon their experiences, document their training. See for example Ivor Gurney, *War Letters* (Hogarth Press, 1984), Part I; Sue Richardson (ed.), *Orders are Orders: A Manchester Pal on the Somme* (Neil Richardson, 1987), ch. 2; George Coppard, *With a Machine Gun to Cambrai* (Papermac, 1986); Ian Hay, *The First Hundred Thousand* (Penguin, 1941). On the theories and uses of basic training, see for example Dixon, *On the Incompetence of Military Psychology*, chs 15–16; Holmes, *Firing Line*, ch. 2.

53. Allfree, p. 23; E.A. Pinks, letter of 9.2.1917; B.W. Hughes, diary entry for 25.1.1916; Copson, p. 3.

54. E.A. Pinks, letters of 24.1.1917, 1.2.1917; Gray, *Confessions of a Private*, p. 30.

55. Thompson, letter of 6.11.1917.

56. Freud offers an interesting discussion of the social suppression of aggression, and the need to exhibit it in time of war, in 'Thoughts for the Time on War and Death: I. The Disillusionment of the War', *Civilization, Society and Religion*, pp. 68–9.

57. W.L. Fisher, diary entry for 1.4.1917; Hughes, diary entries for 20–23.1.1917.

58. W.L. Fisher, diary entries for 6–14.5.1917.

59. W.L. Fisher, diary entry for 20.4.1917; F. Hollingsworth, unpublished account, IWM 82/21/1, p. 1.

60. Simkins, p. 296. Wilson notes that it took seven months to train the first New Army (*The Myriad Faces of War*, p. 250). Only twenty of the conscripts' writings examined here document the element of time in their training experiences.

61. Hollingsworth, p. 1; W.L. Fisher, diary entry for 10.8.1917; Hall, p. 1.

62. B. Davies, IWM 83/31/1, letter of 11.4.1917.

63. Bishop, diary entries for 1–11.1.1917; W.R. Acklam, diary entry for 18.9.1916; Thompson, letter of 24.6.1918; Hall, p. 3.

64. W.L. Fisher, diary entries between 1.5.1917 and 2.7.1917.
65. Copson, p. 3; E.A. Pinks, letter of 12.2.1917; Thompson, letter of 7.12.1917.
66. Taylor, p. 34; R.D. Fisher, IWM 76/54/1, p. 1; S. Pinks, letter of 15.5.1917; W.L. Fisher, diary entries for 18.3.1917, 30.6.1917.
67. Barraclough, p. 1.
68. E.A. Pinks, letter of 17.5.1917; Allfree, p. 24; Cobb, p. 3; W.L. Fisher, diary entry for 20.7.1917; Creek, p. 36.
69. Holmes, p. 36.
70. Thus for example '. . . over one million men [1,138,070] joined the army in the first full year of compulsory military service [1916] despite the many administrative problems'. Grieves, *The Politics of Manpower*, p. 28.
71. Davies, letter of 11.4.1917.

CHAPTER THREE

1. Dunn, *The War the Infantry Knew*, pp. 6–8; E.A. Pinks, letter of 5.6.1917.
2. Henderson, p. 1; Tonkyn, letter of 10.6.1917; J. Bennet, IWM 83/14/1.
3. Henderson, p. 1; W.L. Fisher, diary entry for 11.8.1917.
4. Copson, p. 4; F.R. Jolley, IWM Department of Documents vd., diary entry for 11.6.1917; Tonkyn, letter of 10.6.1917.
5. Henderson, p. 7; Jamieson, p. 5; Jolley, p. 1.
6. Copson, p. 4.
7. Abraham, p. 9.
8. Henderson, pp. 2–3.
9. Hale, p. 131; Acklam, diary entry for 29.9.1916.
10. Bishop, diary entries for 12–13.1.1917; Henderson, p. 9.
11. Cobb, op.cit. p. 5; Jolley, p. 6.
12. E. Holdsworth, IWM 73/147/1, p. 1.
13. W. Fisher, diary entry for 12.8.1917; R.D. Fisher, p. 1; Thompson, letter of 5.7.1918.
14. Holdsworth, p. 1; R.D. Fisher, p. 3; Henderson, p. 9; Jolley, p. 2.
15. Jolley, p. 1.
16. Henderson, p. 4.
17. Cobb, p. 4.
18. R.D. Fisher, p. 2.
19. Hale, p. 133; R.D. Fisher, p. 3; Jolley, p. 2.
20. Henderson, p. 15; Lt W.E. Glasgow, IWM 73/223/1, letter of 27.7.1917.
21. Thompson, letter of 5.7.1918; Graves, *Goodbye to All That* (Penguin, 1979), p. 79.
22. Jolley, pp. 3, 2.
23. Denis Winter, *Death's Men*, p. 72; Taylor, p. 47; E.D. Vaughan, *Some Desperate Glory: The diary of a young officer, 1917* (Frederick Warne, 1981), p. 3.
24. Taylor, p. 47; Jolley, pp. 3–4.
25. Jolley, p. 4.
26. Adams, p. 2.
27. R.D. Fisher, p. 3; Acklam, diary entry for 3.10.1916.
28. Jolley, p. 4.

29. Cobb, p. 4; Bishop, p. 4; E.A. Pinks, letter of 19.6.1917.
30. On 'bullshit', see for example Dixon, *On the Psychology of Military Incompetence*, ch. 16; Holmes, *Firing Line*, ch. 2.
31. R.D. Fisher, p. 4; Jolley, p. 4.
32. Adams, p. 3; Jolley, p. 8.
33. Jolley, p. 7; E.A. Pinks, letter of 12.6.1917.
34. Allfree, p. 59.
35. R. Harris and J. Paxman, *A Higher Form of Killing: The Secret Story of Gas and Germ Warfare* (Chatto & Windus, 1982), p. 16.
36. Hale, p. 134; Acklam, diary entry for 4.10.1916; W.L. Fisher, diary entry for 14.8.1917; Holdsworth, p. 1.
37. Jolley, pp. 4–5.
38. Adams, p. 3.
39. Jolley, p. 5.
40. Bradbury, p. 5.
41. E.A. Pinks, letter of 20.6.1917; R.D. Fisher, p. 5; Lt F. Bass, IWM 77/94/1, diary entry for 16.9.1916.
42. Jolley, p. 6.
43. E.A. Pinks, letter of 25.6.1917; R.D. Fisher, p. 7; Jolley, p. 9.
44. Bass, diary entry for 28.9.1916; ibid; Tilsley, pp. 7–8.
45. Tilsley, p. 8; Acklam, diary entry for 4.10.1916.
46. W.L. Fisher, diary entry for 15.8.1917.
47. E.A. Pinks, letter of 11.6.1917.
48. Adams, p. 2.
49. Clark, diary entry for 15.8.1916, the three dots appear as such in the original diary; Hall, p. 4.
50. Jolley, p. 10.
51. R.D. Fisher, p. 7; Henderson, p. 23; W. Fisher, diary entry for 19.8.1917; D. Winter, *Death's Men*, p. 74.
52. Thompson, letter of 21.8.1918; Abraham, p. 13; E.O. Gale, IWM P 331, letter of 28.7.1916; Bradbury, p. 5.
53. Acklam, diary entry for 5.10.1916; Abraham, p. 13; A.G. Clark, IWM 84/1/1, diary entry for 16.8.1916; C.P. Harris, IWM 87/33/1, diary entry for 17.12.1916.
54. Bradbury, p. 54; Abraham, p. 13.
55. Jolley, p. 11; Allfree, p. 65; W.L. Fisher, diary entry for 19.8.1917; Holdsworth, p. 2.
56. Holdsworth, p. 2; Acklam, diary entry for 5.10.1916; Henderson, p. 18.
57. *Goodbye to All That*, p. 81.
58. Taylor, p. 49; Allfree, pp. 71–2, p. 87, *passim*.
59. Holdsworth, p. 67; Jolley, p. 19.
60. Creek, p. 25.
61 J.T. Lawton, IWM 86/48/1, p. 7; W.L. Fisher, diary entry for 21.8.1917; Harris, diary entry for 20.12.1916; Creek, p. 37.
62. D. Winter, *Death's Men*, pp. 77–8.
63. R.D. Fisher, p. 20; Jolley, pp. 11–12.
64. Harris, diary entry for 20.12.1916; Bass, diary entry for 8.10.1916; G.H. Dixon, IWM 86/57/1, diary entry for 8.1.1917; Adams, p. 7.

65. R.D. Fisher, pp. 16–17; Hughes, diary entry for 6.7.1916; Acklam, diary entry for 26.8.1917.
66. Adams, p. 8.
67. Preston, diary entry for 18.10.1917.
68. E. Blore, IWM 86/36/1, letter of 10.1.1917; Bradbury, p. 62.
69. R.D. Fisher, diary entries for 27–8.3.1918.
70. Bradbury, p. 61.
71. Clark, p. 7; R.D. Fisher, diary entry for 8.4.1918; Thompson, letter of 5.7.1918.
72. Blore, letter of 29.1.1917.
73. Preston, diary entry for 26.7.1917; A.E. Abrey, IWM 84/41/1, letter of 28.3.1917; Thompson, letter of 21.8.1918.
74. Tilsley, p. 10.

CHAPTER FOUR

1. E.A. Pearce and C.G. Smith, *The World Weather Guide* (Hutchinson, 1990), pp. 353–4.
2. Ernst Junger, *The Storm of Steel* (Chatto & Windus, 1929), p. 48.
3. Bishop, diary entry for 12.7.1917; Holdsworth, p. 6; Dixon, p. 3.
4. Abrey, letter of 7.10.1918; Rudge, p. 7.
5. Acklam, diary entry for 19.10.1916; Allfree, p. 171; Thompson, letter of 17.10.1918.
6. C.R.T. Evans, IWM 87/45/1, letter of 12.12.1916; Acklam, diary entry for 4.11.1916; Hughes, diary entry for 4.7.1916; Blore, letter of 10.1.1917.
7. R.D. Fisher, p. 26; Acklam, diary entry for 1.8.1917.
8. Allfree, p. 165; Acklam, diary entry for 1.8.1917; Adams, p. 6; Hughes, diary entry for 29.8.1916.
9. Ditty entitled 'Reminiscences of Rilken Ridge, August 1917', in Bennet, op. cit.
10. J. Fraser, IWM 86/19/1, letter of 1.10.1916; R.D. Fisher, pp. 24–5.
11. Jolley, p. 20.
12. D.N. White, IWM Con Shelf, letter of 4.10.1916; Hall, p. 8; Holdsworth, pp. 6–7.
13. Adams, p. 10; Allfree, p. 160; Dixon, p. 2; R.D. Fisher, p. 26.
14. Allfree, p. 155.
15. Holdsworth, p. 6; Acklam, diary entry for 1.8.1917.
16. Jolley, p. 22.
17. Acklam, diary entry for 26.8.1917; Fraser, letter of 30.8.1916.
18. White, letter of 8.11.1916; F. Carey, IWM 85/43/1, diary entry for 31.7.1917.
19. Harris, letter of 15.1.1918; Hughes, diary entry for 30.8.1916; Jolley, p. 22.
20. E.A. Pinks, letter of 15.6.1917; Jolley, p. 30; Fraser, letter of 12.9.1916.
21. Thompson, letter of 21.8.1918; Gale, letter of 28.7.1916; Voigt (1920 edn), p. 110; Acklam, diary entries for 13.3.1917, 10.5.1917, *passim.*
22. Dixon, p. 2; Acklam, diary entry for 19.12.1916; White, letter of 21.10.1916.
23. L.F. Grant, IWM 87/13/1; Blore, letter of 29.1.1917.
24. IWM Misc. 95/Item 1457; IWM Misc. 263, letter of 11.1.1917.
25. Bishop, diary entries for 13.4.1917, 19.10.1917; R.D. Fisher, p. 44; ibid., p. 42.
26. Acklam, diary entry for 20.3.1917; Fraser, letter of 17.10.1916.
27. Acklam, diary entry for 19.11.1916, *passim*; Bishop, diary entry for 28.6.1917, *passim*; W.L. Fisher, diary entry for 8.10.1917.

28. W.L. Fisher, letter of 8.10.1917; Harris, letter of 21.12.16.

29. R.D. Fisher, p. 46.

30. J. Brent-Wilson, *The Morale and Discipline of the British Expeditionary Force in 1914* (University Of New Brunswick, MA thesis, 1978) p. 32.

31. Acklam, diary entry for 11.10.1916, *passim*; White, letter of 8.11.1916; Lt J. Dale IWM P 272, letter of 10.8.1917.

32. Rudge, p. 8; R.D. Fisher, p. 46.

33. Abraham, pp. 57–8; Blore, letter of 29.1.1917.

34. R.D. Fisher, p. 24.

35. Barraclough, p. 7; Harris, letters of 3.12.1916, 21.1.1917.

36. Blore, letter of 29.1.1917; Gale, letter of 31.10.1917.

37. Rudge, p. 8.

38. For a discussion of the military events leading to the establishment of trench warfare, see for example Wilson, *The Myriad Faces of War*, chs 4, 10. On organisational problems in the supply of men and ammunition at this time, see for example Grieves, *The Politics of Manpower*, ch.1; French, *British Strategy and War Aims, 1914–1916*, chs 8–9. For a full narrative of the events from the combat viewpoint, see for example Dunn, *The War the Infantry Knew*, chs I–V.

39. John F. Lucy, *There's a Devil in the Drum* (Faber & Faber, 1938), quoted in Wilson, p. 63.

40. Graves, *Goodbye to All That*, pp. 85–6.

41. Ibid, pp. 87–8.

42. Barraclough, p. 7; Copson, p. 6.

43. Bishop, diary entry for 6.3.1917; Acklam, diary entry for 30.10.1916; Cobb, p. 7.

44. Harris, letter of 21.12.1916; Adams, p. 3.

45. Bishop, diary entry for 6.3.1917; Copson, p. 6; R.D. Fisher, p. 15; Abraham, p. 26, 31.

46. R.D. Fisher, p. 18; G. Bryan, IWM 80/28/1, diary entry for 1.6.1917; Bishop, diary entry for 21.3.1917; White, letter of 14.10.1916.

47. R.D. Fisher, p. 10; Abraham, p. 59; Thompson, letter of 1.9.1918; R.D. Fisher, p. 23.

48. Bass, diary entry for 3.12.1916; Thompson, letter of 1.9.1918; Abraham, p. 62.

49. Allfree, pp. 129–30; Grant, diary entry for 3.3.1917; Bishop, diary entry for 9.3.1917; White, letter of 28.9.1916.

50. Holdsworth, p. 3; Jolley, p. 14; B.F. Eccles, IWM 82/22/1, letter of 18.9.1916.

51. Jolley, p. 16.

52. Jolley, p. 30.

53. Carey, op. cit.

54. Bryan, diary entry for 7.9.1917; Bass, diary entry for 8.10.1916.

55. Adams, p. 5; Evans, letter of 12.12.1916; Abraham, p. 31.

56. Henderson, Part 5.

57. W.L. Fisher, letter of 12.11.1917; Bradbury, p. 51.

58. Henderson, Part 14; Bishop, diary entry for 28.6.1917; White, letter of 8.11.1916.

59. Henderson, Part 8. On lack of light, see Adams, p. 3; Thompson, letter of 5.11.1918.

60. Jolley, p. 12; R.D. Fisher, p. 9.

61. Bryan, diary entry for 30.5.1917; Thompson, letter of 2.8.1918, *passim*; Bass, diary entry for 25.10.1916. On insects in the structures, see also for example Grant, diary entry for 16.2.1917; Bishop, diary entry for 27.8.1917, *passim*; Acklam, diary entry for 10.11.1916, *passim*.

62. Bryan, diary entry for 30.5.1917; Cobb, pp. 6–7; Preston, diary entry for 23.7.1917.

63. Blore, letter of 10.1.1917; Grant, diary entry for 25.1.1917.

64. See for example: Abraham, p. 6, *passim*; R.D. Fisher, p. 15, *passim*; W.L. Fisher, letter of 25.11.1917.

65. Jamieson, Part III, p. 1; Thompson, letter of 29.9.1918; Evans, letter of 12.12.1916.

66. R.D. Fisher, p. 24; on not removing any clothing, see for example Acklam, diary entry for 11.10.1916, *passim*.

67. Adams, p. 5.

68. Abraham, p. 106; Bass, diary entry for 5.10.1916; Evans, letter of 12.12.1916.

69. Henderson, Part 8.

70. Adams, p. 11.

71. R.D. Fisher, pp. 54, 56.

72. Abraham, p. 106.

73. Thompson, letter of 22.10.1918; Creek, p. 52.

74. Fraser, letter of 20.11.1916.

75. See also for example Acklam, diary entry for 10.5.1917, *passim*; Clark, p. 11 *passim*.

76. Thompson, letter of 12.7.1918.

77. Fraser, letter of 20.11.1916.

78. R.D. Fisher, p. 9.

79. Henderson, p. 3.

80. 'Sing me to Sleep', possibly composed by F. Dixon of B. Company, 19th Middlesex Regt, quoted in Howes, op. cit.

Chapter Five

1. From a comic list of soldiers' superstitions, in Bass, back cover of diary for 1918.

2. Holmes, *Firing Line*, p. 125.

3. Beatrice Webb, unpublished diaries; quoted in David Englander and James Osborne, 'Jack, Tommy, and Henry Dubb: The Armed Forces and the Working Class', *The Historical Journal*, 21, 3 (1978), p. 600.

4. D. Winter, *Death's Men*, p. 147.

5. Clark, diary entry for 25.8.1916. For a discussion of health and food in the First World War, see for example J. Winter, *The Great War and the British People*. On military organisation, see Martin Van Creveld, *Supplying War: Logistics from Wallenstein to Patton* (CUP, 1977); especially chs 1, 4. On the problems of the British wartime economy, see for example Wilson, *The Myriad Faces of War*, chs 11, 13; French, *British Economic and Strategic Planning 1905–1915*; Offer, *The First World War: An Agrarian Interpretation*.

6. Henderson, Part 39.

7. *Lancet*, 27.11.1915, p. 2000.

8. 'Note by the Quartermaster-General to the Forces', *Statistics of the Military Effort*, p. 841.

9. R.D. Fisher, p. 15; Holdsworth, p. 2.

10. On fighting order: Adams, p. 6; on constant appearance of bully: Bass, diary entry for 5.10.1916, *passim*; see also for example Acklam, 9.12.1917, *passim*; Holdsworth, p. 2, *passim*; Thompson, letter of 3.8.1918.

11. Jolley, p. 3; Acklam, diary entry for 9.2.1917; Henderson, Part 39; Abraham, p. 66.

12. Abraham, p. 25; Jamieson, Part II, p. 5.

13. Jamieson, Part II, p. 5; R.D. Fisher, p. 6; Jolley, p. 2; Henderson, Part 39.
14. Abraham, p. 65; 'Note by the Quartermaster-General to the Forces', p. 843.
15. Acklam, diary entry for 23.11.1916; Grant, diary entry for 23.6.1917; Jolley, p. 22.
16. Henderson, op. cit. Part 14.
17. Jolley, p. 30; Henderson, Part 14.
18. Jamieson, Part II, P.5.
19. Adams, p. 5; Bryan, diary entry for 24.8.1917.
20. Acklam, diary entry for 22.4.1918, *passim*; W.L. Fisher, diary entry for 30.8.1917.
21. Bishop, diary entry for 28.1.1917, and *passim* to 12.2.1917; memo written at the bottom of diary page covering 26.2.–4.3.1917; entries for 13.4.1917, 12.7.1917, 31.8.1917, 19.10.1917, 17.11.1917, 19.11.1917, 25.11.1917.
22. *Combed Out* (1920 edn), p. 15; Henderson, Part 15; Jolley, p. 22.
23. Holdsworth, p. 6; Barraclough, p. 4; Hynd, letter of 24.5.1918; W.L. Fisher, diary entry for 29.8.1917; Bradbury, p. 51.
24. Davies, letter of 13.1.1918; Creek, p. 41.
25. R.D. Fisher, pp. 56, 60, 62.
26. F.R. Curtis, unpublished account, IWM 87/17/1, p. 4. On scrounging in villages, see also Adams, p. 8; R.D. Fisher, p. 60.
27. Creek, p. 53; Thompson, letter of 2.10.1918; R.D. Fisher, p. 83.
28. Jamieson, Part II, p. 5; Abrey, letter of 30.10.1916; Carey, diary entry for 13.4.1917; R.D. Fisher, p. 62; Thompson, letter of 2.10.1918.
29. Eccles, letter of 18.9.1916; Bass, diary entry for 10.10.1916; Evans, letter of 28.12.1916.
30. Clark, p. 7; Harris, diary entries for 25.12.1916, 10.1.1917.
31. Acklam, diary entry for 25.12.1916; IWM Misc 263, letter of 11.1.1917; ibid.
32. Clark, diary entry for 23.4.1917; Holdsworth, p. 5.
33. Jolley, p. 41; Acklam, 20.1.1917, *passim*; Harris, diary entry for 26.12.1916. See also for example: Bass, Thompson, Creek, Clark.
34. Bryan, diary entry 23.9.1917; Voigt (1920 edn), p. 36; Henderson, Part 11; W.L. Fisher, diary entry for 17.10.1917.
35. Thompson, letter of 13.9.1918; ibid; Acklam, diary entry for 22.4.1917.
36. Harris, diary entry for 18.12.1916; R.D. Fisher, p. 41; Acklam, diary entry for 9.12.1917.
37. Tonkyn, letter of 10.6.1917; Gale, letter of 28.7.1916.
38. *Statistics of the Military Effort*, p. 875; Bryan, diary entry for 4.9.1917; Thompson, letter of 3.8.1918; Abraham, p. 12.
39. Creek, p. 39; Acklam, diary entry for 25.3.1918.
40. Brent-Wilson, *The Morale and Discipline . . .*, p. 57; W.L. Fisher, diary entry for 11.10.1917; ibid. diary entry for 3.11.1917; R.D. Fisher, p. 12.
41. Eccles, letter of 18.9.1916; Rudge (transcript of an oral history project), pp. 19–20; Acklam, diary entry for 24.2.1917.
42. Clark, p. 10; R.D. Fisher, p. 41; Bishop, diary entries for 30.10.–4.11.1917; Barraclough, p. 2. See also W.L. Fisher, diary entry for 3.11.1917.
43. Rudge, p. 8.
44. Acklam, diary entry for 13.11.1916.
45. Thompson, letter of 5.11.1918; White, letter of 8.11.1916.

46. Acklam, diary entries for 14.11.1916, 16.11.1916, 19.11.1916, 29.11.1916, 1.5.1917, 11.7.1917, 28.9.1917, 2.11.1917, 4.11.1917.

47. White, letter of 14.10.1916.

48. Evans, letters of 28.12.1916, 12.12.1916.

49. White, letter of 21.10.1916; Blore, letter of 10.1.1917.

50. Abraham, p. 90; Thompson, letter of 1.9.1918.

51. Holdsworth, p. 8; R.D. Fisher, p. 44; White, letter of 15.10.1916.

52. Holdsworth, p. 6; Jolley, p. 16; White, letter of 14.10.1916.

53. Henderson, Part 11.

54. White, letter of 28.9.1916; Adams, p. 2; Eccles, letter of 18.9.1916; Thompson, letter of 12.7.1918.

55. Bass, diary entry for 3.12.1916; Abraham, p. 41, 90.

56. Barraclough, p. 8; Creek, p. 47; ibid.

57. Holdsworth, p. 7; Preston, diary entries for 24.6.1917, 3.7.1917, 8.8.1917, 21.8.1917, 5.9.1917.

58. W.L. Fisher, letter of 25.8.1917; Jamieson, Part II, p. 6; R.D. Fisher, p. 23; Acklam, diary entry for 24.2.1918.

59. W.L. Fisher, diary entry for 4.11.1917; Harris, diary entry for 28.3.1917; Bradbury, p. 23.

60. R.D. Fisher, p. 23; Holdsworth, p. 7; Voigt (1920 edn), p. 40; Jolley, p. 20.

61. Bradbury, p. 23; Cobb, p. 9; Misc. 95.

62. Creek, p. 39; R.D. Fisher, p. 40; Rudge, p. 8; Holdsworth, p. 6.

63. Jamieson, Part II, p. 6; Cobb, p. 7; Hollingsworth, p. 8.

64. R.D. Fisher, p. 40; Clark, diary entry for 25.8.1916; Acklam, diary entry for 23.4.1918.

65. Hans Zinsser, *Rats, Lice and History* (George Routledge & Sons, 1935), pp. 177–8; Cobb, p. 7.

66. R.D. Fisher, p. 40; Misc. 95; Creek, p. 38; Abraham, p. 41a.

67. Misc. 95; Acklam, diary entry for 13.3.1917.

68. *The Louse Problem at the Western Front* (HMSO, 1916); Appendix IV, pp. 25–9.

69. Holdsworth, p. 6.

70. Acklam, diary entry for 16.11.1916.

71. Henderson, Part 39.

72. Thompson, letter of 8.10.1918; Tilsley, p. 12; W.L. Fisher, diary entry for 2.9.1917.

73. Abraham, p. 21; Cobb, p. 9.

74. Creek, p. 51; Acklam, diary entry for 3.8.1918.

CHAPTER 6

1. 'Sing me to Sleep', possibly composed by F. Dixon of B. Company, 19th Middlesex Regt; cited in Howes, front of diary.

2. Eccles, letter of 18.9.1916; Fraser, letter of 30.8.1916; White, letter of 4.10.1916; Allfree, p. 6; Dale, letter of 31.5.1917.

3. Creek, p. 42; White, letter of 24.9.1916; see also for example Thompson, letter of 2.8.1918; Abrey, letter of 28.3.1917; Gale, letter of 28.7.1916; Martin Hurvitz, letter of 14.10.1914 (private collection).

4. Creek, p. 42.

5. Henderson, ch. 24.

6. *Censorship Orders and Regulations* (Army Document S.S. 660), p. 5, the emphasis appears on the original document.

7. R.D. Fisher, p. 41; Evans, letter of 12.12.1916; Tonkyn, letter of 10.6.1917.

8. Fraser, letters of 17.10.1916, 30.8.1916.

9. Frequency of correspondence calculated on the basis of the following collections of letters that incorporated envelopes stamped by a censor: Hart, Thompson, Evans. On the mail system, see, 'Behind the Lines 8 – "Letters Up"', *Stand To: The Journal of the Western Front Association*, (1988), p. 4.

10. White, letter of 13/14.10.1916; Abraham, p. 45a.

11. Acklam, diary entry for 29.9.1916; Evans, 12.12.1916; Blore, letter of 10.1.1917.

12. Abraham, p. 45; Eccles, letter of 18.9.1916; Abrey, letter of 30.10.1916; Evans, letter of 12.12.1916.

13. Fraser, letter of 20.8.1916; E.A. Hart, IWM 82/22/1, letter of 3.9.1917; Henderson, ch. 23; Blore, letter of 10.1.1917.

14. Eccles, letter of 18.9.1916; Davies, 13.1.1918; Gale, letter of 25.7.1916; idem, letters of 28.7.1916 and 17.8.1916.

15. *Report on Morale & c. III Army*, January 1917, located in the collection of Cpt M. Hardie, IWM 84/46/1; Dale, letter of 31.5.1917; Canon J.O. Coop, IWM 87/56/1, letter of 22.2.1916.

.16. 2nd Lt J.A. Callum, letter of 6 November (no year), located in Mrs L. Hayman, IWM 88/51/1; Coop, letter of 13.11.1918.

17. Allfree, p. 6.

18. Evans, letter of 12.12.1916.

19. Jolley, pp. 6–7.

20. W.L. Fisher, diary entry for 15.8.1917; Gale, letter of 28.7.1916.

21. Holdsworth, p. 5; Acklam, diary entry for 9.2.1918; Abrey, letter of 28.3.1917, *passim*.

22. Jolley, p. 16; on frequency of pay: Voigt (1920 edn), p. 110; W.L. Fisher, letter of 24.8.1917.

23. Holdsworth, p. 5; Rudge, p. 23.

24. Acklam, diary entry for 9.7.1917; Abraham, p. 17.

25. White, letter of 1.12.1916; on army regulation, see Abraham, p. 21; Davies, letter of 13.1.1918.

26. *Death's Men*, pp. 166, 165; Abraham, p. 21.

27. *Death's Men*, p. 166; on compassion, see for example Jolley, pp. 44, 47; Bishop, diary entry for 17.8.1917; Jolley, p. 22.

28. Bishop, diary entry for 30.6.1917; Rudge, p. 17.

29. Henderson, Part 39.

30. Acklam, diary entry for 30.12.1917; Lt Dale, letter of 10.8.1917.

31. Bishop, diary entry for 20.8.1917; Voigt (1929 edn), p. 180.

32. R.D. Fisher, p. 47; Henderson, Part 48.

33. Adams, p. 9; Bradbury, p. 53.

34. Bradbury, p. 54; Acklam, op. cit.

35. R.D. Fisher, p. 47; Creek, p. 56.

36. Bradbury, p. 54; Jolley, p. 47; Adams, p. 10; Voigt, p. 196.

CHAPTER 7

1.   From a comic list of soldiers' superstitions, in Bass, back cover of diary for 1918.

2.   Michel Foucault, *Discipline and Punish: The Birth of the Prison* (Penguin: Peregrine, 1979), p. 170. On the role of discipline in the training of soldiers and the characterisation of armies, see for example Dixon, *On the Psychology of Military Incompetence*, Part Two; Holmes, *Firing Line*, ch. 8.

3.   Blore, letter of 29.1.1917.

4.   Henderson, part 43.

5.   Rudge, p. 8.

6.   Rudge, p. 8; Voigt (1920 edn), p. 19. See also: Acklam, diary entries for 24.1.1917, 9.2.1917, *passim*; Hale, p. 53, *passim*.

7.   Voigt (1920 edn), p. 20; Henderson, part 43.

8.   Acklam, op. cit.; D. Winter, p. 43.

9.   Henderson, part 43; Blore, letter of 28.10.1916; Acklam, diary entry of 30.1.1917.

10.   Jolley, pp. 39–40.

11.   Beckett, 'The Real Unknown Army', p. 4.

12.   Hale, p. 131; Acklam, diary entry for 29.9.1916; R.D. Fisher, p. 12.

13.   Anthony Babington, *For the Sake of Example: Capital Courts Martial 1914–1918* (Paladin, 1986), p. 4; see also Julian Putkowski and Julian Sykes, *Shot at Dawn: Executions in World War One by Authority of the British Army Act* (Cooper, 1992).

14.   Rudge, pp. 19–21; Abraham, p. 105.

15.   *Statistics of the Military Effort*, Part XXIII – Discipline; Beckett, 'The Real Unknown Army', p. 1; D. Winter, p. 43; Brent-Wilson, p. 52.

16.   Creek, p. 33.

17.   Englander and Osborne, p. 598; Abraham, p. 55.

18.   Brent-Wilson, p. 59; Coop, letter of 3.10.1915; Abraham, p. 62.

19.   Hall, p. 10.

20.   Jamieson, Part 2, p. 5; Jolley, p. 26.

21.   R.D. Fisher, p. 44, pp. 45–6.

22.   Copson, p. 6.

23.   Acklam, diary entry for 30.1.1918.

24.   Hall, p. 4.

25.   Abraham, pp. 10, 12.

26.   Cox, p. 1.

27.   Brent-Wilson, p. 61; on pay deduction: Eccles; Foucault, *Discipline and Punish*, p. 14.

28.   Acklam, diary entry for 15.8.1918; Clark, p. 6.

29.   Prince Rupprecht of Bavaria, diary entry for 21.12.1917; quoted in Babington, p. 247.

30.   Acklam, diary entry for 3.5.1918; Barraclough, p. 3.

31.   Hall, pp. 11–12.

32.   Bryan, diary entry for 1.6.1917.

33.   Voigt (1929 edn), p. 77; Henderson, part 43.

34.   Thea Thompson, *Edwardian Childhoods* (Routledge & Kegan Paul, 1982), pp 54, 92; V.S. Pritchett, *A Cab at the Door* (Penguin, 1971), p. 88.

35.   Henderson, part 43; Abraham, p. 89.

36.   Acklam, diary entry for 9.7.1917; Abraham, p. 17; Bradbury, preface.

37. Jonathan Zeitlin, 'From Labour History to the History of Industrial Relations', *Economic History Review*, XL, 2 (1987), p. 178; the article also offers a comprehensive bibliography on the subject; John Benson, 'Work', in idem (ed.), *The Working Class in England 1875–1914* (Croom Helm, 1985), p. 66; Joseph Melling, '"Non-Commissioned Officers": British Employers and their Supervisory Workers, 1880–1920', *Social History*, Vol. 5, No. 2 (1980), p. 189.

CHAPTER 8

1. Diary of Sir John French, entry for 30.9.1915, Vol. M, French Papers, IWM 75/46/2.
2. Bradbury, p. 1.
3. R.D. Fisher, p. 39.
4. Jamieson, Epilogue.
5. Fraser, diary entry for 20.8.1917.
6. Bradbury, p. 50.
7. Evans, letter of 12.12.1916; Lawton, p. 17.
8. Holdsworth, p. 1.
9. R.D. Fisher, p. 21.
10. Abraham, p. 32; on length and principles of rotations, see for example Hall, p. 5, Adams, p. 6, Abraham, p. 28.
11. Abraham, p. 32.
12. R.D. Fisher, p. 24; Adams, p. 5.
13. Lawton, p. 16; R.D. Fisher, p. 26.
14. Abraham, p. 64.
15. Acklam, diary entry for 11.10.1916.
16. Rudge, p. 18; Creek, p. 37; ibid.
17. Bishop, diary entry for 31.5.1917; Hall, p. 5; W.L. Fisher, diary entry for 15.9.1917.
18. Rudge, p. 18; R.D. Fisher, p. 27.
19. Dixon, diary entry for 25.2.1917; R.D. Fisher, pp. 45–6.
20. Holdsworth, p. 3.
21. Clark, p. 6; Adams, p. 6; Hall, p. 5; Hollingsworth, p. 10.
22. Clark, p. 11.
23. Copson, p. 6; Acklam, diary entry for 18.3.1917; Harris, diary entry for 30.12.1916.
24. Bradbury, p. 51; Gale, letter of 28.7.1916.
25. Gale, letter of 17.8.1916; Clark, p. 5.
26. Acklam, diary entries for 11/12.10.1916.
27. Creek, p. 41; Gale, letter of 17.8.1916.
28. W.L. Fisher, diary entry for 8.8.1917.

CHAPTER 9

1. Blore, letter of 10.1.1917.
2. Erving Goffman, *Asylums: Essays on the Social Situation of Mental Patients and Other Inmates* (Penguin: Peregrine, 1987), pp. 17, 24.

3. John Keegan, *The Face of Battle* (Penguin, 1978), p. 331.
4. F.A.J. Taylor, p. 47.
5. Abraham, p. 86.
6. Lawton, p. 5.
7. Harris, diary entry for 18.12.1916; Blore, letter of 10.1.1917.
8. R.D. Fisher, p. 2.
9. Abraham, p. 45.
10. Bennet, *passim.*
11. Blore, letter of 30.9.1917.

EPILOGUE

1. C. Edmonds (C.E. Carrington), *A Subaltern's War* (Anthony Mott, 1984), p. 17; G. Coppard, *With a Machine Gun to Cambrai* (Papermac, 1986), p. 1; G. Orwell, 'My Country Right or Left', in *Collected Essays, Journalism and Letters*, Vol. I (Secker & Warburg, 1968), p. 538; C.H. Rolph, *London Particulars: Memories of an Edwardian Boyhood* (OUP, 1982), p. 177.
2. Parliamentary Recruiting Committee (PRC), Poster no. 33.
3. J. Bennet, IWM 83/14/1, letter of Ms Estelle Perrett; C.H. Cox, IWM 88/11/1, p. 1.
4. Noel Streatfeild, *A Vicarage Family: A Biography of Myself* (1963; Peacock: Penguin, 1968), pp. 220, 223.
5. Linda Colley, *Britons: Forging the Nation 1707–1837* (Yale UP, 1992), ch.7, *passim*; André Maurois, *King Edward and His Times* (Cassell, 1933), p. 15; Scott Hughes Myerly, '"The Eye Must Entrap the Mind": Army Spectacle and Paradigm in Nineteenth-century Britain', *Journal of Social History*, Vol. 26, No. 1 (1992), pp. 105–31. For discussions of British militarism and associated organisations before 1914, see for example Hugh Cunningham, *The Volunteer Force* (Croom Helm, 1975); John Springhall, Brian Frase and Michael Hoare (eds), *Sure and Steadfast: A History of the Boys' Brigade 1883 to 1983* (Collins, 1983); Anne Summers, 'Militarism in Britain before the Great War', *History Workshop Journal*, No. 2 (1976), pp. 104–23. For the effects of army organisation upon the workplace, see also Joe Melling, ' "Non-Commissioned Officers": British Employers and their Supervisory Workers, 1880–1920', *Social History*, Vol. 5, No. 2 (1980), pp. 183–221.
6. *The Queen's Regulations & Orders for the Army* (HMSO, 1885), p. 85; *Report of His Majesty's Commissioners on the War in South Africa* (HMSO, 1903), p. 4.
7. J. Galsworthy, 'Soames and the Flag 1914–1918', in *On Forsyte 'Change* (1930; Penguin, 1991), p. 266.
8. G.B. Shaw, *Arms and the Man* (Longman, 1977), pp. 16, 27 (spelling is Shaw's); p. 11.
9. Mark Girouard, *The Return to Camelot: Chivalry and the English Gentleman* (Yale UP, 1981), p. 14.
10. Samuel Smiles, *Self Help, with Illustrations of Character and Conduct* (John Murray, 1859), pp. v, 2, 4; pp. 2, 152.
11. Robert Baden-Powell, *Scouting for Boys: A Handbook for Instruction in Good Citizenship* (1908; Arthur Pearson, 1963), pp. 1, 211–38; p. 199.
12. V.S. Pritchett, *A Cab at the Door* (Penguin, 1968), pp. 129, 135; Robert Graves, *Goodbye to*

All That (1929; Penguin, 1979), pp. 38–9. See also J.A. Mangan, *The Games Ethic and Imperialism* (Viking, 1985); esp. chs 1–2. On the importance of voluntarism within middle-class social thought, especially in relation to the concept of duty, and as an ethos to be imparted to the lower classes, see for example Stefan Collini, *Liberalism and Sociology: L.T. Hobhouse and Political Argument in England, 1880–1914* (CUP, 1979), esp. ch. 1; Jane Lewis, *Women and Social Action in Victorian and Edwardian England* (Stanford UP, 1991); Melvin Richter, *The Politics of Conscience: T.H. Green and His Age* (Weidenfeld & Nicolson, 1964), esp. chs 8–10.

13. Lewis, p. 303; Shaftesbury quoted in Gregory Anderson, *Victorian Clerks* (MUP, 1976), p. 75; Arthur H. Dyke Acland & Benjamin Jones, *Working Men Co-operators* (1884), p. 131; Revd Hugh Legge, 'The Education of Democracy', *Economic Review* (July 1901), p. 299.

14. On reasons for volunteering, see for example Simkins, pp. 168–75. For a discussion of the war propaganda, see for example Peter Buitenhuis, *The Great War of Words: British, American and Canadian Propaganda and Fiction, 1914–1933* (University of British Columbia Press, 1987); Cate Haste, *Keep the Home Fires Burning: Propaganda in the First World War* (Allen Lane, 1977); Nicholas Reeves, *British Film Propaganda in the First World War* (Croom Helm, 1986); Michael Sanders and Phillip M. Taylor, *British Propaganda during the First World War* (Macmillan, 1982).

15. The discussion of British war posters is based upon the collection in the Department of Art at the Imperial War Museum. Further images and analysis are taken from J. Barnicoat, *Posters: A Concise History* (Thames & Hudson: World of Art, 1972, repr. 1988); M. Hardie and A.K. Sabin (eds.), *War Posters: Issued by Belligerent and Neutral Nations 1914–1919* (A. & C. Black, 1920); P. Paret, B.I. Lewis and P. Paret, *Persuasive Images: Posters of War and Revolution from the Hoover Institution Archives* (Princeton UP, 1992); M. Rickards, *Posters of the First World War* (1968).

16. PRC 94/IWM 5134 (the entire text is in capitals); PRC 7/IWM 5083; PRC 111/0409; PRC 91, 92/IWM 5163, 5127; PRC 94/IWM 5143; PRC 119/IWM 4887.

17. PRC 75/0313; PRC 108/IWM 0408;

18. PRC 55/IWM 4884; PRC 69/IWM 5118; ibid. The emphasis appears in the original.

19. PRC 144/IWM 5063; PRC 120/IWM 5051.

20. PRC 103/IWM 5041; PRC 127/IWM 5068.

21. PRC 84/IWM 5111; PRC 113/IWM 0309.

22. PRC 140/IWM 5043.

23. PRC 151, 152, 157/IWM 5253, 5052, 5021; PRC 129/IWM 3527; PRC 142/IWM 5054.

24. PRC (no number)/Peter H. Liddle, *Voices of War: Front Line and Home Front* (Leo Cooper, 1988), p. 71; PRC 88/Paret *et. al.* p. 53; Baden-Powell quoted in Springhall, p. 101.

25. Mansion House speech of 19.10.1915; *The Times*, 20.10.1915.

26. *The Times*, 28.10.1915; *Daily Mail*, 14.9.1915, 18.10.1915.

27. The pamphlet is part of the collection of T. Hardman, IWM 84/1/1. The capitals and italics appear as such in the original.

28. John Ellis, *The Social History of the Machine Gun* (Cresset Library, 1987), p. 116.

29. *Statistics of the Military Effort*, p. 237.

30. George Mosse, *Fallen Soldiers: Reshaping the Memory of the World Wars* (OUP, 1990), pp. 6–7.

31. On the national measures for the transformation of the war, see for example Mosse, op. cit.; A. Gregory, *The Silence of Memory: Armistice Day 1919–1946* (Berg, 1994); B. Bushaway, 'Name upon Name: The First World War and Remembrance', in Roy Porter (ed.), *Myths of the English* (CUP, 1992), pp. 136–67.

32. Tilsley, p. xi. On the imaginary status of the war, see for example Samuel Hynes, *A War Imagined* (The Bodley Head, 1990).

33. Voigt, 1929 edn, p. 7; 1920 edn, p. 17.

34. For example in 1926 Herbert Read's *In Retreat* was published, alongside Ford Madox Ford's *A Man Could Stand Up*. 1927 saw the publication of *A Subaltern on the Somme* by Mark VII (Max Plowman), and T.E. Lawrence's *Revolt in the Desert*. Siegfried Sassoon's *Memoirs of a Fox-hunting Man* and Blunden's *Undertones of War* were both issued in 1928. R.C. Sherriff's *Journey's End*, Erich Maria Remarque's *All Quiet on the Western Front*, and Robert Graves's *Good-bye to All That* were all published in 1929. Frederic Manning's *Her Privates We* and Sassoon's *Memoirs of an Infantry Officer* both came out in 1930, *The Poems of Wilfred Owen* in 1931, and Vera Brittain's *Testament of Youth* in 1933. These are but a very few examples of the best-known memoirs. Correlli Barnett, *The Collapse of British Power* (1972), pp. 428–9.

35. Graves, Prologue to the second edition (1957).

36. Basil Liddell Hart, original Preface to the book, in his *History of the First World War* (Pan, 1972).

37. Douglas Jerrold, *The Lie about the War* (1930), p. 10; Cyril Falls, *War Books* (1930), pp. x–xi.

38. Basil Liddell Hart, original Prefaces to both books, in his *History of the First World War*.

39. *Daily Mirror*, 3 July 1963; *Radio Times*, 4 July 1963, p. 2; *Evening News*, 2 July 1963, p. 3. The letters are now lodged in 85 volumes, arranged in alphabetical order, in the Imperial War Museum. For the purposes of this study, ten volumes were sampled, chosen at random from the entire collection.

40. *Radio Times*, 10 August 1964.

41. Telephone interview with Mr Terraine, 10.10.1990; interview with Mr Barnett, 18.10.1990; Terraine; Barnett.

42. It is impossible to encompass the vast output of First World War histories published since 1964. However, for examples of military and social history, see Ian F.W. Beckett and Keith Simpson (eds), *A Nation in Arms: A Social Study of the British Army in the First World War* (1985); J.M. Winter, *The Great War and the British People* (1985); Trevor Wilson, *The Myriad Faces of War* (1986); T.H.E. Travers, *The Killing Ground: The British Army, the Western Front and the Emergence of Modern Warfare, 1900–1918* (1987); J.M. Bourne, *Britain and the Great War, 1914–1918* (1989); J.G. Fuller, *Troop Morale and Popular Culture in the British and Dominion Armies 1914–1918* (1990). For critical discussions of the literature, see for example Bernard Bergonzi, *Heroes' Twilight: A Study of the Literature of the Great War* (1965, repr. 1980); Paul Fussell, *The Great War and Modern Memory* (OUP, 1975); Hynes, *A War Imagined*. For histories based upon oral and written testimonies, see for example Lyn Macdonald, *They Called it Passchendaele* (1978); idem, *Somme* (1983); Martin Middlebrook, *The First Day on the Somme* (1971).

43. Jamieson, Epilogue.

Bibliography

I. MANUSCRIPT SOURCES

All collections are lodged in the Department of Documents in the Imperial War Museum (IWM). Each is presented by name, description of content and catalogue number. 'Official documents' is a general title for items such as a National Registration Card, an attestation certificate or a printed field postcard.

All manuscript sources are reproduced with the permission of the authors' families and the Trustees of the Imperial War Museum.

Conscript and Derbyite collections

Abraham A.J.	account	P.191
Abrey, A.E.	letters	84/41/1
Acklam, W.R.	diary	83/23/1
Adams, H.L.	account	83/50/1
Allfree, Lt E.C.	account	77/14/1
Angel, R.L.	account	88/46/1
Barraclough, E.C.	account	86/86/1
Bass, Lt F.	diary	77/94/1
Bennet, J.	diary	83/14/1
Bishop, E.D.	diary	77/111/1
Blore, E.	letters	86/36/1
Bradbury, S.	account	81/35/1
Bryan, G.	diary	80/28/1
Carey, F.	diary	85/43/1
Clark, A.G.	diary	84/1/1
Cobb, W.	account	73/188/1
Coleman, O.	diary	84/9/1
Copson, P.G.	account	86/30/1
Cox, C.H.	account	88/11/1
Creek, Lt P.	account	87/31/1
Curtis, F.R.	account	87/17/1
Dale. Lt J.L.	letters	P.272
Davies, B.	letters	83/31/1
Dixon, G.H.	diary	86/57/1
Eccles, B.F.	letters	82/22/1
Evans, C.R.T.	letters	87/45/1
Firth, W.H.	letters	88/29/1

Fisher, R.D.	account	76/54/1
Fisher, W.L.	diary	85/32/1
Fraser, J.	letters	86/19/1
Gale, E.O.	letters	P.331
Grant, L.F.	diary	87/13/1
Hall, P.R.	account	87/55/1
Harris, C.P.	diary	87/33/1
Hart, E.A.	letters	82/22/1
Henderson, W.B.	account; draft of autobiographical novel	81/19/1
Holdsworth, E.	account	73/147/1
Hollingsworth, F.	account	82/21/1
Howes, H.G.	diary	79/23/1
Hudson, T.H.	diary	84/58/1
Hughes, B.W.	diary	85/43/1
Hynd, A.	letters	WWI 78/4
Jamieson, A.J.	account	88/52/1
Jolley, F.R.	account	Department of Documents vd
Pinks, E.A.	letters	85/43/1
Pinks, S.	letters	85/43/1
Preston, P.G.	diary	M6/160-167/1
Robb, W.	official documents	85/15/1
Rudge, B.	account, based on an interview to IWM oral history project	85/39/1
Tempest, C.A.	letters	85/39/1
Thompson, J.F.	letters	72/119/1
Tonkyn, W.D.	diary	Con Shelf
White, D.N.	letters	Con Shelf

Non-conscript collections

Binns, J.W.	letter	BBC 'Great War' series
Bird, E.J.O.	letter	BBC 'Great War' series
Clegg, H.	account	88/18/1
Coop, H.D.	diary and official documents	P.448
Coop, Canon J.O.	letters	87/56/1
Cooper, E.R.	diary	P.121
Duckham, A.	official documents	WWI 78/2
Farrow, R.W.	account	75/111/1
Glasgow, Lt W.E.	letters	73/223/1
Gleave, Cpt E.	letters	78/31/1 T
Green, 2nd Lt H.	letters	86/36/1
Hardie, Cpt M.	letters; official reports on morale	84/46/1

Hayman, Mrs L.	letters	88/51/1
Ingrey, F.R.	diary	83/6/1
Lawton, J.T.	account	86/48/1
Pile, A.T.	official documents	83/17/1
Preuss, L.	letter	BBC 'Great War' series
Wilby, G.F.	account	78/31/1 T
Williamson, J.	account	P.443

Ten volumes of letters, selected at random, from the BBC 'Great War' series were read, and sampled for the purposes of Part III of this study.

Other manuscript sources

Hurvitz, M., letters (private collection)
Public Record Office: RG 28/1-4; WO 374/76545

II. PRINTED SOURCES

Censorship Orders and Regulations (Army Document s.s. 660, April 1918).
The Louse Problem at the Western Front (HMSO, London, 1916).
1914-1916 Public General Acts (Eyre & Spottiswoode, London, 1917).
The Queen's Regulations & Orders for the Army (HMSO, 1885).
Report of His Majesty's Commissioners on the War in South Africa (HMSO, London, 1903).
Report on Morale & c. III Army, January 1917, in collection of Cpt M. Hardie, IWM 84/46/1.
Report of the War Office Committee of Inquiry into Shellshock (HMSO, London, 1922).
Statistics of the Military Effort of the British Empire during the First World War, 1914–1920 (HMSO, London, 1922).

III. PUBLISHED PRIMARY SOURCES

Conscripts and Derbyites

Fussell, P. (ed.), *The Ordeal of Alfred M. Hale: The Memoirs of a Soldier Servant* (Leo Cooper, London, 1975).
Gray, F., *Confessions of a Private* (Blackwell, Oxford, 1929).
Taylor, F.A.J., *The Bottom of the Barrel* (Regency Press, London, 1978).
Tilsley, W.V., *Other Ranks* (Cobden-Sanderson, London, 1931).
Voigt, F.A., *Combed Out* (Swarthmore Press, London, 1920; Jonathan Cape, Travellers' Library, London, 1929).

Non-conscripts

Coppard, G., *With a Machine Gun to Cambrai* (Papermac, London, 1986).
Crozier, F.P., *A Brass Hat in No Man's Land* (Jonathan Cape, London, 1930).
Dunn, Capt. J.C., *The War the Infantry Knew 1914–1919* (1938; Cardinal, London, 1989).
Edmonds, C. (C.E. Carrington), *A Subaltern's War* (Anthony Mott, London, 1984).

Graves, R., *Goodbye to All That* (1929; Penguin, London, 1979).

Gurney, I., *War Letters* (The Hogarth Press, London, 1984).

Hay, I., *The First Hundred Thousand* (Penguin, Harmondsworth, 1941).

Junger, E., *The Storm of Steel* (Chatto & Windus, London, 1929).

Lawrence, D.H, *Kangaroo* (1st edn, 1923; Penguin, London, 1973).

Lloyd-George, D., *War Memoirs* (2nd edn, Odhams Press, London, 1938).

Manning, F., *Her Privates We* (1929; Hogarth Press, London, 1986).

James Arthur Salter, *Memoirs of a Public Servant* (Faber & Faber, London, 1961).

Pritchett, V.S., *A Cab at the Door* (Penguin, London, 1971).

Richardson, S. (ed.), *Orders are Orders: A Manchester Pal on the Somme* (Neil Richardson, 1987).

Rolph, C.H., *London Particulars: Memories of an Edwardian Boyhood* (OUP, Oxford, 1982).

Vaughan, E.D., *Some Desperate Glory: The Diary of a Young Officer, 1917* (Frederick Warne, London, 1981).

IV. PUBLISHED SECONDARY SOURCES

Adams, R.J.Q., *Arms and the Wizard: Lloyd-George and the Ministry of Munitions, 1915–1916* (Cassell, London, 1978).

—— and P.P. Poirier, *The Conscription Controversy in Great Britain, 1900–1918* (Macmillan, London, 1987).

Anon., 'Behind the Lines 8 – "Letters Up"', *Stand To: The Journal of the Western Front Association* (1988), pp. 4-5.

Ashworth, A.E., 'The Sociology of Trench Warfare', *British Journal of Sociology*, XIX, 4 (December 1968), pp. 407–20.

——, *Trench Warfare, 1914–1918: The Live and Let Live System* (Macmillan, London, 1980).

Babington, A., *For the Sake of Example: Capital Courts Martial 1914–1918* (Paladin, London, 1986).

Baden-Powell, R., *Scouting for Boys: A Handbook for Instruction in Good Citizenship* (1908; Arthur Pearson, London, 1963).

Barnett, C., *The Collapse of British Power* (Eyre Methuen, London, 1972).

——, *Britain and Her Army, 1509–1970* (Penguin, Harmondsworth, 1974).

Beckett, I.F.W., 'The Real Unknown Army: British Conscripts 1916–1919', *The Great War*, Vol. 2, No. 1, November 1989.

Beckett, I.F.W. and Simpson, K. (eds), *A Nation in Arms: A Social Study of the British Armed Forces in the First World War* (Manchester University Press, Manchester, 1985).

Benson, J. (ed.), *The Working Class in England 1875–1914* (Croom Helm, London, 1985).

Bergonzi, B., *Heroes' Twilight: A Study of the Literature of the Great War* (Macmillan, London, 1980; Constable, London, 1965).

Boulding, K.E., *The Image* (University of Michigan Press, Ann Arbor, 1959).

Brent-Wilson, J., 'The Morale and Discipline of the British Expeditionary Force in 1914' (University of New Brunswick, unpublished MA thesis, 1978).

Brunner, J., 'Psychiatry, Psychoanalysis and Politics during the First World War' (paper presented at the Annual Conference of the Israeli Political Science Association, Tel Aviv University, May 1988).

Bibliography

Buitenhuis, P., *The First World War of Words: British, American and Canadian Propaganda and Fiction, 1914–1933* (University of British Columbia Press, Vancouver, 1987).

Burnet, J., Vincent, D. and Mayall, D. (eds), *The Autobiography of the Working Class: An Annotated Critical Bibliography*, Vol. I (Harvester Press, London, 1984).

Bushaway, B., 'Name upon Name: The First World War and Remembrance', in Roy Porter (ed.), *Myths of the English* (CUP, Cambridge, 1992), pp. 136–67.

Collini, S., *Liberalism and Sociology: L.T. Hobhouse and Political Argument in England, 1880–1914* (CUP, Cambridge, 1979).

Colley, L., *Britons: Forging the Nation 1707–1837* (Yale UP, New Haven, 1992).

Cunningham, H., *The Volunteer Force* (Croom Helm, London, 1975).

Dewey, P.E., 'Military Recruiting and the British Labour Force during the First World War', *The Historical Journal*, 27, I (1984), pp. 199–223.

Dixon, N., *On the Psychology of Military Incompetence* (Futura, London, 1988).

Douglas, R., 'Voluntary Enlistment in the First World War and the Work of the Parliamentary Recruiting Committee', *Journal of Modern History*, 42 (1970), pp. 564–85.

Eksteins, M., *Rites of Spring: The Great War and the Birth of the Modern Age* (Houghton Mifflin, Boston, 1989).

Elliot-Smith, G. and Pear, T.H., *Shell Shock and Its Lessons* (Longman, Green, London, 1917).

Ellis, J., *The Social History of the Machine Gun* (Cresset Library, London, 1987).

Englander, D. and Osborne, J., 'Jack, Tommy, and Henry Dubb: The Armed Forces and the Working Class', *The Historical Journal*, 21, 3 (1978), pp. 593–621.

Falls, C., *War Books* (Peter Davies, London, 1930).

Ferro, M., *The Great War 1914–1918* (Ark, London, 1987).

Foucault, M., *Discipline and Punish: The Birth of the Prison* (Penguin, London, 1979).

——, *The History of Sexuality: An Introduction* (Penguin, London, 1984).

French, D., *British Economic and Strategic Planning, 1905–1915* (George Allen & Unwin, London, 1982).

——, *British Strategy and War Aims, 1914–1916* (Allen & Unwin, London, 1986).

Freud, S., 'Thoughts for the Times on War and Death', in *Civilization, Society and Religion* (Pelican Freud Library, Vol. 12, Penguin, London, 1985).

Fry, M., 'Political Change in Britain, August 1914 to December 1916: Lloyd George Replaces Asquith: The Issues Underlying the Drama', *The Historical Journal*, 31, 3 (1988), pp. 609-27.

Frye, N., *Anatomy of Criticism* (Princeton UP, Princeton, 1957).

Fussell, P., *The Great War and Modern Memory* (OUP, Oxford, 1975, 1977).

Girouard, M., *The Return to Camelot: Chivalry and the English Gentleman* (Yale UP, New Haven, 1981).

Glover, J. and Silkin, J. (eds), *The Penguin Book of First World War Prose* (Penguin, London, 1990).

Goffman, E., *Asylums* (Penguin, London, 1987).

——, *The Presentation of Self in Everyday Life* (Allen Lane, London, 1971).

——, *Stigma: Notes on the Management of Spoiled Identity* (Prentice-Hall, New Jersey, 1963).

Gregory, A., *The Silence of Memory: Armistice Day 1919–1946* (Berg, Oxford, 1994).

Grieves, K., 'Military Tribunal Papers: The Case of Leek Local Tribunal in the First World War', *Archives*, Vol. xvi, No. 70 (October 1983).

——, *The Politics of Manpower, 1914–18* (MUP, Manchester, 1988).

Gunther, M.S. and Trosman, H., 'Freud as Expert Witness; Wagner-Jauregg and the Problem of the War Neuroses', *Annual of Psychoanalysis*, Vol. 2 (1974), pp. 3–23.

Hardie, M. and Sabin, A.K. (eds), *War Posters: Issued by Belligerent and Neutral Nations 1914–1919* (A. & C. Black, London, 1920).

Harris, R. and Paxman, J., *A Higher Form of Killing: The Secret Story of Gas and Germ Warfare* (Chatto & Windus, London, 1982).

Haste, C., *Keep the Home Fires Burning: Propaganda in the First World War* (Allen Lane, London, 1977).

Hayes, D., *Conscription Conflict: The Conflict of Ideas in the Struggle For and Against Military Conscription in Britain between 1901–1939* (Sheppard Press, London, 1949).

Holmes, R., *Firing Line* (Penguin, London, 1986).

Hughes Myerly, S., '"The Eye Must Entrap the Mind": Army Spectacle and Paradigm in Nineteenth-century Britain', *Journal of Social History*, Vol. 26, No. 1 (1992), pp. 105–31.

Hynes, S., *A War Imagined: The First World War and English Culture* (The Bodley Head, London, 1990).

Jerrold, D., *The Lie about the War* (London, 1930).

Jones, E., 'War Shock and Freud's Theory of the Neuroses' (1918), *Papers on Psychoanalysis* (3rd edn, William Wood, New York, 1923).

Keegan, J., *The Face of Battle* (Penguin, London, 1988).

Kennedy, T.C., *The Hound of Conscience: A History of the No-Conscription Fellowship 1914–1919* (University of Arkansas Press, Fayetteville, 1981).

Lamm, D., 'British Soldiers of the First World War', *Historical Social Research*, Vol. 14, No. 4 (1988), pp. 55–98.

Leed, E.J., *No Man's Land: Combat and Identity in World War I* (CUP, Cambridge, 1979).

——, 'Class and Disillusionment in World War I', *Journal of Modern History*, 50 (December 1978), pp. 680–99.

Leri, A., *Shell Shock, Commotional and Emotional Aspects* (University of London Press, London, 1919).

Levi-Strauss, C., *The Raw and the Cooked: Introduction to the Science of Mythology*, Vol. I (Penguin, London, 1986).

Lewis, J., *Women and Social Action in Victorian and Edwardian England* (Stanford UP, Stanford, 1991).

Liddell Hart, B.H., *History of the First World War*, (3rd edn, Pan Books, London, 1972).

Liddle, P.H., *Voices of War: Front Line and Home Front* (Leo Cooper, London, 1988).

Mangan, J.A., *The Games Ethic and Imperialism* (Viking, London, 1985).

Melling, J., '"Non-commissioned Officers": British Employers and their Supervisory Workers, 1880–1920', *Social History*, Vol. 5, No. 2 (1980), pp. 183–221.

Mosse, G.L., *Fallen Soldiers: Reshaping the Memory of the World Wars* (OUP, New York, 1990).

Mott, F.W., *War Neuroses and Shell Shock* (Hodder & Stoughton, London, 1919).

Nissell, M., *People Count: A History of the General Register Office* (HMSO, London, 1987).

Nussbaum, F.A., *The Autobiographical Subject: Gender and Ideology in Eighteenth Century England* (Johns Hopkins UP, Baltimore, 1989).

Offer, A., *The First World War: An Agrarian Interpretation* (OUP, Oxford, 1989).

——, 'The Working Classes, British Naval Plans and the Coming of the First World War', *Past and Present*, No. 107, May 1985.

Paret, P., Lewis, B.I. and Paret, P., *Persuasive Images: Posters of War and Revolution from the Hoover Institution Archives* (Princeton UP, New Jersey, 1992).

Bibliography

Parsons, I. (ed.), *The Collected Works of Isaac Rosenberg* (Chatto & Windus/The Hogarth Press, London, 1984).

Putkowski, J. and Sykes, J., *Shot at Dawn: Executions in World War One by Authority of the British Army Act* (2nd edn, Cooper, London, 1992).

Rae, J., *Conscience and Politics: The British Government and the Conscientious Objector to Military Service, 1916–1919* (OUP, London, 1970).

Reader, W.J., *'At Duty's Call': A Study in Obsolete Patriotism* (MUP, Manchester, 1988).

Rickards, M., *Posters of the First World War* (London, 1968).

Ropp, T., 'Conscription in Great Britain, 1900–1914: A Failure in Civil-Military Communications?' *Military Affairs*, 20 (1956), pp. 71-6.

Sanders, M. and Taylor, P.M., *British Propaganda during the First World War* (Macmillan, London, 1982).

Showalter, E., 'Male Hysteria: W.H.R. Rivers and the Lessons of Shell Shock', in *The Female Malady: Women, Madness and English Culture, 1830–1980* (Virago, London, 1987).

Silkin, J. (ed.), *The Penguin Book of First World War Poetry*, (2nd edn), (Penguin, London, 1984).

Silver, A., 'Vicissitudes of Citizenship and High Military Politics in Liberal Democracies' (paper presented at the annual meeting of the American Political Science Association, September 1990).

Simkins, P., *Kitchener's Army: The Raising of the New Armies, 1914–16* (MUP, Manchester, 1988).

Smiles, S., *Self Help, with Illustrations of Character and Conduct* (John Murray, London, 1859).

Springhall, J., Frase, B. and Hoare, M. (eds), *Sure and Steadfast: A History of the Boys' Brigade 1883 to 1983* (Collins, London, 1983).

Stone, M., 'Shell Shock and the Psychologists', in W.F. Bynum, R. Porter and M. Shepherd (eds), *The Anatomy of Madness* (Tavistock, London, 1985), pp. 242–71.

Suleiman, S.R. and Crosman, I. (eds), *The Reader in the Text* (Princeton UP, Princeton, 1980).

Summers, A., 'Militarism in Britain before the First World War', *History Workshop Journal*, No. 2 (1976), pp. 104–23.

Thompson, T., *Edwardian Childhoods* (Routledge & Kegan Paul, London, 1982).

Travers, T., *The Killing Ground: the British Army, the Western Front and the Emergence of Modern Warfare 1900–1918* (Allen & Unwin, London, 1987).

Van Creveld, M., *Supplying War: Logistics from Wallenstein to Patton* (CUP, Cambridge, 1977).

Waites, B., *A Class Society at War: England 1914–18* (Berg, Leamington Spa, 1987).

Wilson, W., *The Myriad Faces of War: Britain and the Great War, 1914–1918* (Polity Press, Cambridge, 1986).

Winter, D., *Death's Men: Soldiers of the Great War* (Penguin, London, 1987).

Winter, J.M., 'Military Fitness and Civilian Health in Britain during the First World War', *Journal of Contemporary History*, 15 (1980), pp. 211–44.

——, *The Great War and the British People* (Macmillan, London, 1986).

Wolff, L., *In Flanders Field* (Readers Union: Longmans, Green & Co., London, 1960).

Yealland, L.R., *Hysterical Disorders and Warfare* (Macmillan, London, 1918).

Zeitlin, J., 'From Labour History to the History of Industrial Relations', *Economic History Review*, XL, 2 (1987), pp. 159–84.

Zinsser, H., *Rats, Lice and History* (George Routledge & Sons, London, 1935).

Index

Due to the focus on the collective experience and identity of the conscripts, the index contains no personal names or specific locations. The conscripts quoted in the text are identified in the notes.